The Boundaryless Organization

Breaking the Chains of Organizational Structure

Revised and Updated

Ron Ashkenas, Dave Ulrich,

Todd Jick, Steve Kerr

Forewords by C. K. Prahalad and Lawrence A. Bossidy

JOSSEY-BASS
A Wiley Company
www.josseybass.com

Published by

JOSSEY-BASS
A Wiley Company
989 Market Street
San Francisco, CA 94103-1741

www.josseybass.com

Jossey-Bass books and products are available through most bookstores. To contact Jossey-Bass directly, call (888) 378-2537, fax to (800) 605-2665, or visit our website at www.josseybass.com.

Substantial discounts on bulk quantities of Jossey-Bass books are available to corporations, professional associations, and other organizations. For details and discount information, contact the special sales department at Jossey-Bass.

Library of Congress Cataloging-in-Publication Data

The boundaryless organization : breaking the chains of organizational structure / Ron Ashkenas . . . [et al.] ; forewords by C. K. Prahalad and Lawrence A. Bossidy.— 2nd ed.
p. cm. — (The Jossey-Bass business & management series)
Includes bibliographical references and index.
ISBN 0-7879-5943-X (alk. paper)
1. Organizational change. 2. Industrial organization. 3. Interorganizational relations.
4. Partnership. I. Ashkenas, Ronald N. II. Series.
HD58.8 .B675 2002
658.4'063—dc21   2001006128

SECOND EDITION
HB Printing 10 9 8 7 6 5 4 3

Contents

Foreword

C. K. Prahalad

The new business environment imposes new demands on managers. They have to engage in a fundamental reexamination of strategies, both at the corporate and at the business levels, as well as reassess the capabilities of their organizations to execute the new and often complex strategies. Most managers have little appetite for either fundamentally rethinking strategy or creating radically new organizational capabilities. Both tasks require a capacity to forget as well as a capacity to learn; they require tools for honest assessment of where one is and a capacity to conceive where one ought to be.

The process of reexamining and reinventing the company demands a new organizational theory and, at the same time, a critical evaluation of the limits of existing theory. It requires the capacity to think long term and, at the same time, create the financial and the organizational space for change through efficiencies. It is the appetite for this process of reexamining and reinventing that will separate the builders (leaders) from caretakers and the undertakers (managers and cautious administrators).

The Search for High Performance

Under pressure for performance in a changing competitive environment, managers seem to gravitate toward improving the efficiency of existing organizational arrangements and implementing existing strategies. This is "doing what I know" better. Hence, the current managerial preoccupation with "implementation." However, in different companies, a focus on implementation means different things, from downsizing to reengineering to various forms of "cultural change" programs. In the absence of clear guideposts, we see a wide proliferation of tools and fads that promise a simple cure-all. Yet the evidence is that even very popular implementation tools have not been unqualified successes. Moreover, all these initiatives consume an enormous amount of organizational energy.

The need for a comprehensive framework, a theory, to sort out fads from useful initiatives is obvious. Managers building a high-performance firm need a framework that enables them to evaluate initiatives, sequence them, and recognize the risks and time frames they involve.

The Boundaryless Organization provides an excellent start to the process of discovering the essential building blocks of organizations that can cope with the complex strategies needed in the future. Implicit in the message of this book is the strategic imperative of competitive success: traditional notions of efficiency, such as quality of asset management, are not enough. We need to go beyond them and develop a new managerial scorecard.

From Asset Management to Resource Leverage

Beset by the new competitive reality, firms typically start to focus on better asset management (reduction of working capital) as well as on reduction of investment requirements by selective outsourcing. However, vitality in the medium to longer term comes not from asset reduction but from resource leverage. Managers must be able to get a bigger bang for the buck, better commercial results from the infrastructure in which they have invested. The brands, patents and technology, global supply base, physical infrastructure, and competencies that the collective and shared learning of the organization represents—that is, the physical and the invisible, intellectual resources of the firm—need to be leveraged. The reusing of intellectual assets to create new businesses and new sources of competitive advantage is a process of discovering hidden wealth and requires a new management process. *The Boundaryless Organization* implicitly accepts the need for resource leverage. The authors suggest four dominant themes that are critical to such leverage: speed (not size), flexibility (not rigidity, often disguised as role clarity), integration (not specialization), and innovation (not control).

Most often, the reason managers do not move beyond asset management to resource leverage is that the latter requires new ways of managing. The essence of such leverage is learning, sharing knowledge, redeploying knowledge, and bundling physical and intellectual assets in new and creative ways. Therefore, the capacity to transcend current administrative boundaries is a critical precondition for resource leverage. That boundary spanning, or creating of "boundaryless" behavior, is the substance of this book. *The Boundaryless Organization* is about the "how" of strategy.

Creating the Organization of the Future

Basing their findings on their extensive experience in working with senior managers of some of the best-known firms, the authors identify four essential boundaries to be spanned. These include hierarchical levels (breaking the tyranny of the vertical, status-driven boundaries), interunit divisions (breaking functional, business unit, and other horizontal boundaries driven by specialization, expertise, and socialization), barriers between internal and external organizations (breaking the boundary between the customer and the organization), and finally, global differences (breaking the boundaries between geographic markets and cultures). In large, well-established organizations such as GE, General Motors, Sears, and IBM, each one of these boundaries was an integral part of the management process. Call them bureaucracy, internal governance, or administrative heritage, these boundaries were real, and implicitly defined the range of competitive options available to each firm. It is no surprise, therefore, that these organizations were unable to adapt speedily to the changing competitive realities. A lack of organizational capacity to reconfigure physical and intellectual resources in new and creative ways—not as resources per se—had become their primary source of competitive weakness. GE was one of the first to realize the suffocating effects of the traditional boundary-based approaches to managing, effects that inhibited the organization's ability to leverage resources. GE initiated a process for systematically creating a "boundaryless" organization. The authors' experience is derived significantly from their work on this process, initially at GE and subsequently at other firms as well.

Boundaryless behavior is not about eliminating all administrative procedures and rules. It is about reducing the threshold of pain when creating new patterns of collaboration, learning, and productive work. It is about removing the restrictions, real and imaginary, imposed on individuals and teams by formal structures. Boundarylessness is about boundary spanning; it is about substituting permeable structures for concrete walls.

The Boundaryless Organization is organized in a user-friendly manner. The authors follow a simple structure to articulate their complex message about each of the four boundaries:

1. A logical reason for the need to reexamine the effects of a specific kind of organizational boundary (for example, vertical boundaries, or the hierarchy).
2. A method (an instrument) with which you can assess the state of your company along this dimension (for example, how hierarchy-bound your organization is).
3. A brief history of how this kind of boundary evolved. What were the theoretical underpinnings behind the organizing idea?
4. The consequences of the condition. When does an organizational practice become a pathology? (For example, hierarchy-based management was fine in slow-moving businesses, but in businesses that need quick response time and flexibility, hierarchies can become pathologies.)
5. The steps that can be taken to break old patterns and create the new patterns of boundaryless behavior (for example, creating a shared mindset).
6. The benefits to the organization from this approach.

Two themes dominate the book. First, creating a boundaryless organization takes time and perseverance. It takes repetition. It takes small acts, symbols, course corrections, coaching, and celebrations. It is not without pain. It takes training. It should involve all people in the organization. Most often, these simple and, at the same time, profound lessons are not well understood by leaders. Reinventing the company is not about a single initiative; neither is it an off-line activity. It is on-line, involves multiple initiatives, and is cumulative.

The second theme is that success in current business is critical to provide necessary space and confidence to the organization. Focusing on business results is critical as a management group attempts to reinvent itself. Change not anchored in business results is likely to drift. Strategy provides the anchor and the rationale for reinventing the company.

These two underlying themes, so often missing in books on change and transformation, make this a book for line managers as much as a guide for HR professionals. The focus is on general management in a changing marketplace.

The Boundaryless Organization is a very important contribution to the emerging thinking on preparing for competing in the future.

Ann Arbor, Michigan
July 1995

C. K. PRAHALAD
Coauthor of Competing for the
Future; *Harvey C. Fruehauf Professor
of Business Administration and Professor of Corporate Strategy and International Business, Graduate School of
Business Administration, University
of Michigan*

Foreword

Lawrence A. Bossidy

Nobody argues anymore with the notion that what it takes to succeed today is radically different from what it took yesterday and that tomorrow's success factors will be different as well. The speed of changes in the global market in an age of accelerating technological innovation means that there are no longer any certainties. New products and competitors emerge almost overnight, and the half-life of market strategies shrinks almost daily. It is the kind of environment in which great companies can be humbled very quickly—but where nimble, creative, and courageous organizations can thrive as never before.

To succeed in this environment, leaders need to rethink the traditional ways that work gets done. Whoever can contribute value—whether he or she is a production worker, middle manager, specialist, vendor, customer, or senior executive—needs to be encouraged to collaborate with others and make things happen, without waiting for some central authority to give permission. The old questions of status, role, organizational level, functional affiliation, and geographic location, all the traditional boundaries that we have used for years to define and control the way we work, are much less relevant than getting the best people possible to work together effectively.

For many organizations, this concept of boundaryless behavior sounds threatening and risky. After all, it means transferring decision-making authority away from executives and out to frontline workers; it means listening to customers and changing our products and delivery systems to meet their needs; it means forming partnerships with suppliers rather than just telling them what to do; and it means establishing coalitions with other parts of the

company rather than defending turf. And when all this is taken together, it means that the role of manager, executive, and leader
changes drastically—from controller and authority figure to stim-
ulator, catalyst, cheerleader, and coach. So it is not an easy shift.
However, in the environment of the twenty-first century, making
such a shift is no longer a choice.

During my years as CEO of AlliedSignal, and now Honeywell,
we have been working to make this kind of boundaryless transformation, not only in our management team but throughout the
company. It has not painless or easy. Nor is the transformation complete. We still get hung up on titles, status, roles, rules, functions,
and geographic differences that divide us rather than bring us together with each other and with our customers. But by becoming
more boundaryless, we have been able to establish and achieve new
standards of excellence. And most important, we are becoming far
more capable of succeeding in an unpredictable future.

If your organization is ready for this kind of transformation,
The Boundaryless Organization will provide a simple but provocative
framework either for getting started or for accelerating the pace.
At AlliedSignal, I asked all of our managers to read it, to learn from
the rich cases that it contains, and to use the tools that might be
helpful to them, and I am doing the same at the new Honeywell. But
make no mistake, this is not a cookbook or a how-to guide. Too
many managers today are looking for the quick-fix elixir that will
make them winners overnight. It does not exist, either in this book
or elsewhere. The authors of *The Boundaryless Organization* rightly
argue that we do not need new buzzwords about organization but
new ways of thinking about our organizations. As such a new way of
thinking, this book is not a solution but a set of ideas that should
cause all managers to rethink how they get work done.

In the final analysis, there is no substitute for your own creativity and leadership, for your creation of your own boundaryless
agenda. And that is the uniqueness of *The Boundaryless Organization*. It is not a prescription but a challenge. It is up to you to take
advantage of it.

Morristown, New Jersey
October 2001

LAWRENCE A. BOSSIDY
*Chairman and Chief
Executive Officer,
Honeywell Corporation*

Preface

In the five years since *The Boundaryless Organization* first appeared, we have seen the themes it describes play out time after time on the organizational stage. Firms that managed to loosen their boundaries and operate with greater speed, flexibility, and innovation have tended to be more successful at navigating the white water of the global economy. Conversely, organizations that have maintained more rigid internal and external boundaries have struggled.

At the same time, the world continues to change with lightning speed. When we wrote *The Boundaryless Organization* in 1993 and 1994, the Internet was just beginning to enter our consciousness. E-mail had not yet become a way of life, and globe-spanning wireless communication was only a dream for most people. Since then, thousands of dot-com companies full of entrepreneurial energy have burst on the scene. And though many have fallen by the wayside, together they have heralded the dawn of a new economic and organizational era. People struggling to define the new reality constantly refer to virtual, networked, wired, horizontal, knowledge-based organizations.

Also in the past five years, the tiger economies of Asia emerged with a roar that influenced firms everywhere, then collapsed in the midst of currency crises, and then recovered faster than anyone thought possible. And while regional conflicts continue to flame across the world, a truly global economy has become a reality. In today's world, a consumer in Boise might easily talk to a customer service representative in India about a product manufactured in Mexico—without realizing that the transaction has spanned the globe.

Pushed by the burgeoning global economy and the technological innovation rate, the pace of mergers, acquisitions, and alliances has climbed to unheard-of levels, with trillions of dollars worth of deals reshaping the corporate landscape and dislocating millions of people. Yet at the same time, even as companies connect more with each other, they are simultaneously engaged in an unprecedented war for talent as human capital becomes one of the scarcest resources on the planet.

So clearly, in the past five years, the pace of change has accelerated. Yet in the midst of this new environment, the fundamental capabilities of human beings have not changed. Human brains have not grown larger to be able to absorb the Web-based sea of information, and the ability to engage in dialogue has not grown along with all the technologies that could support it twenty-four hours a day. Thus organizations still need to function at the human scale—to take advantage of technology and globalization while basing themselves on human capabilities. And in that context, we firmly believe that the concepts and principles laid out in *The Boundaryless Organization* are still on target.

The Essence of a Boundaryless World

For those who are picking up the book for the first time, here are the key ideas:

1. Success factors in the twenty-first century include speed, flexibility, integration, and innovation—*in addition to* the traditional success factors of size, role definition, specialization, and control—even when these factors seem to contradict each other. Managers must create organizations with sufficient critical mass that can also move quickly and nimbly through the changing business terrain.
2. To achieve these success factors, every firm needs to reshape four types of boundaries:
   - *Vertical boundaries* (the floors and ceilings of organizations), which separate people by hierarchical levels, titles, status, and rank.
   - *Horizontal boundaries* (the internal walls), which separate people in organizations by function, business unit, product group, or division.

- *External boundaries* (the external walls), which divide companies from their suppliers, customers, communities, and other external constituencies.
- *Geographic boundaries* (the cultural walls), which include aspects of the other three but are applied over time and space, often across different cultures.

3. Each of these boundaries needs appropriate permeability and flexibility—so that ideas, information, and resources can flow freely up and down, in and out, and across the organization. The idea is not to have totally permeable boundaries or no boundaries—that would be "*dis*organization." Rather, you want sufficient permeability to allow the organization to quickly and creatively adjust to changes in the environment.

4. Leaders can use a number of levers to foster appropriate permeability—almost like fine-tuning the dial on a radio. These are the four most powerful levers:
   - *Information:* Foster access to information across all boundaries.
   - *Authority:* Give people the power to make independent decisions about action and resources.
   - *Competence:* Help people develop the skills and capabilities to use information and authority wisely.
   - *Rewards:* Provide proper shared incentives that promote organizational goals.

5. Leaders themselves need to adopt new ways of working to lead boundaryless organizations. They need to shift from command and control to methods that rely more on creating shared mindsets, stretch goals, and empowered colleagues. They need to shift from having the right answers to asking the right questions. But at the same time, they need to keep the focus on results, maintain clear accountability for performance, and make tough decisions.

Origins of the Concept

The first edition of this book grew out of our experiences with one of the largest and most ambitious organizational change efforts ever attempted, the General Electric Work-Out process. Late in 1988, GE CEO Jack Welch asked Dave Ulrich to pull together a team of academics and consultants who could help GE transform the way it did business. Among others, Ulrich enlisted Ron Ashkenas, Todd Jick (then at Harvard University), and Steve Kerr (then at the University of Southern California). For the next several years, we worked intensively with a variety of GE businesses to reduce bureaucracy, shorten cycle times, and increase capabilities for change. Periodically, we met with others involved in Work-Out to share experiences and learn from each other.

It was at GE that we first heard the term *boundaryless organization,* which Jack Welch had been using since 1990. It sounded like just another buzzword at first, but we kept encountering aspects of the boundaryless theme. For example, in the early days of Work-Out, we conducted hundreds of "town meetings"—attempts at direct dialogue between managers and their employees—and we saw how hard it was to overcome these vertical boundaries. At the same time, we began to see the disconnections, the horizontal boundaries, between functions and departments.

As Work-Out progressed and GE's internal boundaries became increasingly permeable, we began to focus on relationships with customers and suppliers, the external boundaries. Dave Ulrich had written extensively on how human resource practices could create greater customer commitment. Building on these ideas, we began helping GE businesses hold town meetings with customers and suppliers. Todd Jick conducted the first one, between GE Appliances and Sears, and it was followed by many more.

By 1991, we were looking at global linkages, as GE businesses shifted from domestic to worldwide concerns. For example, Ron Ashkenas took part in an extended effort to integrate GE Lighting's domestic business with its European acquisitions—including its new Hungarian partner, Tungsram Ltd., the first major acquisition of an Eastern bloc company by a Western concern.

By 1992, we realized that GE was engaged in a paradigm shift, altering multiple organizational boundaries at the same time. With that shift in mind, Kerr, Jick, and Ulrich began creating a conceptual framework that would shape managers' understanding of the boundaryless organization and what they could do to achieve it. This framework became the GE program known as the Change Acceleration Process (CAP). Since 1992, hundreds of GE managers and many of their customers and suppliers have used CAP to break down boundaries of all sorts.

By 1993, we realized that more and more organizations were struggling with the same issues, and that the insights we had gained could form an action framework for them. To make the framework useful, we set out to create not only a conceptual model of the boundaryless organization but also a set of simple tools that managers could tailor to their individual requirements. The first edition of this book was the result.

Nonetheless, the framework we have created is not based on GE, nor is *The Boundaryless Organization* a book about GE. Since GE was a leader in creating a boundaryless organization and a formative learning site for all of us, we have drawn on its experience and a number of GE examples. However, we have also drawn on the experience of numerous other organizations, and GE examples form only a small part of the total.

In the five years since writing the original book, we've observed that boundaryless organizations—or those that strive to be so—improve their chances of success in the global Internet era. Indeed, organizations *must* have some degree of boundarylessness to function effectively today. And that applies equally to a large firm trying to shake free from long-standing bureaucracy and to a start-up firm struggling to find an organizational model that can support its growth.

One Boundaryless Organization

Consider the case of Charles Schwab & Co., the San Francisco–based brokerage founded in 1974 with the then-radical mission of giving ordinary people greater access to investment opportunities. Inspired by this mission, the firm grew rapidly while it maintained a boundaryless start-up culture where everyone did everything and everyone knew everyone else.

In 1983, to fund further expansion, Charles Schwab sold the firm to Bank of America, hoping that being part of a global financial services organization would allow it to achieve the mission more quickly. Unfortunately, BofA's culture at the time, combined with strict banking regulations, constrained Schwab's ability to expand into a full range of products and services.

But Schwab did not give up on his dream. Instead, in 1987 he bought back the firm and then took it public to raise funds for expansion and growth. By 1996, riding the wave of a thriving U.S. and global economy, the firm was again experiencing double-digit growth rates and had added thousands of staff to keep up with the demand. The price of this rapid growth, however, was incredible stress on the underlying boundaryless culture. It is one thing to have rapid and informal networked decision making when everyone is close together; it is quite another to maintain these patterns when people are scattered far and wide, do not share the same history, and are too busy to get together.

Nowhere was this level of stress more apparent than in Schwab's information technology organization, which was the backbone of the firm's success. Chief Information Officer Dawn Lepore, a thirteen-year Schwab veteran, had made sure that the IT organization's capacity had grown along with Schwab's customer base. However, the demands of managing hundreds of people, multiple data centers, and dozens of applications and databases—and keeping it all running perfectly—had driven out much of the ability to think, innovate, and plan ahead. Every day was a new crisis. And because of the incredible growth, most members of her management team were relatively inexperienced, many of them never having run large organizations before.

Lepore wanted to avoid the traditional solutions of greater structure, hierarchy, and management control. Thus she began a two-year effort to build a boundaryless IT organization that could keep up with—even get ahead of—Schwab's growth. Using a number of concepts from *The Boundaryless Organization,* she drove home the idea of creating a "shared mindset" about the mission of the IT organization and its place in the firm. She created communication mechanisms and interactive forums to educate all the IT people about what was needed. She focused on strengthening processes that cut across units, with clear owners, checkpoints, measures of performance, and reviews. She standardized and centralized services wherever it made sense, and tailored and decentralized support where that was appropriate. She created decision processes that included her clients and other key stakeholders. And she did all of this while building a team of managers that could work collaboratively as well as independently—and could even function without her for two months during her maternity leave.

In the midst of this transformation, Schwab spawned an entire revolution in the investment industry. Late in 1995, a technology team in Lepore's organization built a Web-based trading application. When the technology proved to be sound and reliable, co-CEOs Charles Schwab and David Pottruck established a new electronic brokerage unit, e.Schwab, headed by Beth Sawi with support from Lepore's organization through Gideon Sasson. Kept separate from the Schwab mainstream so that it could develop quickly and flexibly, the new unit was an immediate success with customers, growing from nothing to 1.2 million accounts by the end of 1997. Eventually, Schwab was faced with the question of whether e.Schwab should be kept separate, competing with other Schwab channels such as telephone reps and branches, or be integrated into and perhaps even transform those channels. Early in 1998, Pottruck made the call to bring e.Schwab into the fold, and to integrate Web trading into all of Schwab's business. Although this decision had significant short-term revenue implications (Web-based trading had lower commissions), it proved to be a major success. Within a year, trading volume and customer accounts had increased dramatically, while costs had actually been reduced—so that revenue shortfalls were more than made up by profitability increases. And Schwab was now the industry leader in Web-based trading across all of its channels.

Flexibility Across Boundaries

Companies today need to keep reinventing themselves—and the flexibility of a boundaryless organization is almost a prerequisite for that process. Thus traditional companies need to become more boundaryless to succeed in the new economy, and companies already in the new economy need to stay boundaryless to keep up with it.

The continued success of GE, one of the largest old economy companies, illustrates the importance of this constant reinvention. In the first half of the 1990s, GE used Work-Out and other processes to build a highly flexible, boundaryless culture. In the second half of the 1990s, GE transformed itself over and over again to keep up with—and ahead of—the global Internet economy. Thus GE was able to acquire and integrate dozens of organizations and become a world leader in the process of acquisition integration.[1] Using Six Sigma quality processes, GE was then able to streamline its work and reduce costs by millions of dollars. At the same time, GE was shifting many of its businesses more toward services and toward the development of global markets. And finally, using the mentality of "destroy your business.com," all GE businesses focused on how to best exploit the Internet for competitive advantage—leading to many more millions of gains and even greater boundaryless capability.

But what are the new realities today that require boundaryless capability? Why is it even more critical today to make sure that boundaries are permeable than it was five years ago? We have seen four shifts, all accelerated by the explosion of Internet and communications technologies, that make boundarylessness not just a nice-to-have but a requirement for successful firms in the twenty-first century.

A New Relationship with Customers

No matter how much companies have hitherto focused on customer service—on being "close to the customer" or "customer-centered"—they never really bridged the gap between themselves and those who bought or used their products or services. In some cases, the supply chain between producer and consumer was too long; in others, it took too long to get customer input to the decision makers; in still others, the customers never had any effective contact with many parts of the producing company.

One of the most striking shifts in the past five years is the way the new technologies make it possible for companies—in fact, require companies—to interact with customers in a much more personal, ubiquitous, real-time, and constant manner. Customer feedback, ideas, complaints, and comments are available (whether you want them or not) at all times. Customers can send e-mail directly to producers and service providers, at all levels throughout the value chain, at all times—and they expect an almost instantaneous response. And since customer input has no lag time, customers expect response to that input—real product and service changes—to be rapid or even immediate. In fact, customers now expect to be involved in the design of the product and service itself—so that it is tailored to their specific needs. This can range from specifying the mix of songs on a downloaded CD to selecting customized features and colors on an automobile.

These new possibilities have led to whole new business paradigms based on different needs and expectations of customers. For example, many Web-based companies do not actually produce anything—they bring together offerings from competing companies and help customers sort out what they need and put together the right suite of products and services. This has led many traditional producers to offer customers a choice of competitors' products along with their own. And it has shown these producers that customers are usually willing to pay as much or more for the service of putting things together—for tailoring, delivering, maintaining, and refreshing the mix—as they are for products themselves. With this insight, for example, GE has transformed itself in the past five years from a diversified manufacturing company to much more of a services firm.

This focus on tailored service also means that companies have the potential to know much more about their customers than ever before. Within the limits of privacy, they can know their preferences, ordering patterns, lifestyle requirements, and so forth. Thus promotions can be more targeted, products and services can be aimed at narrower customer groups (or even tailored to individual customers), and relationships can be developed over a lifetime. The new metric is increasingly *customer share* instead of *market share*—meaning that the goal is not just to have a chunk of the market but to have an increasing share of the individual customer's potential purchasing space. As such, for example, Coke goes after a customer's "share of stomach," Fidelity competes for "share of wallet," Amazon looks for "lifetime sales."

A New Relationship with Employees

Just as the boundaries between companies and customers have become more permeable, so have the boundaries between managers and employees. Employees coming into the workforce today have largely grown up in the Internet age. They barely remember when information was not accessible at all hours from around the globe. Many of them have had cell phones and pagers since before they were in high school, and they expect important information to come to them whenever it is needed. They have been raised on CNN and e-mail and are capable of multiprocessing at Internet speed. In many corporations, starting with GE, it is these net-savvy youngsters that are teaching the old-timers how to navigate in the new information world.

Organizations can no longer maintain the traditional notions of power and information, where people at the top were the only ones in the know. Almost all employees have come to expect full disclosure of financial information, strategic decisions, customer wins and losses, and organizational changes. Open book management, informational town meetings, informational Web sites, and other means of information sharing have become commonplace rather than isolated, innovative experiments.

More and more today, even more than five years ago, employees at all levels expect to have a voice in the firm's key decisions. They expect to be engaged as informed adults, able to discuss bad news and good. More than anything, they expect to be told the truth, without protective secrecy or sugarcoating. After all, if they don't get the information from management, they can get it just as easily elsewhere.

In addition, many employees—particularly in service, knowledge, and key skill industries—regard themselves as free agents or volunteers who support the company and are entitled to information about it rather than as employees who exchange work for pay. The psychological balance of power has subtly shifted from employer to employee, partly because a booming economy in many parts of the world has created a labor shortage and provided increasing numbers of workers with investment portfolios. Even more, however, the shift stems from the unlimited sense of opportunity evoked by the information economy. With thousands upon thousands of start-ups, coupled with the e-transformation of traditional firms, more and more people feel—often rightfully so—that they can make it on their own, that they do not need the safety net of a company to work for. The barriers to entry for someone with a good idea and access to a computer are virtually nil, so why not take a shot?

With this attitude—reinforced by the idea of a "war for talent"—the shift from a control-based relationship between manager and employee to more of an information-based relationship has accelerated in the past five years. Not all managers have learned to operate in this way (regardless of age), but the need to do so has certainly increased.

A New Relationship with a Network of Alliances and Partners

When we first wrote *The Boundaryless Organization,* the idea of a vertically integrated organization that could function independently—like the old Ford Motor Company—had already broken down. Thus we focused on the importance of being part of a value chain, and of making the external boundaries between value-chain members more permeable.

In the past five years, this trend has accelerated exponentially. Today's companies don't just form value chains, they form value networks that can include many dozens of players around the globe. For example, a traditional manufacturer today might purchase raw materials and components through an Internet-based bid process that widely expands the potential supplier base. Alternatively, the same organization might dramatically improve its purchasing power by joining its competitors in a consolidated buying site, perhaps managed through a joint venture owned by dozens of firms. Once the product is produced, the manufacturer might sell it through its own sales force, through alliances with a variety of distribution channels, or through an assortment of Web sites. These Web sites might be designed or run by other organizations, and the financial transactions might be managed through a variety of partners as well. In short, though most transactions move much faster now, the network of players that touch, expedite, or influence these transactions has multiplied.

At the same time, organizations in the past five years have engaged in a frenzy of structural realignment that has led to trillions of dollars worth of acquisitions, divestitures, joint ventures, outsourcing, and alliances. On one hand, many firms have realized that they cannot do everything—that they need to concentrate on core competencies and focused missions. Thus, for example, a number of automotive companies spun off or divested themselves of divisions that make components, leading to new companies such as

Delphi Automotive (from General Motors), Visteon (from Ford), and Meritor (from Rockwell). On the other hand, once firms have created this focus, they have tried to gain critical mass in their competency area through purchases of similar firms. For example, since its creation, Meritor has bought Volvo's axle business, Lucas-Varity's brake business, and the Euclid Aftermarket Company, and then merged with Arvin Industries, another automotive supply company.

In other cases, whole industries have undergone consolidation because of the belief that larger firms could compete more effectively in the global marketplace. This has been the case in sectors such as aerospace, pharmaceuticals, and financial services. At the same time, in many of these sectors, the creation of critical mass has been proceeding almost hand in hand with the proliferation of alliances that offer opportunities, capabilities, or innovations that don't exist in the larger firm. For example, large pharmaceutical firms such as Pfizer (which acquired Warner Lambert) and Glaxo-SmithKline (a merger between Glaxo-Wellcome and SmithKline Beecham), have hundreds of research alliances, co-marketing ventures, and clinical trial arrangements with outside partners. These alliances are facilitated—or even made possible—by electronic collaboration tools that are a result of Internet technology.

One other form of structural change that has occurred is an acceleration of outsourcing of functions previously considered part of the firm. Many firms now rely on partners to take care of all or part of their purchasing, information technology, finance, customer service, and human resources. For example, the outsourcing firm Exult handles all HR transactions and basic HR functions for Bank of America. Similarly, an Indian IT firm called Wipro manages data processing and application development for a number of U.S. and European Fortune 500 firms.

Taken together, these structural realignments have required firms to reexamine both their internal and external boundaries. While outsourcing is cost-effective, to be business-effective a relationship needs to be well managed, collaborative, and even evolutionary. The same is true for alliances—which need constant recalibration and dialogue. Acquisitions and mergers also generally require fundamental or even revolutionary rethinking about how parts of a firm fit together—rethinking that cannot be done without effective dialogue across boundaries. Thus boundaryless-ness has become a precondition for success for firms undergoing these structural shifts—which perhaps is why so many acquisitions and alliances have been less successful than planned.

A New Relationship with Time and Space

A final shift that has made the concepts of *The Boundaryless Organization* even more critical in the past five years has been the total breakdown of time and space as a limiting factor in organizational interactions. Business can now take place anytime, anywhere. There is no place to hide and no place where communications can't reach. Cars, planes, trains, homes, restaurants, markets, and street corners are just as accessible as the office. And even though Motorola's Iridium project was a commercial disaster, the dream of communicating anywhere on the planet is close to reality as even the least developed countries of the world employ wireless and cellular technologies.

On a personal level, these developments have dramatically increased the productivity of most individual managers and employees. Decisions are faster, data more accurate, key people better informed. On the other hand, personal stress levels have increased as the expectations for constant availability and immediate response have grown almost out of control. Managers in most firms now routinely receive hundreds of messages per day—through e-mail, voice mail, telephone, fax, and in person. Sorting through this drift and finding ways to keep up and respond has become a major managerial challenge.

From an organizational perspective, the advent of anytime-anywhere communications has made almost all boundaries more permeable. Dialogue across levels can take place now not just in special town meetings but through chat rooms, e-mail forums, and interactive on-line events. Cross-functional and cross-organizational teams can work together through electronic collaboration spaces, easily sharing databases, ideas, work plans, and more—without needing more than an occasional telephone or in-person meeting. And team members from different continents can participate with total equality since the electronic space is not limited by time zones and geographic borders.

Yet even though all these capabilities are more available than they were five years ago, they're far from fully deployed and used in most organizations. And that is where the boundaryless levers still come into play. Having the capability to share information still does not mean that the right information is transmitted. In fact, often too much of the wrong information is sent, clogging the human bandwidth for response and action. Similarly, cross-boundary teams still require clarity about how much authority they can exert. Who makes decisions and on what basis? How do they get rewarded? What is their incentive for working at all hours of the day and night, at home or at the office?

The developments of the past five years have created enormous opportunities for more permeable boundaries in organizations, but leaders must still find the right ways to use these capabilities to achieve results. The technology alone is not enough. Leadership at a human scale is still required.

A New Edition of *The Boundaryless Organization*

Given these realities of the twenty-first century, we felt that it would be important to senior executives to take a fresh look at the concepts of *The Boundaryless Organization,* and to find ways of incorporating them into their continually transforming firms. Thus we have not changed our basic messages, nor the tools and diagnostic materials that go along with them. We have, however, refreshed the book by updating many of the cases and even replacing some of them with more current examples.

To make the information accessible, we have continued to organize the book into four parts. Segments devoted to vertical, horizontal, external, and geographic boundaries describe how these barriers both help and hinder organizations and how managers can loosen them or break them down where necessary. Each part contains a pair of chapters, one to explain the boundary in question, and the other to provide specific action levers—the tools and techniques you can use to implement permeable boundaries and overcome the forces resisting the change.

Added to this edition, world-class executives start off each part with personal views of how the opening of boundaries has changed their organizations for the better. These accounts emphasize that creating the boundaryless organization does not happen by itself—it is, and always will be, a function of leadership, and there is no better way to learn about leadership than to listen to those who have struggled with it themselves.

Throughout the text, detailed examples from many organizations show the real difficulties that boundaries cause in today's businesses and the practical solutions that managers and consultants are currently applying. Brief questionnaires help readers evaluate their organizations' own structural boundaries and need and readiness for change. Finally, our concluding chapter is designed to help executives examine the nature of their personal boundaries and identify the specific leadership challenges they will meet as they take their organizations into the twenty-first century.

Is This Book for You?

Organizations of all sizes have boundaries that increase costs, slow production, and stifle innovation, so our model and related tools for loosening and permeating boundaries can be used by executives and managers in large, midsized, or small businesses of all kinds. And since all levels of management affect how organizational boundaries operate, and since those boundaries in turn affect the work of everyone in an organization, managers at any level can apply appropriate selections of the tools we describe.

We realize that changing the nature of organizational boundaries is a challenging task. *The Boundaryless Organization* was written to make that task a little easier.

Acknowledgments

Many contributors helped us transform this book from an embryonic idea to a finished product. First and foremost are the many clients and management colleagues who asked us to work alongside them in breaking down boundaries and who were willing to share their experiences in this book. We are particularly grateful to the four managers who provided first-person accounts of their boundaryless journeys. It is always easier to give advice from the outside, knowing that others have the ultimate responsibility for implementation and for dealing with the consequences. We have immense respect for the organizational pioneers and leaders noted in this book and for the countless other managers who have trusted our ideas and valued our experiments. We have learned much from them. Credit for results is all theirs. Any inaccuracy regarding their stories is our responsibility.

A number of consultant colleagues also helped to make this book possible. In particular, several members of Robert H. Schaffer & Associates provided cases and read drafts of the manuscript, including Keith Michaelson, Suzanne Francis, Harvey Thomson, Matthew McCreight, Robert Neiman, Rudi Siddik, Elaine Mandrish, Richard Bobbe, and Nadim Matta. Matta also created much-appreciated first drafts of several of the self-diagnostic questionnaires. Robert Schaffer provided not only cases but also general wisdom about the persistence needed to complete a book. Katy Paul-Chowdhury and Wes Siegal of RHS&A coordinated much of the editing, new research, and revisions for the second edition. Sumantra Ghoshal, now of the London Business School, offered insights and encouragement during Todd Jick's two years of on-site research and teaching at INSEAD about what globalization really means. Wayne Brockbank and Dale Lake, both at the University of Michigan, and Warren Wilhelm of Global Consulting Alliance also provided invaluable feedback.

Jossey-Bass editor Sarah Polster, who passed away this July after a nine-month battle against cancer, was the first to recognize that the concept of the boundaryless organization could be expanded into a management book. Through many months of rough drafts, she maintained her belief in our ability to create a good book, always reminding us that "there's a book in there somewhere." We hope readers will agree with her assessment. Susan Williams and Byron Schneider provided editorial guidance for the second edition.

To produce the final draft of the original book, we relied heavily on Rick Benzel, our development editor, surrogate writer, and sometime conscience. More times than we care to remember, Rick took our collective thoughts and structured them, helping us convey them clearly and concisely. We owe him an enormous debt of gratitude. Hilary Powers provided similar guidance and support on the second edition.

Emilieanne Koehnlein, administrative assistant at Robert H. Schaffer & Associates, was also critical to our project. She provided word-processing support for both editions of the entire manuscript, pulling together multiple documents in different formats, tracking down all the endnotes, and generally keeping the project together. We could not have completed this book without her. We also wish to acknowledge the contributions of Ginger Bitter, who provides administrative support for Dave Ulrich.

Finally, in any project that requires work beyond the already overstretched boundaries of professional life, families are the real heroes. For all their unconditional support, despite our many missed evenings at home and our weekends away, we wish to acknowledge and thank our wives and children: Barbara, Eli, Shira, Ari, Wendy, Carrie, Monika, Michael, Rose, Zoe, Adina, and DJ.

We promise not to do it to you too many more times without asking.

October 2001

Ron Ashkenas
Stamford, Connecticut

Dave Ulrich
Ann Arbor, Michigan

Todd Jick
Cambridge, Massachusetts

Steve Kerr
New York, New York

The Authors

Ron Ashkenas is the managing partner of Robert H. Schaffer & Associates, a management consulting firm based in Stamford, Connecticut. For many years, Ashkenas and his colleagues have pioneered results-driven approaches to organizational change, using many of the methods described in *The Boundaryless Organization*. His clients have included Motorola, JP Morgan-Chase, Pfizer, Charles Schwab & Co., the World Bank, and many other public and private firms. Ashkenas was among the original group of consultants that designed and implemented GE's Work-Out process, and has consulted with GE for over a decade.

Ashkenas also has worked extensively with corporate staff specialists and internal consultants to help them improve the bottom-line impact of their professional contributions. He has lectured on this subject for the Institute of Management Consultants and has run numerous workshops for corporate staff groups. He has been a member of the New York Human Resource Planners board of directors and currently serves on the editorial board of the *Human Resource Management Journal*.

Prior to joining Schaffer & Associates in 1978, Ashkenas received a B.A. degree (1972) from Wesleyan University, an Ed.M. degree (1974) from Harvard University, and a Ph.D. degree (1979) in organizational behavior from Case Western Reserve University, where he also held several research and teaching assignments. He has published dozens of book chapters and articles on organizational change and improvement and on the dynamics of acquisition integration, as well as *The Boundaryless Organization Field Guide* (Jossey-bass, 1999; coauthored with Urich, Jick, and Paul-Chowdhury). His articles have appeared in the *New York Times* and in such journals as the *Harvard Business Review*, the *National Productivity Review*, *Leader to Leader*, and *Human Resource Management*. Ashkenas can be reached at ron@rhsa.com.

Dave Ulrich is professor of business administration at the University of Michigan, where he is on the core faculty of the Michigan Executive Program and codirector of Michigan's Human Resource Executive Program and Advanced Human Resource Executive Program.

His teaching and research addresses the question of how to create an organization that adds value to employees, customers, and investors. He studies how organizations change fast, build capabilities, learn, remove boundaries, and leverage human resource activities. He has generated multiple award-winning national databases on organizations, assessing alignment between strategies, human resource practices, and HR competencies. He has published over ninety articles and book chapters, along with numerous books, including *Organizational Capability: Competing from the Inside/Out* (with Dale Lake), *Human Resource Champions: The Next Agenda for Adding Value and Delivering Results,* and *Tomorrow's (HR) Management* (with Gerry Lake and Mike Losey).

He currently serves on the editorial boards of four journals, participates in board and advisory work for consulting and professional firms (Herman Miller, McKinsey, Provant, Exult), and is a fellow in the National Academy of Human Resources. He was editor of *Human Resource Management Journal* from 1990 through 1999. Ulrich was co-founder of the Michigan Human Resource Partnership. He has been listed by *Business Week* as one of the world's "top ten educators" in management and the top educator in human resources and by *Forbes* as a leading business coach, and has received professional and lifetime achievement awards from the World Federation of Personnel Management, Society for Human Resource Management, International Association of Corporate and Professional Recruitment, International Personnel Management Association, and Employment Management Association. He has consulted and done research with over half of the Fortune 200.

Ulrich received his B.A. degree (1979) from Brigham Young University and his Ph.D. degree (1982) from the University of California at Los Angeles. He has taught at Brigham Young University, UCLA, and Pepperdine University. Ulrich can be reached at dou@umich.edu.

Todd Jick is a managing partner of the Center for Executive Development. He has been actively involved in executive education and consulting in such areas as leadership, organizational change and transformation, new organizational paradigms, service management, customer-supplier partnerships, and human resource management. He has taught in executive programs at Harvard and INSEAD, and worldwide under the auspices of the Asian Institute of Management, Euroform (Spain), Ambrosetti (Italy), the Australian Institute of Management, and the Jerusalem Institute of Management. He has carried out executive education or consulting at numerous companies such as General Electric, AT&T, IBM, Honeywell, General Motors, and Merck. His European-based clients have included Unilever, Philips, Ciba-Geigy, and Alcatel Bell.

Jick has been published widely. His books include *The Challenge of Organizational Change*, with Rosabeth Moss Kanter and Barry Stein (1992); *Managing Change: Cases and Concepts* (1993); and *Management Live!* with Bob Marx and Peter Frost (1991). He has written more than thirty business school cases. He earned a B.A. degree (1971) in social anthropology from Wesleyan University and M.S. (1976) and Ph.D. (1978) degrees in organizational behavior from Cornell University. He was a professor at the Harvard Business School for ten years and a visiting associate professor, organizational behavior–human resource management, at INSEAD. He also taught at the Columbia University Graduate School of Business and York University in Toronto. His e-mail address is tjick@cedinc.com.

Steve Kerr is chief learning officer and a managing director of Goldman Sachs. Until March 2001 he was vice president of leadership development and chief learning officer for General Electric, including responsibility for GE's renowned leadership education center at Crotonville. He was formerly on the faculties of Ohio State University, the University of Southern California, and the University of Michigan, and was dean of the faculty of the USC business school from 1985 through 1989. He is also a past president of the Academy of Management.

Kerr earned his B.A. degree (1961) from Hunter College and his Ph.D. degree (1973) from the City University of New York. He is the author of dozens of articles and book chapters and two textbooks on organizational behavior. His writings on leadership and "on the folly of rewarding A, while hoping for B" are among the most cited and reprinted in the management sciences. During the last five years he has been the subject of interviews in *Forbes, ASAP, Fortune, Human Resource Executive, Intranet, Investors Business Daily,* the *New York Times, Organizational Dynamics, Knowledge Management, Organization Science,* and the *Wall Street Journal.*

Chapter One

A New World Order

Rising to the Challenge of New Success Factors

A new world order is replacing generations-old patterns of power and privilege. Leaders have been replaced, centers of governance have been renamed, new patterns for distributing wealth and influence have been created. And we're not talking about the demise of the Soviet Union, the construction of the International Space Station, and the end of apartheid in South Africa.

We're talking about business. Twenty-first-century business is in the midst of a social and economic revolution, shifting from rigid to permeable structures and processes and creating something new: the *boundaryless organization*.

Consider these developments, once thought unimaginable and now almost taken for granted:

- GlaxoSmithKline Pharmaceuticals has cut months out of the drug development process by replacing sequential clinical data collection, analysis, and regulatory reporting with cross-functional teams composed of statisticians, biometricians, clinical trials experts, data management experts, and others.
- General Electric managers routinely have fifteen to twenty direct reports. Often, there are no more than three or four layers of management between the CEO and frontline workers in a company of more than 300,000 people.

1

- Fidelity Investments, Charles Schwab, CSFB Direct, and Spear, Leads & Kellogg—brokerage competitors—have formed a joint venture to develop an electronic communications network for trading NASDAQ stocks online.

Business authors have described hundreds of similar innovations, declaring the rise of a "new organization" to which they have given many names: virtual organization, front/back organization, cluster organization, network organization, chaotic organization, ad hoc organization, horizontal organization, empowered organization, high-performing work team organization, process reengineered organization, and the list goes on.

However, underlying all these descriptions, theories, and experiments, we believe, is a single deeper paradigm shift. In our view, that shift—the emergence of the boundaryless organization— is the driving force that makes all these new organizations possible, the underpinning that lets them move from theory to reality. Emerging organizations may take a variety of forms, but the constant is that they evoke different kinds of behavior. Specifically, behavior patterns conditioned by boundaries between levels, functions, and other constructs are replaced by patterns of free movement across those same boundaries. Rather than using boundaries to separate people, tasks, processes, and places, organizations are beginning to focus on how to get through those boundaries—to move ideas, information, decisions, talent, rewards, and actions where they are most needed.

In that context, our purpose here is not to herald yet another new organization. Rather, it is to describe the boundaryless structures behind all the new labels and to lay out their underlying assumptions, the changes in behavior they generate, and the results they can yield. To do this, we delineate four types of boundaries that characterize most organizations.

- *Vertical* boundaries between levels and ranks of people
- *Horizontal* boundaries between functions and disciplines
- *External* boundaries between the organization and its suppliers, customers, and regulators
- *Geographic* boundaries between locations, cultures, and markets

We also describe the leadership challenges that the new structures pose. Most important, we provide leaders with a practical set of tools for moving their own organizations toward useful and practical boundaryless behavior.

Boundaryless Behavior: The Art of the Fluid

Organizations have always had and will continue to have boundaries. People specialize in different tasks, and thus boundaries exist between functions. People have differing levels of authority and influence, so boundaries exist between bosses and subordinates. People inside a firm do different work than suppliers, customers, and other outsiders do, so boundaries exist there as well. And people work in different places, under different conditions, and sometimes in different time zones and cultures, thus creating additional boundaries.

The underlying purpose of all these boundaries is to separate people, processes, and production in healthy and necessary ways. Boundaries keep things focused and distinct. Without them, organizations would be *dis*organized. People would not know what to do. There would be no differentiation of tasks, no coordination of resources and skills, no sense of direction. In essence, the organization would cease to exist.

Given the necessity of boundaries, making a boundaryless organization does not require a free-for-all removal of all boundaries. That would be silly. Instead, we are talking about making boundaries more permeable, allowing greater fluidity of movement throughout the organization. The traditional notion of boundaries as fixed barriers or unyielding separators needs to be replaced by an organic, biological view of boundaries as permeable, flexible, moveable membranes in a living and adapting organism.

In living organisms, membranes exist to provide shape and definition. They have sufficient structural strength to prevent its collapse into an amorphous mass. Yet they are permeable. Food, oxygen, and chemical transmitters flow through them relatively unimpeded so that each part of the organism can contribute to the rest.

So it is with the boundaryless organization. Information, resources, ideas, and energy pass through its membranes quickly and easily so that the organization as a whole functions effectively. Yet definition and distinction still exist—there are still leaders with authority and accountability, there are still people with special functional skills, there are still distinctions between customers and suppliers, and work is still done in different places.

Like a living organism, the boundaryless organization also develops and grows, and the placement of boundaries may shift. Over time, the levels between its top and bottom may decrease, functions may merge to combine skills, or partnerships may form between the firm and its customers or suppliers, changing the boundaries of who does what.

Because the boundaryless organization is a living continuum, not a fixed state, the ongoing management challenge is to find the right balance, to determine how permeable to make boundaries and where to place them. But why should anyone make this effort? What is so important about becoming boundaryless?

A Changing Paradigm for Organizational Success

In recent years, almost all organizations have experimented with some type of change process aimed at creating more permeable boundaries. Whether it was called total quality, reengineering, reinvention, or business process innovation, organizations have invested untold resources in trying to make change happen.

The impetus behind many of these efforts has been the astounding fall from grace, or actual demise, of some of the most highly regarded and revered organizations in the world: IBM, Lloyd's of London, Eastern Airlines, General Motors, Eastman Kodak, and many others. Each experienced severe financial difficulties, crises in leadership, and major changes in direction. Nor is membership in this fallen-angels club limited to a handful of fields. The phenomenon crosses all lines from retail sales to automotive manufacturing, publishing to air travel, financial services to computers. It crosses geographic boundaries, with troubled giants found not only in North America but also in Europe, Asia, and Latin America.

The difficulties in these companies cannot be explained by lack of long-range strategy or intelligent planning. IBM, Kodak, and many of the others had and continue to have world-class planning functions and capabilities. They have not stumbled due to lack of technology or investment. In the past twenty years, GM probably invested more in automation than any other company in the world. IBM's research investment was, for many years, far beyond the business norm.

Naturally, individual explanations can be provided. IBM was too wedded to mainframe computers; TWA was unable to cope with deregulation; Xerox mismanaged the reorganization of its sales force. But such explanations miss the larger pattern. The stark reality is that each company slipped from invincible to vincible when it faced *a rate of change that exceeded its capability to respond.* When their worlds became highly unstable and turbulent, all these organizations lacked the flexibility and agility to act quickly. Their structures and boundaries had become too rigid and calcified.

It is against this backdrop of highly visible failures and falls that most organizations have launched their change efforts. And though each effort has unique characteristics, conditions, and drivers, they tend to share a common theme: the attempt to retool the organization to meet an entirely new set of criteria for success.

Out with the Old—In with the New

For much of the twentieth century, four critical factors influenced organizational success.

- *Size.* The larger a company grew, the more it was able to attain production or service efficiencies, leverage its capital, and put pressure on customers and suppliers.
- *Role clarity.* To get work done efficiently in larger organizations, tasks were divided and subdivided, clear distinctions were made between manager and worker, and levels of authority were spelled out. In well-functioning organizations, everyone had a place, accepted it, and performed according to specifications.
- *Specialization.* As tasks were subdivided, specialties were created or encouraged to provide fine-grained levels of expertise. Thus finance, planning, human resources, information technology, inventory control, and many other tasks all became disciplines in their own right.
- *Control.* With all these specialized tasks and roles, most organizations needed to create controls to make sure the pieces

performed as needed, coming together properly to provide whole products or services. Therefore, a major role of management throughout the twentieth century was to control the work of others to ensure that they were doing the right things, in the right order, at the right time.

With these success factors in mind, managers and organizational theorists focused on organizational structure as their primary vehicle for achieving effectiveness. They debated such questions as these:

- How many layers of management do we need?
- What signing authority will different levels have?
- What is the proper span of control?
- What is the best balance between centralization and decentralization?
- How do we describe and classify each job and set pay levels?
- How do we organize field locations and international operations?

Their goal was to create the organizational structure and attendant processes that would let a company maximize the four critical success factors. What has happened, however, is that microprocessors, high-speed information processing and communications, and the global economy have conspired to radically shift the basis of competitive success. To a large extent, an exclusive focus on the old success factors has become a liability. Instead—as shown in the box—the old success factors need to be combined with a new and sometimes paradoxical set of factors that look very different from the old.

The Shifting Paradigm for Organizational Success

Old Success Factors	*New Success Factors*
Size	Speed
Role clarity	Flexibility
Specialization	Integration
Control	Innovation

- *Speed.* Successful organizations today are increasingly characterized by speed in everything they do. They respond to customers more quickly, bring new products to market faster, and change strategies more rapidly than ever before. While size does not preclude speed, large organizations are like tankers. Compared to smaller firms, they take longer to change direction because they have a greater mass to be informed, convinced, and channeled. Their challenge is to act like a fast-moving small company while retaining access to the large company's broader resources.
- *Flexibility.* Organizations that move quickly are flexible. People do multiple jobs, constantly learn new skills, and willingly shift to different locations and assignments. Similarly, the organization pursues multiple paths and experiments. Role clarity can constrain flexibility—people locked into specific roles and responsibilities become unwilling to jump in at a moment's notice and do whatever is needed. Conversely, flexible organizations revel in ambiguity, throw out job descriptions, and thrive on ad hoc teams that form and reform as tasks shift.
- *Integration.* Organizations adept at shifting direction have processes that carry change into the institutional bloodstream, disseminating new initiatives quickly and mobilizing the right resources to make things happen. Instead of breaking tasks into pieces and assigning specialists to perform those pieces with precision, the organization creates mechanisms to pull together diverse activities as needed. It focuses more on accomplishing business or work processes and less on producing specialized pieces of work that management will eventually pull together. It still needs specialists, but the key to success is often the ability of those same specialists to collaborate with others to create an integrated whole.
- *Innovation.* A world of rapid change makes innovation essential. Doing today's work in today's way becomes outdated quickly, so boundaryless organizations constantly search for the new, the different, the unthinkable. They create innovative processes and environments that encourage and reward creativity, rather than stifling the creative spirit with the systems of approvals and double-checks needed to preserve standard operating procedures in organizations that focus on control.

In short, organizations designed to meet the old set of critical success factors alone are increasingly incapable of thriving or even surviving in the new world. Consider the contrast between retailers Sears and Wal-Mart.

The Giant and the Upstart

Sears, for many years the world's largest retailer, succeeded with a management process based on structure and control. As the company grew, Sears leveraged its buying power through strong centralized functions. Almost all key decisions were made in its Chicago headquarters. The stores mirrored the control philosophy, allotting different levels of approval to various managerial levels, with all really important decisions traveling far up the chain of command. This approach succeeded for many years, as long as size, role clarity, specialization, and control were what drove competitiveness.[1]

Then, in the 1980s, the rules of the retail game changed. Consumers wanted lower prices, better service, and a constantly changing array of merchandise. In this environment, speed mattered more than size. Customers wanted goods on the spot; they weren't willing to place orders and wait. At the same time, flexibility and integration proved able to drive out costs. Successful retailers gave people multiple jobs and designed integrated service functions. Innovation became critical to maintaining the edge in merchandise, service, and store layout.

In this new world, Sears began to slip. At first, management asked the traditional questions, looking to structure for answers and repeatedly restructuring, closing stores, and changing leaders. Nothing worked. It was not until Sears started trying to become a more "customer-focused company" and asked each store to find ways of identifying and serving customer needs that things began to turn around. Once it shifted focus, Sears was able to reduce corporate staff dramatically, moving decision-making responsibility to stores and store managers. The new success factors compelled Sears to redesign itself.

In contrast, upstart Wal-Mart, from the beginning of its existence, focused on the new success factors. Founder Sam Walton's philosophy was to find out what customers wanted and provide it quickly, at lower cost than any competitor. This meant designing fast, flexible processes for gathering and using consumer and competitive intelligence. One such process is the weekly "quick market intelligence" (QMI) exercise that is at the heart of Wal-Mart's success.

QMI works like this: every Monday morning, two hundred or more of Wal-Mart's senior executives and managers leave Bentonville, Arkansas, to visit Wal-Mart stores and competitors in different regions of North America. For three and a half days, they talk to store managers, employees, and customers, learning about what is and is not selling. On Thursday evening, the fleet of Wal-Mart planes returns these executives to Wal-Mart headquarters. On Friday, in what they call the "huddle," they examine the quantitative data (computer-based reports of what is selling) and match the data with their field observations to make decisions about products and promotions. Each Saturday morning, a teleconference shares these ideas with over three thousand stores and gives everyone the game plan for the next week. The cycle time for ideas at Wal-Mart is measured in days, not weeks or months. Boundaries that would have led to committee meetings, task forces, and reporting up the chain of command in the old Sears have been replaced by executives who collect information from the source and act.

Even Wal-Mart store managers can move with speed, flexibility, and creativity. They can set up their own "corners" with merchandise they think will sell to their local customers. If an idea works, it gets a larger test and sometimes expands nationwide. Similarly, managers can make pricing changes on the spot if they think a change is warranted or if a competitor has a lower price. They do not need to call Bentonville for permission.

This kind of speed, flexibility, integration, and innovation has helped Wal-Mart continue to grow and thrive, even during downturns in the retail industry.

Similar contrasts can be made between Microsoft and Digital Equipment (now part of Compaq), between Southwest Airlines and TWA, and between Enron and most public utilities. Organizations preoccupied with the old success factors and the attendant questions about organizational structure are struggling, while those that focus on the new factors for success and the corresponding boundaryless behaviors are poised to win.

Four Boundaries

In their quest to achieve the success factors of the twenty-first century, organizations must confront and reshape the four types of boundaries we mentioned earlier: vertical, horizontal, external, and geographic.

Vertical. Vertical boundaries represent layers within a company. They are the floors and ceilings that differentiate status, authority, and power: span of control, limits of authority, and the other manifestations of hierarchy. In a hierarchy, roles are clearly defined and more authority resides higher up in the organization than lower down. You can track the intensity of vertical bounding by the number of levels between the first-line supervisor and the senior executive and by the differences between levels. Hierarchical boundaries are defined by title, rank, and privilege. The classic example is the military, where clear symbolic and substantive differences exist by rank: officer clubs differ from enlisted clubs, officers have privileges not available to enlisted personnel, generals have more status and staff than colonels, and so on. When rank has its privilege, it is a clear symbol of vertical boundaries.

In contrast, boundaryless organizations focus more on who has useful ideas than on who has authority and rank. Good ideas can come from anyone. These organizations make no attempt to dissolve all vertical boundaries—that would be chaos—but their permeable hierarchies give them faster and better decisions made by more committed individuals.

Horizontal. Horizontal boundaries exist between functions, product lines, or units. If vertical boundaries are floors and ceilings, horizontal boundaries are walls between rooms. Rigid boundaries between functions promote the development of local agendas that may well conflict with each other. In the traditional firm, engineering usually wants to create more innovative products and looks for technologically hot ideas, marketing wants more varied and customized products, and manufacturing wants long, stable production runs with little innovation and few variations. Each of these functional areas then maximizes its own goals to the exclusion of overall organizational goals.

Processes that permeate horizontal boundaries carry ideas, resources, information, and competence with them across functions, so that customer needs are well met. Quality, reengineering, and high-performing work team initiatives often foster such processes. Once managers begin to move work quickly and effectively across functions or product lines, horizontal boundaries become subservient to the integrated, faster-moving business processes.

External. External boundaries are barriers between firms and the outside world—principally suppliers and customers but also government agencies, special interest groups, and communities. Traditional organizations draw clear lines between insiders and outsiders. Some of these barriers are legal, but many are psychological, stemming from varied senses of identity, strategic priorities, and cultures. These differences lead most organizations to some form of we-they relationship with external constituents. Business involves negotiation, haggling, pressure tactics, withholding of information, and the like. When there are multiple customers or suppliers, one may be played off against another.

While external boundaries do provide positive identity for insiders ("I work for X!"), they also diffuse effectiveness. Often, customers could help a firm resolve internal problems—and have a keen interest in solutions. They know the output of the firm and need high-quality products and services. Similarly, suppliers want to see their customers succeed because successful customers buy more. With thinner boundaries between firms and customers and suppliers, the resulting confluence of interests can produce much more efficient operations.

Geographic. Geographic, or global, boundaries exist when firms operate in different markets and countries. Often stemming from national pride, cultural differences, market peculiarities, or worldwide logistics, these boundaries may isolate innovative practices and good ideas, keeping a company from using the learning from specific countries and markets to increase overall success.

With information technology, workforce mobility, and product standardization, global boundaries are quickly disappearing. Traditional work differences in Europe, Asia, and North America are being driven out by the need for more globally integrated products and services. Yet at the same time, firms that succeed across global boundaries respect and value local differences as a source of innovation. Colgate Palmolive, for example, has worked to establish brand equities throughout the world. Its brand of toothpaste and tooth powder, for example, while adapted to local preferences for taste, color, and so on, has become global. Consumers in Europe, Australia, North America, and Asia can recognize the brand and find value in it. Creating global brand equities requires companies to think across global boundaries.

When vertical, horizontal, external, and geographic boundaries are traversable, the organization of the future begins to take shape. When these four boundaries remain rigid and impenetrable—as they so often do today—they create the sluggish response, inflexibility, and slow innovation that cause premier companies to fall.

Permeability in Action

To get an overview of boundaryless behavior, consider the case of GE Capital's private label credit card business, a business whose permeable boundaries have allowed it to continually reinvent itself.

The Turnaround Kids

GE Capital's private label credit card business is composed of two organizations, Card Services (CS) in the U.S. market, and Global Consumer Finance (GCF) outside the United States. Headquartered in Stamford, Connecticut, they provide private label credit card services to retail chains. GCF also provides a variety of consumer lending and banking products. CS and GCF customers include such retail chains as Macy's, Wal-Mart, Harrods, IKEA, and hundreds more.

In both revenue and human capital, CS and GCF are two of GE Capital's largest businesses, employing over twenty thousand people worldwide in a diverse range of functions and disciplines, including systems, telecommunications, customer service, marketing, finance, risk management, and product development. The businesses have state-of-the-art processing centers around the world, providing almost instantaneous customer service to retailers and millions of their cardholders.

Based on year 2000 data, GE Capital is the world's largest provider of private label credit cards. Assets total over $50 billion, and both CS and GCF are among the highest net income generators in GE Company, growing at a double-digit rate each year. In addition, the company continues to expand aggressively, looking for major acquisitions in Europe, Latin America, and the Far East, while continuing to bring on major new customers in the United States.

In short, CS and GCF are enviable, successful businesses—financially sound, providing attractive rates of return, and satisfying their customers while also growing aggressively. And they're both boundaryless organizations. For example, when an associate in any of GCF's thirty-one countries turns on a computer, a "GCF Workplace" screen appears—in one of twenty-five languages. Using this intranet, GCF associates can provide the same kinds of services, using the same measures and tools, with access to the same resources and knowledge banks, from almost anywhere in the world. And if managers or associates in different parts of GCF need to work together, they can take advantage of "Same Time," which allows them to hold meetings while sharing visuals and data in real time across the globe.

Customer service teams in the centers are responsible for credit card approvals, problem resolution, and accounts receivable for a portfolio of stores. In most cases, frontline associates in these teams have the authority and the tools to make decisions on the spot for customers, without having to check with supervisors or managers for approval.

From the standpoint of the credit card holder, these services seem to be provided by the retailer. CS and GCF thus function as invisible partners, responsible for managing the retailer's financial relationship with all credit card holders. In addition, a marketing group also works closely with each retailer to agree on standards to apply to potential cardholders, rates to charge, and marketing programs and promotions to offer.

Seeing this level of success, few remember that in the early 1980s, GE was trying desperately to sell its credit card organization, then named Private Label. It had been in business for fifty years, yet its market share was a mere 3 percent. It was an old, tired business—a mediocre performer in a declining market—and its own strategic planners did not believe it had much of a future. They were convinced that private label credit cards would go the way of the dinosaurs, displaced by universal cards such as Visa, MasterCard, and

American Express. "Why," they reasoned, "would consumers want to carry multiple credit cards when they could carry just one or two? And if that's the case, we don't have a business here!"

So Private Label's outlook was bleak. Holding fast to his pledge to sell off businesses that could not become the number one or two performers in their industries, in 1982 GE's new chairman and CEO Jack Welch put it on the block. Fortunately for GE, potential buyers agreed that Private Label was a dying business. They stayed away. With little choice other than to make the best of it, GE Capital promoted Private Label insider David A. Ekedahl to run the business. His mission: keep it going as long as you can without losing money. Ekedahl did better than that. He created a successful boundaryless corporation that has continued to grow for almost two decades.

Reformulating External Boundaries

Private Label's transformation did not begin with a grand plan. In fact, as Ekedahl describes it, the objective was to keep the wolves at bay by adding new customers. However, Ekedahl and his managers first had to decide who the customers were and how to win their business. That analysis led to an important insight—the company needed to concentrate not just on the consumer (the end user of private label cards) but on the retailer as well. The doom-and-gloom planning assumptions were based on the belief that Private Label's customers were consumers, who would not want to carry multiple cards. But if the first customer was the retailer, maybe there were different needs to be met.

By changing the long-standing external boundary that defined the customer, Ekedahl began a transformation that was to take Private Label light years forward. He realized that fast and flexible processing, at a lower cost than could be provided by universal cards, would be the critical success factor for retailers. If Private Label could get the retailers on board quickly, manage the volume of business efficiently, provide error-free processing, and manage customer databases, it would have tremendous leverage with retailers. And the information about customer buying patterns would then pay off even more in purchasing, promotions, and marketing decisions. But at this time, Private Label's procedures for setting up a new retailer and working with an existing one were all incredibly cumbersome. To achieve fast and flexible processing, another boundary needed to be opened up.

Loosening Horizontal Boundaries

Dave Ekedahl's description of what happened next illustrates how key insights open up the path to the boundaryless organization.

> We had just signed up a new company to do their private label credit cards, and I wanted to go through the process of getting that client on board. I found that in order to do that, I had a lot of people in the room, but none of us had any idea what to do by ourselves. We needed dozens of other people. So I figured if this was what it took to get something done, I might as well organize around these kinds of processes. So we began to recreate our own organization around the major processes that needed to get done rather than just do it ad hoc all the time.

Making organizational structure mirror the way work actually got done, Ekedahl gradually transformed Private Label, leveling horizontal boundaries between systems and other business functions. The change was complex because the systems resources were all part of GE Capital, centralized and well defended by solid functional walls. No systems people were dedicated to Private Label; different resources were brought to bear whenever there was a particular need. Ekedahl was determined to change this functional dynamic.

But by no means was the transition smooth. Early in 1989, Ekedahl tried to bridge the functions by sponsoring a joint conference with the central systems organization. At a rancorous concluding meeting, the systems people complained that they were not consulted soon enough in new customer conversions and were given unrealistic requirements and deadlines. Meanwhile, Ekedahl's marketing people accused the systems professionals of not delivering on their promises. Ekedahl found himself caught in the middle, wanting to create a cross-functional team yet forced to arbitrate between functions with walls too high for collaboration.

Ekedahl did not give up. First, he influenced the head of GE Capital's systems to dedicate a group of professionals to his business. Then he insisted that the systems and marketing people find new ways of working together, and he encouraged them to rethink their basic work processes. Although reluctant, the two groups eventually responded to Ekedahl's continuing pressure.

In 1990, Rich Nastasi, head of the systems group, began to work with the other business functions to cut the time required to bring a new retailer on board. A small cross-functional team mapped the typical process, which was averaging eight weeks. Nastasi then brought together a group of systems, marketing, finance, and customer service people and challenged them to do the job in a matter of days, not weeks. To everyone's amazement, solutions began to emerge: earlier systems involvement in customer negotiations, standardized data collection procedures, ways of training customer personnel to help in the conversion, structured conversion procedures, and technical means of transferring electronic files more quickly.

Over the next few months, as the solutions were implemented, elapsed times began to drop dramatically, to less than a week for all but the largest new customers. Equally significant, the different functions put the solutions in place together. The walls were coming down. Less than a year later, Nastasi and his people were reporting directly to Ekedahl, as full-fledged members of the business team for what was now called Retailer Financial Services (RFS).

Flattening Vertical Boundaries

As RFS organized around key processes, a different organization took shape. Gradually, the company shifted from a centralized model where systems, credit, marketing, and customer service were all run out of Stamford to a hybrid model with both centralized and decentralized processes. The guiding idea was that processes to support specific customers should be managed in the field, close to those customers. Processes requiring consistency and control—financial reporting, credit scoring, systems processing, and telecommunications—should be handled by the head office. Additional head office roles were to facilitate sharing of best practices, movement of key personnel, acquisition of new customers, and allocation of investment resources.

To shift processes to the field, RFS created "regional business centers." Retailer customers in each region looked to the centers for training in systems and procedures, development of mailing and promotional programs, management information, and the whole range of cardholder customer services, both through the mail and on the phone. The centers also managed credit risk—allowing better balance between how much to market and how much risk to allow. The key and single focus of these centers was to help retailer customers become more successful.

Setting up regional centers, however, was expensive. Ekedahl was under pressure to reduce costs by increasing productivity. Although the business was willing to invest in automated dialers and on-line information systems, new technology did not improve productivity enough to pay for the added cost of the centers. This cost-cutting pressure led to a radically new organization. As Ekedahl explains: "We originally came at it from a productivity point of view. We figured maybe we could save costs by not having so many management levels. So we asked a group of our associates how to do this. The exempt and the nonexempt people got together for a week and went way beyond what we had been expecting. They recommended that we organize around teams, with no managers whatsoever. I said, 'what the heck, let's try it,' So we did, starting with one business center in Danbury."

Setting up business centers without hierarchical boundaries was a fundamental revolution. And as in any revolution, there were casualties—managers who couldn't adjust, supervisors who couldn't find a place, and in particular, frontline associates who couldn't handle the increased accountability. For the first few years, several centers suffered high levels of associate turnover. It turned out to be hard to find employees able to function effectively as team players with no supervision and high responsibility. Despite careful screening and orientation, many still opted out after less than a year.

Eventually, through a dialogue helped along by a few outside experts in team processes, a pattern for success emerged. Teams were set up to serve all the needs of one large or several small retailers and the retailers' customers. All team members were cross-trained in all the skills needed for effective service, including handling billing problems and collections, changing credit lines, and changing customer data. The more senior or experienced people (in most cases, former supervisors) became roving trainers, documenters of procedures, and problem solvers.

The payoff from the first boundaryless business center was so great that Ekedahl and his team never seriously considered restoring the traditional vertical organization. Even with the turnover, productivity was still many times greater and overall costs far lower. And the customers loved the service they were now getting from a dedicated team that knew their business, their consumers, and their systems. They began to see the business teams as extensions of their own companies and not just as service providers.

Given this success in existing business centers, Ekedahl decided that all new business centers should be set up in teams from the beginning. Thus when RFS bought the Macy's credit card and servicing portfolio in the early 1990s, the entirely new business center established to handle it was organized without managers from the start.

The Flexibility to Reinvent

By 1995, when Dave Ekedahl retired, RFS was considered a model of a successful, high-performance, boundaryless organization. But RFS was also facing a test of its capacity not just to thrive but to survive—the retail industry was slowing down overall, and RFS's largest customer, Montgomery Ward, was about to go under.

For many years, Wards (as it was called) had an entire RFS division—based in Merriam, Kansas—dedicated to serving its cardholders. By 1998, Wards represented almost 40 percent of RFS's net income. So when Wards began to spiral into decline during a nationwide credit squeeze, RFS's own profitability plummeted. To fix that situation, GE Capital asked Edward Stewart, one of its executive vice presidents, to focus his efforts on restoring RFS to profitability. Stewart found that he had to reinvent the private label business, now called Card Services, all over again.

Obviously, Stewart's first step was to look for a solution to the problems with Wards. By exchanging debt for equity, Stewart helped GE Capital take a controlling interest in Wards and forced a series of moves—first taking the company into bankruptcy, and then bringing it out in a much-reduced form. Unfortunately, even the scaled-down Wards could not survive, and by the year 2000, the painful decision was made to close the doors and liquidate. Fortunately, a series of business plays mitigated the financial consequences of this decision. Stewart was able to strike a deal with Wal-Mart to take on its private label card business and, as part of the deal, flipped all the

Wards cardholders to Wal-Mart. This dramatically reduced the level of credit write-offs, and maintained (and even added to) CS's volume. Stewart also engineered a trade of Bank One's private label business for GE Capital's bankcard business, which also led to some much-needed financial gains. During this period, Stewart also "triaged the entire portfolio" with a more rigorous risk screen, which led to a reduction in nonperforming assets and a scaling down of the entire business.

These financial moves, though, were not enough to restore CS to the needed levels of growth and profitability. In particular, the smaller (though better-performing) portfolio required costs to be reduced dramatically—but in ways that did not diminish customer service or destroy the vitality of the business.

Because CS was already a flexible, boundaryless organization, Stewart was able to take a page out of Ekedahl's book and refocus the organization once again around core processes—but this time to use new technologies as an enabler of productivity.

Throughout most of the 1990s, the old RFS had been a hybrid organization with some centralized functions along with regional units that each managed a separate P&L. At the end of the 1990s, Stewart consolidated all the units into one P&L. He built strong, centralized process organizations for customer service, marketing, and collections, and then closed 40 percent of the existing sites. Within this framework, Stewart asked each of his managers to use Six Sigma quality tools to achieve high levels of performance and service at much reduced costs. He then created a "digital dashboard" on the company intranet to track performance against agreed-upon standards. Down the side of this dashboard is a list of clients; across the top are the performance standards in areas such as computer up time, card authorization speed, call answering times, and so forth. The dashboard pulls data directly from the computer systems and telephone networks and displays it in real time—highlighting any metric that falls outside the variance standard. Functional managers can use it to track their processes; "client leads" can use the very same data to look at the performance for their customer. And associates themselves can look at their own performance and see where they stand and where they need to improve.

To take this streamlining one step further, Stewart began to move whole processes to India, where they could be performed effectively at half the cost. Using telecommunications technology and Internet-based tools, by the beginning of 2001, over a thousand people in India were performing collections and customer service functions for clients in the United States. For the digitally enabled, boundaryless organization, location had become less relevant than customer-focused process efficiency. But the real payoff was a return to profitability and growth.

Crossing Geographic Boundaries

Until 1991, RFS was largely a U.S. business. With the acquisition of the credit card portfolio of Burton—a major U.K. retailer—in 1991, Ekedahl and his team were thrust into global management. At first, the Burton organization was kept intact, reporting to Stamford as one more business center with only a minor exchange of ideas and systems technology. To people in Stamford, Burton was interesting but not critical. That soon changed.

Two factors propelled RFS into a global role. First, the traditional domestic market for growth was clearly full of uncertainties: retailers (such as Wards) were struggling and even going out of business, there was pressure to reduce credit card interest charges, and competitors were introducing new strategies such as co-branded cards. Second, Burton's processing capacity was underused. If RFS took on new portfolios in Europe, the Burton operations center could handle them with little incremental cost. By applying its world-class technology expertise, RFS could have a significant competitive advantage in Europe.

So RFS began an acquisition binge in Europe. In less than two years, it had signed up dozens of new retail customers and purchased whole portfolios from banks and other financial institutions. Suddenly, RFS had a major presence in Europe.

The question was how to manage that new presence. Given its strategic importance, should it be closely managed from Stamford? Or should it be managed locally, from within Europe? Should its procedures and processes mirror the U.S. organization? Or should RFS Europe be allowed to develop its own way of doing things based on what worked in Europe and in each individual country? And how should European and U.S. personnel interact—as representatives of different divisions or as members of a synergistic team? And what would happen if RFS went on beyond Europe?

Early in 1993, Ekedahl appointed Dave Nissen, a seasoned RFS manager who had run both Private Label and the MasterCard program, to oversee the European expansion. Ekedahl hoped that putting someone who was completely familiar with U.S. operations in charge of the European acquisitions would combine the best thinking from the U.S. side with a deeper understanding of what worked in Europe. By the end of 1993, Ekedahl had appointed Nissen to head RFS International. Essentially, Nissen's charge was to create a European version of the RFS domestic operation—a series of regional business centers serving specific clients in their own languages, joined with a central processing facility (Burton) that achieved scale in operations. A small central staff, headquartered in Europe, would provide coordination, technical support, and best practices from both Europe and the United States. Nissen was also to search for acquisitions in other parts of the world.

Growing a business outside the United States, however, is not the same as building a domestic business, and RFS International was split off from RFS in 1994 to form an independent business called Global Consumer Finance. Freed from the U.S. parent, Nissen decided to shift the business model. He could not build enough scale in private label credit cards in any one country, so he diversified the business to include a range of consumer lending products such as personal loans, auto loans, and second mortgages. The myriad regulations meant that in many countries he needed to buy or open local banks to support these products.

With this model, Nissen was able to grow GCF rapidly, not only in Europe but in Asia as well. By encouraging cross-selling across a half-dozen key products, he built volume and scale in each country—and then applied the best process management and technology to make it efficient. But how do you manage across dozens of countries and languages—and thousands of branches—each of which has different regulations, cultures, and business quirks? Without a common framework, Nissen found that his own time was fragmented, and the business was becoming a "tower of Babel."

To overcome this aspect of the geographic boundary, Nissen convened his senior management team at a hotel in Tarrytown,

New York, in early 1999. Together the team developed what came to be known as the "Tarrytown 21"—a set of twenty-one measures that each country in GCF would use to manage the business. As Nissen says, "We had lots of local CEOs running their businesses by gut. We needed to have all of them focusing on the same things. And if they are focusing on those measures, they will be successful. Then I can focus on acquisitions, sharing best practices, and hiring the best talent."

Since 1999, each GCF country manager has implemented the Tarrytown 21, which is now accessible through their intranet, "GCF Workplace." There is also a management rhythm for reviewing this data—all of which is displayed as variations on control charts— each month and quarter. And soon all of the data will be provided in real time through AIM, an automated information management system that will allow managers and associates to see how they did against the key measures every day.

From its beginnings as an offshoot of RFS, GCF has grown into a business almost double the size of its parent—and poised to continue growing around the world.

So, that, in broad outline, is how GE Capital's private label credit card business became a true boundaryless organization, continually inventing new ways to function across all four boundaries with speed, flexibility, integration, and innovation.

Get Ready for Resistance

GE Capital's private label business journeyed successfully from the traditional structure to the boundaryless organization of the twenty-first century. But that journey took more than a decade. At times, it was marked by pain, struggle, and doubt. And any organization that intends to become boundaryless must prepare itself for resistance, both from within and without. The trip is not easy, for many reasons.

To start with, many people find the mere thought of a boundaryless organization terrifying. After all, boundaries *are* organizations; they define what's in and what's out, who controls and who has status. Changing the nature of boundaries is akin to removing your own skin. So people feel threatened at an almost unconscious level.

Some related threats are more consciously felt. For example, much has been written over the years about middle managers' resistance to employee empowerment efforts. In our view, such resistance is entirely rational. After all, in most organizations, the core of the middle-management job has been to maintain the barriers between senior management strategy and workers' implementation of that strategy. In this construction, middle managers have a series of vital roles: translating strategy into specific tasks, sequencing work, establishing measures of progress, controlling resources, and assessing performance. Workers generally do not interact directly with senior management and vice versa, except in ceremonial or other circumspect ways.

When senior managers talk about empowerment, middle managers see their roles as boundary controllers vanishing. If employees can translate senior management strategy into decisions and interact directly with senior managers, what is left for middle managers to do? Some new roles open up for middle managers, but the ratio is not one-to-one—there aren't enough to go around. So the threat middle managers face is not only loss of power but actual loss of jobs.

Such threatened losses exist throughout organizations when barriers become more permeable or are moved. For example:

- Functional specialists may fear losing their technical edge if forced to spend much time as generalists in cross-functional team activities.
- Individuals from different cultures may not want to team with one another or work for one another due to biases and stereotypes and the fears they generate.
- Individuals from different cultures may simply have trouble communicating, due not only to different languages but to different ways of viewing the world.
- People at all levels may fear having to learn new rules of the game if traditional methods of advancement and career tracking change.
- Managers may fear embarrassment if information once typically hidden becomes shared with other levels.
- Former competitors within an organization or between organizations may find it difficult to learn how to collaborate.

In addition, two overriding psychological barriers block acceptance of the boundaryless organization. One function of boundaries is to supply protection, a sense of security. Boundaries resemble the solid walls around your house. If people could not only see through your walls but actually pass through them, your sense of security would vanish.

Boundaries also give people a place to hide. In an organization with permeable boundaries, ineffective performance is highly visible, not just to a few people but to many. This can trigger enormous anxiety, especially in those who feel (as everyone does at times) somewhat unsure about their ability to do a job or learn new skills.

Given these threats to job, status, and security, it is no wonder that attempts to make boundaries more permeable trigger an organization's immune system. All kinds of resistance, overt and covert, begin to emerge.

Several years ago, for example, an executive at what was then the American Can Company decided that the workers in a newly acquired plant should be reshaped into a "high-performance/high-involvement" workforce. Essentially, he wanted to create an organization with much more permeable vertical and horizontal boundaries. To do so, he brought in a new plant manager who believed in empowerment, and as a gesture of goodwill to the workforce, he removed the time cards and put all workers on salary. He then instructed his staff to double the size of the plant, in the belief that this newly motivated workforce would become the core of his most productive machine-building site.

Within days, the forces of resistance went into play. Workers objected strenuously to the removal of time cards, pointing out that they could no longer use overtime to earn extra money. When the new plant manager tried to convince them that the time clocks were removed because he "trusted them," they concluded that the argument was merely camouflage for cutting their pay. While this debate was going on, headquarters staff arrived and began a thorough inventory of machinery and personal tools in preparation for the expansion. The presence of staff people counting their equipment further fueled the workers' mistrust of management. When the new plant manager tried to stop the inventory until he got things sorted out with the workforce, he found himself in a power struggle with the corporate head of facilities and engineering. Eventually, the battle escalated to the executive who had initiated the "model plant," who was shocked to see his experiment founder so quickly. However, before he could resolve the issues between his staff colleagues and his new plant manager, the International Machinists Union instigated an organizing campaign that the corporate human resource function determined to fight.

Within months, what had started out as a promising, well-intentioned experiment meant to serve as a model for the corporation had gone down in flames. The new plant manager was gone, the workforce was alienated from management, and relations between corporate manufacturing and engineering were strained. The vertical and horizontal boundaries, far from becoming more permeable, had been reinforced. The immune system had done its work, surrounding and engulfing the foreign body of change before it could infect the rest of the organization.

The shift to permeability is fraught with such threats, barriers, and resistance. Nonetheless, it is possible to identify and then overcome resistance and make the boundaryless organization a reality.

Making It Happen:
Getting the Most from This Book

Organizations can transform themselves. They can develop more permeable boundaries despite the immune response. And thanks to such pioneer organizations as GE Capital, the transformation no longer has to take a decade or be based on trial and error. Nor does it have to wait until external or environmental crises force the issue. Our accumulated experience in helping dozens of organizations of all types to journey toward boundarylessness has identified effective tools and techniques for change. There are frameworks that can be applied, questions that can be asked, and lessons that can be learned to help managers accelerate their progress toward the boundaryless organization.

The four main parts of this book each focus on one of the four types of organizational boundaries: vertical, horizontal, external, and geographic. Without doubt, much has been written about each of these boundaries individually, and many companies have experienced great success in permeating or loosening one or two of them. But few have been able to put together an entire package, to create permeability across all four boundaries. One of our purposes, then, is to show boundaryless transformation from an integrated perspective, one that deals with all four boundaries, so that leaders can complete their paradigm shift.

At the same time, we have made the practical assumption that different organizations and units within organizations are on different places on the continuum and that different strategies and tactics will be useful to them at different times. Thus we do not advocate a frontal assault on all four boundaries at once, nor do we advocate a particular sequence of assaults. Each organization must determine how far it has gone toward permeating boundaries and assess where greater permeability will make the most impact most quickly. Organizations just setting out on the journey may need to employ strategies very different from those of organizations that have been traveling awhile. Similarly, organizations in different industries or facing different competitive threats may need to move relatively faster or further along the continuum than others.

To help you manage these differences, we provide diagnostic instruments that assess where you are and where you want to be. To start with, your responses to the questionnaire at the end of this chapter will give you an overall picture of where you stand in relation to each boundary and each of the new success factors. More specific questionnaires in each section assess your progress on permeating a particular boundary. In essence, this will allow you to view this book not as a cookbook with a fixed menu but as a self-paced learning guide. Through the self-assessments, you can set the pace, select the boundaries most in need of change in your organization, and determine which actions might be most useful in fostering that change.

Useful as they are, these brief instruments cannot provide a statistically valid measure of boundaryless behavior. In addition, your ratings themselves will be highly subjective, conditioned by your unique perspectives on your organization. A major purpose of each questionnaire is to stimulate discussion with your colleagues, both within your organization and outside it, and to help you select the actions that might do most for you.

A second assumption we make is that creating the boundaryless organization is, at its heart, a leadership challenge. It is more than applying a series of tools and techniques. The transformation of the traditional organization also requires the transformation of the traditional leader. Leaders of a boundaryless organization differ from traditional managers. They spend their time differently; possess a different set of skills, beliefs, and attitudes; judge themselves differently; and view their careers in different ways. Chapter Ten talks about these transformational challenges explicitly, but our assumption throughout is that this shift requires leaders from the CEO to the first-line supervisors to have the fire to make it happen.

A final assumption is that we need to share with you real cases and illustrations of organizations struggling with changes in boundaries. As much as possible, these cases are based on our personal experiences. Whenever we can, we identify companies by name, with the understanding that we are reporting only parts of the overall company experience and that we are doing so through the filter of our own eyes.

As we noted in the Preface, General Electric was the breeding ground for many of our ideas. It is a diverse mixture of separate businesses, each of which is a Fortune 100 company on its own. GE started explicitly on the boundaryless journey in 1988 and is further along than many other organizations, so it is a rich source of learning for others. As Jack Welch stated in his 1993 letter to shareholders: "Boundaryless behavior is the soul of today's GE. . . . People seem compelled to build layers and walls between themselves and others. . . . These walls cramp people, inhibit creativity, waste time, restrict vision, smother dreams, and above all, slow things down. . . . The challenge is to chip away at and eventually break down these walls and barriers, both among ourselves and between ourselves and the outside world."[2]

Our intent is to support organizational leaders as they chip away at their own boundaries—so that more organizations can experience the speed, excitement, and energy of the boundaryless world.

Questionnaire #1 will gauge approximately how far your organization has evolved toward the boundaryless paradigm. More specifically, it will help you determine where you might most profitably concentrate your change efforts.

Questionnaire #1

Stepping Up to the Line: How Boundaryless Is Your Organization?

Instructions: The following sixteen statements describe the behavior of boundaryless organizations. Assess the extent to which each statement characterizes your current organization, circling a number from 1 (not true at all) to 5 (very true).

	Speed	Flexibility	Integration	Innovation	Total Score
Vertical boundary	Most decisions are made on the spot by those closest to the work, and they are acted on in hours rather than weeks. 1 2 3 4 5	Managers at all levels routinely take on frontline responsibilities as well as broad strategic assignments. 1 2 3 4 5	Key problems are tackled by multilevel teams whose members operate with little regard to formal rank in the organization. 1 2 3 4 5	New ideas are screened and decided on without fancy overheads and multiple rounds of approvals. 1 2 3 4 5	
Horizontal boundary	New products or services are getting to market at an increasingly fast pace. 1 2 3 4 5	Resources quickly, frequently, and effortlessly shift between centers of expertise and operating units. 1 2 3 4 5	Routine work gets done through end-to-end process teams; other work is handled by project teams drawn from shared centers of experience. 1 2 3 4 5	Ad hoc teams representing various stakeholders spontaneously form to explore new ideas. 1 2 3 4 5	

External boundary	Customer requests, complaints, and needs are anticipated and responded to in real time. 1 2 3 4 5	Strategic resources and key managers are often "on loan" to customers and suppliers. 1 2 3 4 5	Supplier and customer reps are key players in teams tackling strategic initiatives. 1 2 3 4 5	Suppliers and customers are regular and prolific contributors of new product and process ideas. 1 2 3 4 5
Geographic boundary	Best practices are disseminated and leveraged quickly across country operations. 1 2 3 4 5	Business leaders rotate regularly between country operations. 1 2 3 4 5	There are standard product platforms, common practices, and shared centers of experience across countries. 1 2 3 4 5	New product ideas are evaluated for viability beyond the country where they emerged. 1 2 3 4 5
Total Score				

Questionnaire Scoring

After you have rated each statement, total your scores across the rows and down the columns. Each row and column score should be a number between 4 and 20.

Column scores represent your organization's relative achievement of the new success factors. A score of 12 or less on any one factor suggests significant work may be needed, especially if the factor will be critical in your industry or type of organization. A score of 16 or higher suggests your organization already has achieved significant strength in the factor. It will be important to build on that strength. Overall, your scores can help you and your colleagues begin to think about the overall urgency for change facing your organization.

Row scores represent your organization's relative success at achieving permeability of the four boundaries. Again, a score of 12 or less on any one boundary suggests an opportunity for significant improvement, and a score of 16 or higher probably indicates an area of strength.

Questionnaire Follow-Up

With these scores in hand, you may want to begin your reading with the section on the boundary where you find most urgency or opportunity for change. Or you may want to begin with a section that covers your area of strength to find ways of building on that success.

Though you can certainly complete the questionnaire by yourself, you might find it valuable to ask others in your organization to complete it as well. It can then be the basis of a group discussion that will help you and your team develop a shared view of your organization and a more common understanding of changes that might be needed. Developing this common understanding is, in itself, one step toward becoming a boundaryless organization.

Free Movement Up and Down

Crossing Vertical Boundaries

First Person: **Cesar Guajardo,
General Director, Praxair Mexico**

Praxair Mexico is that country's top producer and distributor of industrial gases. It has three divisions (Industrial Gases, Packaged Gases, Specialty Products) and employs approximately fifteen hundred people in more than a hundred locations throughout Mexico. Since becoming General Director in 1995, Cesar has transformed Praxair Mexico from a traditional hierarchical company with average performance to a high-performing, boundaryless organization. Under his leadership, Praxair Mexico has realized a 17 percent annualized growth rate and a 22 percent annualized improvement in profitability.

Cesar joined Praxair in 1975, working his way up through the management ranks. In 1986, he left to run his own company, where he developed his ideas about how to tap into the potential of employees. He returned to Praxair Mexico to head the Industrial Gases Division in 1994. Following are his reflections on what has been involved in transforming Praxair Mexico:

I strongly believe in people. If you free up people, things can change dramatically. When you create true empowerment, you can improve productivity not by just a percentage but exponentially. That is what happened in Mexico.

When I became head of the company, I knew we had people with a lot of experience—good people who knew the business and knew what to do. But they were waiting for orders. I wanted to change the culture so that they would do what they thought was right for the company without waiting to be told.

In management, we normally want to tell people what to do. That used to be what it meant to be a boss. But now we need to learn how to coach from the bench. The only way for the organization to run faster is to let people go as fast as they want.

To get started, I immediately gave people the responsibility and authority to do what they needed to improve performance in their areas. I did ask them to share large-scale decisions with me. But otherwise, I gave them the authority to make the decisions on their own. I also tried to get committees of two, three, or five persons to share ideas and get points of view. People needed to learn how to encourage other people to learn. Sometimes, I had to let them learn on their own by making mistakes. And at times, I had to support ideas that were not very good at the beginning, but at the end they worked just fine.

When I became general director, we established a vision in those years. Since then, I've kept sharing my vision and giving direction as needed, and I continually encourage people to tell me about their improvement ideas and the things they can do to improve performance. I travel across the country and in every place I stand in front of a group and tell them the same thing: "I want to hear from you about what we can do. We can be the number one country in the entire Praxair Corporation. You tell me what we can do to accomplish our vision. Tell me what we can improve and we will do it." You have to develop a trusting atmosphere between people and the leaders of the organization—that is the most important issue.

Let me give you an example. We used to buy a lot of product from our competitors because our plants weren't producing enough to meet customers' demands. So we went to the manufacturing people and asked them what they could do. They said, "make this and that change and we can be more productive." We told them to go ahead, and that launched a lot of small productivity projects—and started generating a culture where employees told bosses what needed to be done. That let us go from buying three hundred metric tons per month from competitors to selling three hundred metric tons per month to them in less than a year. And all the ideas about how to do this came from employees in the division. Managers just needed to listen. They didn't need to do a big economic analysis.

A critical issue was to make people grow their jobs. I wanted to keep people from being robots. Here's an example from the Cylinder Division. We reduced our turnover—the time it takes cylinders to leave the plant full and come back empty—from seventy days to forty days in one year. Reducing turnover lets us get more use of the assets. So we started by analyzing the data and then we asked our people what we could do. We found that empty cylinders sometimes sat at customer sites for months. We told the salespeople they would get an incentive if they brought the cylinders back into use sooner. Up until then they focused only on sales of cubic meters, never on cylinder turnover and asset management and pricing and services—and making money. When we focused on making money, we got focused on costs, expenses, accounts receivable, and cylinder turnover.

In essence, we turned salespeople into businesspeople. Everyone has to think about making the business more effective, not just the managers. It doesn't really matter where you sit in the company—sales, HR, finance. You are not there just to do a functional job, but to help make money. This is what I call a boundaryless organization.

The key question was how to get people involved in their jobs. If they are not motivated, then they just wait to go home at the end of the day. That's why I engage them in projects, and in realizing the vision of making Praxair Mexico the number one country in the corporation. We had to get them alive again. I believed they had the potential to do it, they just needed to be energized.

For a lot of people in Praxair Mexico, and in Mexico overall, this is radical thinking. But it was common sense for me. When I was out there running my own business, I realized that I was responsible for the sales, receivables, accounting, tax, everything. The problem was how to make it run properly when we got bigger. It's harder when the responsibilities are split between different people. People with big egos don't want to share information or even know how things work elsewhere. So to overcome this, we have to work to change attitudes and have good, candid discussion.

With this in mind, when I came back to Praxair, I knew I needed to select good leaders for my team—self-secure people who are not afraid to accept mistakes. Good leaders are honest and tell the truth. They respect others and recognize the efforts of others.

Good leaders work together for the good of the overall business and are not afraid to contain their own egos. To cascade this spirit throughout the organization, everyone needs to see the top leaders collaborate. But when I arrived, too often the top people wouldn't share information; they were enemies. And consequently, there was no cross-selling of products, no sharing of assets, and little efficiency across the country. When the top group didn't work together well, it was no wonder the rest of the organization also didn't.

It was only when we could get leadership at the top to share and work together that the changes really cascaded throughout the organization. But this was not an easy process. When I started as General Director, I had twelve direct reports. Some of them were more concerned with their status, cars, stock options, and egos than with the performance of the business. But I only had to relieve one of them. By making it clear what was expected, I inspired five others to leave on their own over the next two years.

I decided not to replace them. Instead, each of the remaining senior leaders has a broader scope of responsibility, in addition to the challenge of working as a team. And this has worked beautifully. For example, instead of four regions for cylinders, we now have someone who oversees the entire business and can make sure that customers get products from the closest plant. Before, in the fragmented organization, a customer might have to wait for products that were coming from four hundred miles away even though there was a much closer plant in a different region. In other words, we operated like four companies instead of one. Similarly, we probably reduced our truck fleet by half by sharing trucks across divisions. Now we see each other as partners instead of competitors—we have been erasing the boundaries as much as we could. Obviously, there is a lot more that can be done.

To summarize, I draw two lessons from this experience: First is to give power to the people. Empower them to do the job they were hired to do. Second, erase all the boundaries in the organization. They divide people and get in the way of having a great company. But all this must be done through good leaders who also are humble. As leaders, we are here to serve our people—not to be served by them.

| Toward a Healthy Hierarchy

Like Napoleon's troops keeping busy in Egypt by shooting at the Sphinx, modern organizational critics have found the concept of hierarchy an easy target. Hierarchies have been blamed for all manner of organizational ills—slow decision making, isolation from customers, inequality in compensation, and more. Yet despite the barrage of criticism, hierarchies, like the Sphinx, endure.

We have no wish to add to the chorus proclaiming that hierarchical organizations are outmoded or dangerous or ineffective. On the contrary, we see hierarchies as necessary, inevitable, and desirable fixtures of organizational life. As long as resources are limited and perspectives differ, organizations will need some people to be leaders and make decisions for others. So our goal is not to persuade you to eliminate hierarchies but to show you how to make them work in a boundaryless world.

The Persistent Vertical Organization

Like multistory buildings, organizations are commonly thought of first and foremost as vertical structures. Managers are at the top and workers are at the bottom. Orders flow down the chain of command, and production takes place below. At the top is the head, and at the bottom are the hands. In between are multiple layers that translate orders, provide materials, measure output, make corrections, and report to the top on the final results.

This is an oversimplified, inaccurate picture of organizational life, yet it is what most people imagine when they hear the word *organization,* and it is reinforced by the language everyone uses to describe organizations and their dynamics. *Headquarters* implies that the central office houses the brains of the organization. *Managers* and *workers* suggest that management and work are different things, and *exempt* and *nonexempt* suggest that workers themselves fall into scaled categories. *Rolling up the numbers* indicates a belief that results need to be aggregated to be useful for those "at the top." *Superiors* and *subordinates* suggest that some people are of higher status or better than others, and *career ladders* evokes a picture of successful careers as moving upward from rung to rung.

People think of organizations in vertical terms because the concept of hierarchy (of an up-down arrangement) is an archetype, a first principle that underlies the way they think about the world. It is an almost unconscious sense of how things should be, perhaps stemming from the fact that family life is, at least temporarily, a hierarchy. Infants begin life helpless and dependent upon their parents. Parents have total authority and responsibility; they control information, make decisions, and direct their children's actions. It is a natural order that makes survival and growth possible. As families grow, members' experience with hierarchies expands. Older siblings are given authority over younger ones; in some extended families, grandparents or older relatives provide another layer of deference and are given the status of patriarch or matriarch.

A Structure That Works

Given the biological underpinning of hierarchy, it is no wonder that vertical organizations are so prevalent. It is difficult to find any organization with no trace of a structure in which some people have more authority than others to make decisions and set direction, some people direct others in how to do work, and rewards are based not only on contribution but also on vertical position.

Hierarchical organization is not only natural, it is also an effective tool for getting things done. One of the earliest instances of management consulting—in the Bible—recommended it: Jethro, Moses' father-in-law, suggested that Moses set up a hierarchy of judges to govern the children of Israel in the wilderness.[1] Most religions, both Eastern and Western, employ some form of vertical structure, with high priest, acolytes, attendants, and followers. Military organizations have long structured themselves with levels of power cascading down from generals through the ranks to privates.

And almost all governments have relied on elected, appointed, or self-appointed rulers to provide leadership and direction through layers of officials and followers.

Basic work units have been hierarchically organized for thousands of years, often using slave or conscript labor supervised by taskmasters and "owners." Skilled workers also organized themselves into hierarchical structures of apprentices, journeymen, and master craftsmen.

Given this long history, the industrialists of the early twentieth century clearly didn't invent hierarchy. They did, however, raise it to new levels. Frederick Taylor's time and motion studies and his development of the field of industrial engineering provided tools for harnessing newfound technology and organizing to maximize its impact. By breaking work into small components and creating controls to integrate the components "up the line," scientific management led to amazing gains in efficiency. In many cases, it did not just double or triple production but obtained tens or hundreds of times greater output.

The implementation of these concepts by industrialists such as Henry Ford, Andrew Carnegie, and John D. Rockefeller took the industrial revolution to new heights. The ability to manage mass production and distribution of goods and services by building huge hierarchical organizations fueled an unprecedented period of worldwide economic growth and a rise in standards of living far beyond what had ever been achieved before.

Equally important, the application of scientific thinking to vertical organizations led to the evolution of a management morality and the gradual reduction of personal abuse, nepotism, and corruption. Rules of behavior, legal mechanisms for the protection of workers, and workers' unions to counter the power of senior management all became commonplace. In short, the modern hierarchy was an unqualified success.

But Continuing Criticism, Too

Despite hierarchies' effectiveness, they have always been subjects of criticism and intense debate. Frederick Taylor himself appeared before congressional committees to explain scientific management to skeptical lawmakers who were concerned that too much power would be concentrated in the hands of industrial barons. In 1905, a prominent industrial engineer named H. Fitz John Porter wrote passionately that effective organizations needed collaboration between managers and workers and needed to incorporate workers' ideas into managerial direction—the opposite of Taylor's view. Taylor's studies led him to believe that workers should take no initiative but just do their jobs the scientifically proven one best way. Porter's observations were decidedly different:

> I have never failed to see a marked change come over the entire organization . . . as soon as the members felt they were accorded recognition as rational beings and to be consulted on matters of common interest. Generally, the rank and file of the working organization is considered in the same category as privates in an army; they are not supposed to think, but to do as someone above them has planned. The usual result, as might be expected, is that they do not use their brains for the benefit of the concern. . . . The operative, if encouraged to think, will soon effect great savings in the work at which he is more of an expert than anyone else who is not constantly engaged at it.[2]

The "industrial democracy" movement of the 1920s called for worker committees and councils and even worker representation on boards of directors. In a 1923 government report, eighty firms were cited as having formal mechanisms for management and employees to participate in decisions.[3] Even President Woodrow Wilson supported the concept, saying, "the genuine democratization of industry [is] based upon a full recognition of the right of those who work, in whatever rank, to participate in some organic way in every decision which directly affects their welfare or the part they are to play in industry."[4]

In the 1930s, the now famous Hawthorne experiments, led by Harvard professor Elton Mayo at the Chicago Hawthorne Plant of Western Electric, proved that workers' productivity increased dramatically when management paid attention to them and did not treat them like cogs in a machine.[5] But the Depression and the subsequent world war distracted most mainstream Western management from Mayo's findings. Instead, the strict vertical hierarchy prevailed as organizations focused on maximizing production through massive assembly lines and top-down direction.

After World War II, criticism of vertical hierarchies resurfaced as people began to look beyond production to quality of life and the ability of workers to feel greater personal fulfillment on the job. The clearest expression of this movement was voiced by Douglas McGregor, the MIT professor who made the now classic differentiation between Theory X and Theory Y. Theory X, of course, was management through the traditional vertical hierarchy with power concentrated at the top. It was based on the assumption that average people worked as little as possible and were mostly concerned with their own well-being. Therefore, the job of management was to counter these tendencies with clear direction and firm control. Theory Y was a much more benign system in which managers consulted workers and took their views and needs into consideration. It was based on the assumption that people want to do a good job both for themselves and for their organizations. In other words, Theory Y offered a much more permeable structure than Theory X. Ideas, information, and even rewards flowed more freely up and down the organization. McGregor viewed the more permeable organization as far more conducive both to productivity and to employee satisfaction, and he declared that "the essential task of management is to arrange organizational conditions and methods of operation so that people can achieve their own goals best by directing their own efforts toward organizational objectives. This is a process primarily of creating opportunities, releasing potential, removing obstacles, encouraging growth, providing guidance."[6]

McGregor and other human relations theorists received a great deal of attention, but the basic vertical structure of most organizations remained unchanged—largely because it continued to work. After McGregor, an almost unrelenting chorus continued to rail against the evils of hierarchy: the pecking order of positions, titles, and reporting relationships based on rank rather than on competence; the internal competition for power, influence, and rewards; the slow pace of decision making; the senior management out of touch with day-to-day happenings in the field; the focus on internal issues and requirements rather than customer needs.

In response to these criticisms, countless programs have taken aim at vertical boundaries and hierarchical distinctions in organizations. Every generation trumpets anew the discovery that a magical alternative is just around the corner. Compare these two declarations:

There are at lease four relevant threats to bureaucracy: (1) rapid and unexpected change; (2) growth in size; and (3) complexity of modern technology. . . . A fourth factor is a new concept of power, based on collaboration and reason, which replaces a model of power based on coercion and threat.

As the power of position continues to erode, corporate leaders are going to resemble not so much captains of ships as candidates running for office. . . . Call it whatever you like: Post-heroic leadership, servant leadership, distributed leadership or, to suggest a tag, virtual leadership. . . . It's real, it's radical, and it's challenging the very definition of corporate leadership.

The first statement was written in the mid-sixties by well-known professor of organizational development Warren Bennis.[7] The second statement, predicting the very same demise of hierarchical leadership, appeared in *Fortune* magazine in 1994—almost thirty years later.[8]

Yet hierarchical organizations persist. All the predictions of their death have not come close to realization. And as long as hierarchies have their roots in family life, form the basis of most human social structures, and continue to work, they will have immense staying power. We suggest it is time to stop trying to eliminate them or pretend they will somehow go away. Instead, we propose asking a new question about them.

Reframing the Debate

In our view, the question that should concern companies today is not how to eliminate hierarchies but how to have healthy hierarchies, structures that meet the success requirements of organizations for the twenty-first century: speed, flexibility, innovation, and integration.

Most organizations have hierarchies designed around the old success factors: size, role clarity, specialization, and control. These hierarchies have become dysfunctional in a world of exponentially accelerating rates of change. For example, few people realize that the first developers of the personal computer were not Apple's Steve Jobs and Steve Wozniak but researchers at Xerox PARC, who developed their PC, the Alto, in 1973—a full three years before Apple's first product. They were unable, however, to sell their idea up the chain of command. Since their idea was not about copiers, the company's mainstream product, it received little attention and funding. Frustrated by the vertical barriers, many of the key developers left Xerox, taking their technology with them. Some joined the less hierarchical start-up company that became Apple.[9]

Warning Signs in Unhealthy Hierarchies

Most organizations, large and small, have similar stories of innovation or change slowed down by too many approvals, of wrong decisions made for lack of information known at lower levels, of well-meaning and motivated employees disheartened by silence from superiors, or of personal incentives not aligned with the organization's goals. All these situations are warning signs, red flags signaling dysfunctional hierarchies. Here are other warning signs:

Slow response time. When an organization takes too long to make decisions, respond to customer requests, or react to changes in market conditions, it is signaling its dysfunctional hierarchy. For example, one quasi-governmental development bank had dozens of review points in its core lending process, each generating mounds of paperwork. The result was a process so cumbersome that the bank could not lend out all the money it had available for certain country development projects.

Rigidity toward change. When organizations insist "we've always done it this way," or spend more effort finding ways not to change than on changing, their vertical boundaries have probably become calcified. This happened in a large pharmaceutical company. Facing new competitive and regulatory threats, senior management decided to focus research on a limited number of disease categories where chances of success were greatest—a radical shift for a company where research funding had been almost unlimited. For months after that decision was made, however, more energy went into justifying existing research than into pursuing the new categories.

Underground activity. Another sure sign of a dysfunctional hierarchy is that creativity and innovation are driven underground. For example, although one large financial organization stressed innovation, very few requests for funding of new projects came to the senior management group. When asked why, middle managers said the only way to get things done was to keep new ideas "under the radar screen" until they were fully formed.

Internal frustration. Yet another sure sign of a dysfunctional hierarchy is that employees and managers feel dissatisfied with the organization, the way it works, and the way it treats them. Often, this indicates that people are not being listened to. In severe cases, it also can suggest that people do not feel a sense of equity in such areas as pay, promotions, and recognition. They're often correct in this, as in a large insurance company with unexpectedly high turnover of talented women middle managers. In interviews, it came out that many middle-management women perceived that men in comparable jobs were paid more and had greater opportunities for promotion. When the human resource manager ran the numbers, he found this perception was borne out, to the great surprise of the male-dominated management team.

Customer alienation. A final warning sign is that customers feel frustrated and angry. The warning is especially acute when customers feel they are not listened to. Often, it is sales and service people who catch the brunt of this dissatisfaction when they are unable to respond immediately because they have to kick customer complaints and special requests up the line. For example, a specialty chemicals manufacturer shared the customer service people of a sister commodity chemicals group. Service people had strict instructions to respond only to requests for information about orders or to accept routine sales information, a system that was perfectly appropriate for a cost-driven commodity business. For the specialty business, however, the system was a disaster. Anything out of the ordinary—and in specialty chemicals almost everything is out of the ordinary—required a second, third, or fourth call to a more senior person who could expedite an order or put in a special request. Naturally, customer response time was poor, morale among the customer service people was low, and the overall growth of the business was severely constrained.

Acting on the Warning Signs: Four Leverage Points

The red flags described here usually indicate that an organization's vertical boundaries are too tight. But what to do about it is a judgment call that depends on the immediate situation—loosening vertical boundaries is a continuum, not an on/off duality. Gary Wendt, former CEO of GE Capital, drove home this point during a discussion of the approval cycle for a certain type of deal: "We can speed up the cycle by not having an approval process—just let each person approve his or her own deals. But that would give us an unacceptable degree of risk. What we need to do is find the right balance so that we can approve deals quickly but still feel confident that we've looked at all the different angles."

Finding the right balance of freedom and control is a central task of leadership in the boundaryless organization. Moreover, the balance must be struck on multiple dimensions. Think of adjusting the various switches to select the right levels of bass and treble for each kind of music you play. Similarly, in adjusting vertical boundaries, leaders will move switches from controlled to loose on four critical dimensions:[10]

- *Information* moves from closely held or integrated at the top to open sharing throughout the organization.
- *Competence* moves from leadership skills exercised at senior levels and technical skills exercised at lower levels to competencies distributed through all levels.
- *Authority* moves from decisions concentrated at the top to decisions made all along the line, at whatever points are appropriate.
- *Rewards* move from position-based to accomplishment-based.

Information: How Much Should Be Shared?

In a traditional hierarchy, information filters up the organization to those in power. Only at the top of the pyramid is information from lower levels collated, analyzed, and interpreted. Senior managers stay senior because they are the only ones with complete information, and that information gives them power. In the extreme case, the system resembles a spy network in that no one but the topmost manager knows all the sources of information and can put all the pieces together. As in secret government projects, each lower-level person works in a separate area, unaware of others' areas or the end product.

The traditional process is most effective for extremely confidential or sensitive issues. For example, planning a major acquisition, merger, or stock offering or determining a significant personnel or organizational change often requires a closed, centralized, and highly controlled flow of information to promote an effective result or prevent harmful speculation. Day-to-day business, however, can grind to a near standstill if all information is treated as confidential.

In a hierarchy with permeable vertical boundaries, data and ideas are shared widely throughout the organization. This shared information helps all employees gain a common sense of purpose and an understanding of organizational goals. They are therefore more accepting of organizational directives. Understanding the *why*, they are more likely to accept the *what*. Shared information makes the boundaryless hierarchy like a hologram in that every part of it has all the attributes of the whole. Each employee or team can set goals consistent with the organization's goals.

Competencies: Who Has Skills and Ability?

In traditional hierarchies, the leadership competencies of knowledge, skill, and ability reside at the top, and it is assumed that the leaders have the know-how to create a competitive corporation. At lower levels, people have narrower technical skills, mostly directed to producing products or services. The implicit boundary assumption is that every player in the hierarchy has a clearly defined role and that senior managers are orchestrators of the multiple roles.

In hierarchies with loose boundaries, competencies reside throughout the organization. Regardless of title or position, the people with the skills to do a job are encouraged to pitch in and do it. No one can say, "It's not my job." Thus, ability to act comes from skill, not just position, and actions are taken by trained and talented individuals wherever they sit. People's competencies are also reinforced through training at all levels. Contrast this with the findings of Lee Dyer and his colleagues at Cornell that 80 percent of the training budget in traditional organizations went to middle and senior managers and just 20 percent to lower-level employees.[11]

In boundaryless hierarchies, training is not only given across all levels of the organization but focused on similar things across levels. Traditional organizations give lower-level employees skills training while senior employees receive strategic education, but boundaryless organizations offer all employees similar strategic education. For example, training courses for new professional hires at General Electric examine career development and what it takes to succeed at GE. However, in the same course, senior managers are invited to talk about business conditions and business strategies. The reasoning is that all employees, even new ones, need a shared view of what it takes for GE to succeed.

Gaining competence throughout an organization results from more than training; it also comes from changes in staffing and recruiting philosophy. Rather than viewing employees as cogs that can be repaired or replaced, the organization with loosened vertical boundaries sees the workforce as the engine that drives the firm—perhaps the single most significant asset the company holds. Thinking about employees as long-term investments or capital assets forces firms to think about hiring practices, job rotation programs, developmental assignments, performance management, and a host of other HR practices in a new light. In essence, the aim is to establish higher performance standards and then do everything possible to build capability, commitment, and retention among those who meet those standards.

This does not mean that traditional organizations do not have competent people. They do, but they deploy them differently. Consider the contrast between a symphony orchestra and a jazz band. In the orchestra, all the musicians are talented. Each is expert in one instrument, and the conductor makes sure they all interpret the music in the same way. The orchestra succeeds when competencies are integrated and coordinated. The jazz band also has talented individuals expert in playing their instruments. But coordination is shared among band members rather than assigned to a conductor. A jazz band is a boundaryless organization, with the musicians individually internalizing the feeling and mood of the music and then harmonizing their instruments with one another.

It doesn't matter whether one prefers classical music or jazz. The point is that a classical orchestra requires a predefined and fixed score, with room for improvisation or change only in prearranged solos, while a jazz band requires people who can blend their talents without a fixed score. For most modern organizations, the world of fixed scores is gone. Constant improvisation is the rule, not the exception, in today's rapidly changing environment.

Improvisation requires both independent judgment and a range of competencies. That is another reason to diffuse all kinds of competency throughout an organization. As the demand for speed increases, more decisions need to be made on the spot rather than through a hierarchy. Customers are rarely willing to wait for a problem to be resolved, a price to be quoted, an inquiry to be answered. They expect to deal with competent, empowered employees on the front line.

Authority: Who Decides What?

Traditional hierarchies make decisions at the top and draw clear lines to prescribe limits of signing authority and approvals. Senior levels make decisions because the information and competencies needed for successful choices of action have been restricted to these levels.

Boundaryless hierarchies leave decisions to the person closest to the issue, the one who has to live with the consequences of the decision. Authority is less a function of position or title and more a function of information and competence. As decision making moves down the organization, the distance between decision and implementation is shortened.

The traditional rationale for centralized decision making was that the higher the number of individuals reviewing a decision, the higher the quality of that decision. This was the logic behind one case we found, where sixteen signatures were required for approval of a project. (The seniormost manager even complained that there was no room left on the paper for his name.) In reality, when too many signatures are required, decision quality actually drops. The first few reviewers tend to sign off casually, assuming that later ones, having more authority and insight, will do the requisite serious analysis. However, if the project is approved by many lower-level managers, the senior managers assume that those closer to the work have checked the details. So they sign perfunctorily, too. In the end, the project may never receive thorough analysis because no one owns the decision. All the sign-off process has produced is wasted time. In one small study, we found that each approval signature took an average of five working days. So a sixteen-signature approval might take four months to come up with a poorer decision than three or four reviewers could have reached in less than three weeks.

Moving decision-making authority down the organization requires trust that employees at lower levels will make accurate, well-informed decisions. This trust is directly linked to the loosening of boundaries surrounding competence and information. Employees are more trustworthy when they have accurate information and are competent to make decisions.

Sometimes people inadvertently let decision making creep upward. When a senior executive talks about a program or policy, others tend to assume that such talk equals a decision. A costly example of this occurred at Cummins Engine in the late 1960s. J. Irwin Miller—the chairman—was also known to be a shareholder in a truck company that bought engines from Cummins. Miller once looked over a mock-up of an ad with pictures of trucks that had Cummins engines but were made by a different truck company. He approved the campaign but wrote in the margin, "Why this truck?" At considerable cost, all the ads were rephotographed using politically correct trucks. Miller later ruefully remarked, "I was just asking."

Rewards: Do Incentives Match Goals?

Traditional hierarchies carefully scale rewards by vertical position. In essence, such organizations pay jobs rather than people, typically assigning points to jobs on an evaluation plan that emphasizes such factors as span of control, budgetary authority, and scope of responsibility. This plan leads to much higher pay for senior managers than for entry-level employees. In recent years, a number of studies have compared compensation of CEOs to that of new hires or to median pay rates within a firm. Most of these studies found huge differences, with pay ratios of several hundred to one not uncommon. A few critics of these studies have pointed out that they deal with a relatively small number of highly visible corporate giants and that the situation is much less severe in firms with sales between one-half and one billion dollars.[12] Nevertheless, nearly all studies have concluded that the ratio of CEO to low-level employee compensation continues to grow in the United States, and that the gap is growing in Europe and Japan, too.

But that is only the perceived tip of the actual iceberg. In addition, high-level people receive other benefits: first-class or company plane travel, deferred compensation and stock options, use of company cars and preferred parking spaces, meetings in five-star resorts, larger offices, better furniture, higher-caliber secretarial support, and more. So there is no real incentive to become the best programmer, financial analyst, or production worker. The incentive is to get the next job up. When rewards are based on position, they send the message that what counts is vertical advancement up the hierarchy.

When rewards exist to recognize and encourage superior performance regardless of level, boundaries loosen and the hierarchy's health improves. People in healthy hierarchies are still motivated by money or power, but they can earn those rewards by being high performers and by managing important processes effectively. They can benefit from staying in one job and doing it well. They do not feel compelled to get promoted or moved, often to something they may do less competently.

The desire to move up in traditional hierarchies often gets in the way of healthy organizational functioning. For example, a large insurance company once promoted one of its best claims examiners to supervisor. Basically an introvert who enjoyed detailed paperwork and fact-based phone calls, this person did not relish dealing with people face to face. But the claims supervisor role required direct interaction with other claims examiners, extensive discussions with irate customers, and presentations to senior management. These were areas where no amount of training would create comfort. As a result, the new supervisor gave customers short shrift and ignored the need to coach the staff, and the overall performance of the claims processing area suffered. The company had lost one of its best claims examiners and gained a terrible supervisor.

To an outsider, this kind of Peter principle promotion makes little sense. But if a corporation ties rewards to vertical position, then the promotion of people ill-suited to their new jobs is almost inevitable. In a traditional organization, how could an excellent worker be rewarded other than by a move into supervision? Without a promotion to recognize fine work, even a happy introvert is likely to become embittered, start to perform poorly, and even leave, requiring the company to spend money recruiting and training someone else. To further the dilemma, if such a company does promote someone who would do a very good job as a supervisor but has not earned the promotion by high performance in hands-on work, the resulting perception of inequity would probably undercut morale and performance in the whole unit. And this phenomenon of inappropriate promotion occurs at all levels, up to and including that of CEO—it's far from limited to frontline workers and their supervisors.

Organizations' need for an alternative is growing exponentially. Delayered and downsized organizations have far fewer promotion opportunities than their predecessors. At the same time, the population looking for promotion is soaring—as they reach middle age, many baby boomers feel frustrated as they compete for ever-smaller numbers of executive slots.

To create healthy hierarchies, organizations must change the basis of their rewards. In the boundaryless organization, rewards have two objectives: to recognize past performance and to stimulate competent (or different) performance in the future. These objectives change the logic. Rather than paying jobs and motivating people to get the next job up, boundaryless organizations pay people for expanding their capabilities so as to make the maximum contribution to the organization. People who make a good contribution and add to their skills are rewarded; people who do not make a sufficient contribution and do not advance in competence are either not rewarded or rewarded to a much lesser degree than others.

With pay systems that reward added skills and tie pay closely to performance, healthy hierarchies have more than superficial distinctions between high- and low-performing individuals. In addition, healthy hierarchies continue to reward people who remain in productive jobs as long as they continue to grow and contribute. No one needs to become a supervisor or manager or to take on any other unwelcome role simply to get more pay.

The classic example of an organization in which employees succeed by being high performers rather than ladder-climbers is the university. Educators come into the university as assistant professors and may receive one or two promotions during an entire career. Their rewards are tied to instructional quality as indicated by student evaluations or teaching awards, quality and quantity of research and publications, and election to professional associations, not to moving along to more senior positions. Nor is title or rank singularly important. At most universities, every instructor, whether a junior or senior faculty member, is referred to as "professor."

Sticky Switches: Myths About Creating a Healthy Hierarchy

Even though there are only four principal switches that can be moved to shift an organization toward a healthy hierarchy, calibrating these switches is complex—especially when the environment is constantly changing. Not only does each dimension need to be aligned properly with varying business and competitive needs, the dimensions must also be coordinated with one another.

Yet many organizations ignore the complexity and attack hierarchical dysfunctions unsuccessfully through simplistic or unidimensional means. We've observed seven common myths about ways to permeate vertical boundaries and create healthy hierarchies.

Myth 1: Delayering creates healthy hierarchies. Many firms have downsized and claimed to have vanquished vertical boundaries. This is like cutting back on football scholarships and then claiming you have changed the game. Limiting the number of scholarships limits the number of players, but it does not ensure that the game is played differently. Similarly, removing layers does not mean that vertical boundaries are loosened and that information, competence, decision making, and rewards are now spread through lower levels of the organization.

Many prominent companies fell prey to this myth during the last twenty years, thinking that flattening their hierarchies would automatically change their organizational dynamics. It just isn't so. One of the most dramatic examples of acting on this myth occurred when GE Lighting acquired Hungary's Tungsram Ltd., Eastern Europe's largest lighting company, in 1989. After forty years of control by a government that guaranteed full employment, Tungsram was heavily overstaffed. When GE began removing layers of management, laying off thousands of people, it found that the old habits remained. Tungsram had fewer layers, but much more was needed to make its hierarchy healthy.

Myth 2: Training creates healthy hierarchies. Some organizations spend enormous amounts training all employees. As a result, employees are more competent, but if they cannot apply that competence, they are not operating in a more effective hierarchy. Acquiring competence and using it are two separate matters. If employees want to act and are trained to act but then are not allowed to act—to make decisions with good information—they become frustrated.

This happened at Chase Manhattan Bank (now JP Morgan-Chase) in the mid-1980s. The bank's vice chairman realized that traditional corporate lending was becoming less profitable and that the bank needed to shift from standard commercial banking products such as loans to more sophisticated investment banking products such as trading, advisory services, and financial engineering. To accelerate this change, he insisted that every corporate lending professional go through a required curriculum on various investment banking subjects. After spending millions of dollars on this training, the bank had lots of relationship managers who understood investment banking products. Unfortunately, it also had an information system that couldn't support the new products, a measurement and reward system geared to corporate lending, and a decision-making process that evaluated deals using commercial credit-risk parameters. In short, Chase bankers were all dressed up with nowhere to go. It was not for another five years that changes on many of the other dimensions needed for Chase to succeed in the investment banking markets were put in place.

Myth 3: Shared decision making creates healthy hierarchies. One of the most widely used levers for organizational change is moving decision making to lower levels on the assumption that employees will automatically become more satisfied and empowered and overall decision making will speed up. The reality is that lowering decision-making levels, as a change by itself, may be more entrapment than empowerment.

Entrapment occurs when employees are made responsible for decisions they don't understand. In many organizations, managers are given authority to reach decisions but not adequately trained to do so. When empowered but untrained managers make poor decisions, it may not be their fault but the fault of those who gave them authority without ability.

This lack of training was probably one of the underlying reasons for the disastrous real-estate portfolios that plagued many commercial banks in the early 1990s. For example, at Ameritrust, an Ohio-based regional bank (since merged with Society Bank, now known as Key Bank), lending officers had the authority to make deals but were given very little guidance and few standards for acceptable deals. As a result, lending officers used their own judgment and put the numbers together in ways that would make the deal look attractive. Later, when trying to clean up the portfolio, management realized that each lending officer was using different evaluation standards, which meant that the bank had *no* standards. Decision making was dispersed, but tools for making good decisions were not in place.

In a similar vein, decision-making authority may be moved down the organization without shared rewards and risks. Managers assume that employees will make effective decisions for the greater good alone, but simply desiring altruism and a sense of organizational interest among employees does not make it so. The invisible hand of self-interest is also at work. For example, if Ameritrust bankers had been given their share of the real-estate lending profits over time, they would have had an incentive to reduce medium and long-term lending risks. But because they were paid up front on the basis of production (volume of loans), their focus was almost exclusively on this short-term result.

Myth 4: Sharing information creates healthy hierarchies. Giving employees more information without opportunity to act on the information is like telling them they won the lottery but not where to collect the money. Expectations rise, but people who cannot act on their expectations soon see information as a liability, not an asset. Similarly, without competence to act and authority to make decisions, employees are informed but unable to deliver.

A classic example comes from analysis of the *Challenger* space shuttle disaster. In this case, employees of the key subcontractor, Morton Thiokol, as well as many NASA engineers, had extensive reports about potential O-ring failures in the shuttle engine assembly. But top management of the space agency had a deadline to meet and did not want to hear probable causes of delays. So the information was laundered as it went up the chain of command, being made to appear less threatening than it was. In short, having subordinates with information but no authority led to a disaster.

This myth is especially prevalent today, when most employees have access to virtually unlimited information through the Internet. Yet without the competence, authority, and incentive to act on that information, employees just drown in data instead of making something happen. For example, a consumer products company with quality problems had an Internet-accessible defect tracking system that listed thousands of product failures under dozens of defect categories—but employees had no authority or ability to make improvements. Nothing happened until management empowered and trained cross-functional teams to tackle some of the most critical categories of problems.

Myth 5: Broad sharing of rewards creates healthy hierarchies. It's often said that the way to employees' hearts is through their pocketbooks. If you give people enough money and recognition, the myth goes, then they will perform effectively and create a healthy hierarchy. The reality, however, is that rewards can encourage random or even counterproductive behavior. People also require competence, information, and appropriate authority to act.

Rewards alone are not enough because incentive structures are never crystal clear. They always have gray areas that require subjective judgment, no matter how many performance measures and standards and formulas are employed. In addition, employees usually have multiple paths for achieving rewards. That's why sales representatives spend so much time studying their commission structures. They are looking for new income-adding angles—perhaps they can push one product over another or trade off margin for volume or focus on after-sales services. If salespeople make these decisions without a thorough understanding of company strategy and the ability to execute in line with that strategy, their sales efforts may miss the mark.

Another reason why rewards alone can't create healthy hierarchies is that individuals' satisfaction is a function of their subjective expectations, while rewards reflect objective measures of success. Without widely shared information about company performance, people often judge their compensation against fantasies or incomplete pictures of how the company is doing. Such comparisons may well lead to low morale no matter how big the reward. For example, following the Time Inc.—Warner Pictures merger, the combined companies' operating performance stayed quite healthy. However, a series of events flowing from the merger forced the new Time Warner to cut back on stock options for a couple of years. This move left many executives and managers feeling they would have been better off without a merger.

Myth 6: All employees want to be empowered in the healthy hierarchy. Hopeful consultants maintain that all employees want to be empowered, unleashed, and liberated. Management simply needs to pass out information, authority, training, and rewards to everyone; let people loose, and good things will happen. But life is not so simple.

People hold jobs for many reasons: to earn a paycheck, to get away from home, to contribute to society, to make friends, to master particular skills, to get recognition, and the like. Some even come to work because they enjoy being told what to do, or they feel most secure in a structured, well-ordered environment, or they get satisfaction out of doing one thing well, over and over. Some people don't want to be empowered to make their own decisions, and assuming they do can create dysfunction.

The American Can Company plant mentioned in Chapter One is a classic example of the empowerment myth in action. In that case, management pulled out time clocks unilaterally, assuming that workers would welcome the freedom to come in late or leave early as long as they accomplished their work for the day. Many workers, however, did not want that freedom—they wanted the structure inherent in clocking in and out, and they wanted to know that if they took a day off to go hunting, they would be docked for it instead of having to make up the work the next day.

A world with unlimited resources or unlimited cooperation would not need vertical hierarchies. Everyone would agree on how to use machines, apply skills, sell products, and allocate rewards. But in the real world, people need leaders to resolve conflicts, allot resources, and make decisions about how to proceed. At every level, people need to know who is in charge, who represents them, who speaks for them to the organization and the outside world. Although much of that leadership can be shared and distributed, and everyone can contribute to it, it still must exist. The assumption that it is not needed produces either anarchy (everyone decides what to do separately) or a sense of resentment ("Why doesn't someone make decisions around here?")—and anarchy and resentment do not reflect a healthy hierarchy. The assumption that leadership is not needed is akin to what Randall Tobias, former CEO of Eli Lilly & Company, called "anarchic empowerment"—an abnegation of leadership rather than a mobilization of organizational resources.

Myth 7: Middle managers resist healthy hierarchies because they will lose power. The common wisdom is that middle managers do not want to strengthen competence and share information, decisions, and rewards because they will then lose power and status. To a degree, this is true—if power and rewards are still being distributed according to hierarchical position. But if the power and reward structure is aligned with performance and skills, as suggested earlier, why do middle managers still resist?

In this situation, the issue for middle managers is less the power they lose and more the things they have to learn how to do differently. A healthy hierarchy, with shared information and authority, puts middle managers in a whole new role. Instead of controlling, directing, evaluating, and ordering, they must facilitate, coach and counsel, mentor, translate strategies into goals, and design processes for joint assessment. Their resistance comes from the fear—often well-founded—of not being able to make the transition.

A prime example of this dynamic occurred a number of years ago at a small university in Los Angeles where a manager wanted help in making his team "more innovative." After observing interactions for a while, one of the authors suggested that the manager learn some new behaviors and skills to stimulate his people to come up with creative answers. Currently, he was just tossing out a problem and waiting for a solution, and that was not working—people assumed that he knew the answer already. The manager replied, "That's the same thing the last consultant told me—and I fired him too, just like I'm firing you." This middle manager was intellectually willing to share power, to gather creative input, but he was unwilling to retool himself to make that sharing possible.

Getting Started: How Healthy Is Your Hierarchy?

When organizations avoid the seven myths and calibrate the four dimensions of vertical boundaries correctly, matching the calibration to the external requirements for success, they can create powerful, effective, and healthy boundaryless hierarchies. The boundaryless hierarchy is not an oxymoron—an inherently contradictory condition—it's necessary for today's business. Leaders are still needed to resolve conflicts, allocate resources, set direction, and represent the organization to the outside world. But healthy hierarchies have an

Questionnaire #2

Stepping Up to the Line: How Healthy Is Your Organization's Hierarchy?

Part 1: Success Factors

Instructions: Determine how critical the four new success factors are in your organization, circling High, Medium, or Low for each factor.

1. Speed	High	Medium	Low
2. Flexibility	High	Medium	Low
3. Integration	High	Medium	Low
4. Innovation	High	Medium	Low

Part 2: Red Flags

Instructions: Evaluate how often the following five danger signs appear in your organization, circling a number from 1 (too often) to 10 (seldom).

	Too often		Sometimes		Seldom
1. Slow response time	1 2 3	4 5 6 7	8 9 10		
2. Rigidity to change	1 2 3	4 5 6 7	8 9 10		
3. Underground activity	1 2 3	4 5 6 7	8 9 10		
4. Internal employee frustration	1 2 3	4 5 6 7	8 9 10		
5. Customer alienation	1 2 3	4 5 6 7	8 9 10		

Part 3: Profile of Vertical Boundaries

Instructions: Assess where your company stands today on the four dimensions of information, authority, competence, and rewards, circling a number from 1 (traditional) to 10 (healthy).

	Traditional Hierarchy	Healthy Hierarchy	
Information closely held at top.	1 2 3 4 5 6 7 8 9 10	Information widely shared.
Authority to make decisions centralized at top.	1 2 3 4 5 6 7 8 9 10	Authority to make decisions distributed to wherever appropriate.
Competence specialized and focused—people do one job.	1 2 3 4 5 6 7 8 9 10	Competence widespread— people do multiple tasks as needed.
Rewards based on position.	1 2 3 4 5 6 7 8 9 10	Rewards based on skills and accomplishments.

appropriate two-way flow of information, widely distributed competencies, authority to act settled close to where decisions need to be made, and rewards that reinforce performance. When these conditions are appropriately met, organizations can realize significant gains in speed, flexibility, integration, and innovation.

For example, the St. Louis branch of the AgFirst Farm Credit Bank once got into trouble because its loan portfolio exceeded the value of the farmland on which the loans were based. In a striking instance of hierarchical health, the branch did not blame the loan agents. Instead, it gave them what they needed to work in the best interests of both sides: detailed information about the status of each loan, so they could stay in constant contact with their customers and work with them to meet the obligations. It also provided training in working cooperatively with customers in crises, so the agents could get both the bank and the farmer out of the difficult situation. In addition, it gave agents the authority to devise individual plans to help each farmer work out a solution to the financial trouble. If agents saw foreclosure as the only option, they also had the authority to do that. Finally, they were rewarded not only by how quickly they resolved loan issues but also by their relationships with the farmers. As a measure of agent performance, customers completed surveys rating loan agent fairness and attitude. After taking these steps, the bank discovered that farmer morale around St. Louis was much better than in the bank's other markets. Through the move to a healthy hierarchy, the St. Louis branch had not only managed the short-term crisis, it had also built relationships for future business.[13]

Your organization, too, may have opportunities to strengthen performance, making its vertical boundaries more permeable through recalibrating the four dimensions of a healthy hierarchy. In the next chapter, we outline a number of specific steps you can use to move in this direction. We also define some overall principles for creating a strategy for healthy hierarchy. Before you begin that chapter, however, we recommend that you assess the health of your hierarchy today and where it needs to change if you are to meet the success criteria most important to you.

Questionnaire #2 will give you a baseline snapshot of your organization and its hierarchy. Use the first two sections to assess the extent to which your company needs to be driven by the new success factors and to consider how often the warning signs of dysfunctional hierarchy appear in your organization or unit. The third section allows you to assess your current vertical boundaries against the four dimensions of the healthy hierarchy and produce an organizational profile.

Questionnaire Follow-Up

We suggest that you complete the questionnaire by yourself first. Then ask a group of colleagues to complete it. In a group forum, compare your answers and discuss the following questions:

- How important is it to our organization's success that we loosen our vertical boundaries? In other words, do we really need to operate faster and more flexibly?
- Are the red flags serious and recurrent? Which ones are most worrisome?
- To what extent is our current vertical profile dragging us down and causing us problems?
- In the current profile of our hierarchy, which dimensions are strongest? Where do we most need to change to be more successful?
- What is our desired profile of vertical boundaries? Where would we like to be on each of the four dimensions in the next year or two—that is, what profile do we need to compete successfully now and into the future?

Chapter Three

Rewiring and Retuning the Hierarchy

Developing a healthy hierarchy is like developing a healthy body—it takes a personal fitness plan. As in a fitness plan, success does not come from fad diets and exercise-of-the-month programs. Rather, it requires a sustained process that puts carefully chosen change activities together properly. For a healthy hierarchy, the process we recommend is what we call *wiring and tuning* the system.

Wiring the system (even in a wireless world) involves putting in place components such as management commitment and alignment between structure and strategy that are prerequisites for permeable vertical boundaries. A fine music system requires speakers, a receiver, a tuner, a CD player, a tape deck, an equalizer, and an antenna all connected together in the right way—otherwise, no amount of electricity or digital input will make all the elements produce audio output on demand. In just the same way, an organization's key components must be wired together and integrated—otherwise, no amount of delayering, empowering, profit sharing, or training will produce a truly healthy hierarchy.

Wiring the system, however, is only half the job. In a music system, music is not an inevitable outcome of stringing the electronic components together properly. The sound may still be discordant, too loud, full of static, or unsuited to the room. Only a system tuned and calibrated to the needs of the moment produces wonderful music. In organizations, too, once the components are in place, they need constant tuning—especially along the four dimensions described in Chapter Two: information, competence, authority, and rewards. Without such tuning, organizations are likely to succumb to one or more of the seven myths, resulting in further calcification of the vertical boundaries.

Although wiring and tuning sound straightforward, we have seen all too many organizations fail for lack of concentration on *both*. For example, we have seen many managers take care of wiring by writing mission and vision statements extolling the virtues of employee involvement, participative management, empowerment, and other healthy hierarchy initiatives. They put a key component in place—conceptual alignment between business strategy and organizational structure. But these mission statements became fodder for cynicism when employees saw no tuning, no actions to bring the practices to life.

Conversely, we have seen managers grasp at current fads and so-called cutting-edge management tools such as Six Sigma quality or delayering. They dive into the tuning without thought to the wiring, the choice of components to be tuned. Their actions are parachuted into the organization, and the effect is short-lived at best. Again, the result may be greater rigidity in the vertical boundaries than before.

We believe that loosening vertical boundaries takes both wiring, to provide the framework for the long term, and tuning, to generate momentum for the short term. Once you have a set of wiring steps and enough information about tuning information, competence, authority, and rewards, you'll be able to put together your own plan for loosening your organization's vertical boundaries.

Wiring the Components for Vertical Boundary Change

Company after company has poured resources into seemingly powerful change programs, only to leave participants disappointed in the meager or even counterproductive results.[1] One major reason for these failures is that managers often skip the process of wiring the system.

All four of the components shown in the box need to be wired together to loosen vertical boundaries within an organization.

System Components for Loosening Vertical Boundaries

- Align healthy hierarchy concepts with business strategy.
- Develop a sustained and visible management commitment through constant actions, big and small.
- Take a cumulative approach.
- Develop a shared mindset.

Align Healthy Hierarchy Concepts with Business Strategy

For concepts like empowerment, involvement, participation, and joint problem solving to be more than slogans, you need alignment between business strategy and change efforts to implement these concepts. In particular, change efforts must be means of reaching business ends—not just window dressing to make everyone feel good.

This alignment means that the practices for creating and maintaining healthy hierarchies must be critical to the day-to-day accomplishment of the business's goals. Managers must connect activities that dismantle rigid hierarchies to business results, and initiatives such as employee involvement, participative management, empowerment, or reengineering must affect strategy and not be just ends in themselves.

Without such alignment, you can talk about reengineering, reinventing, or redesigning your organization until you run out of breath, but you won't get action. Instead, managers at each level will see a bifurcation between organizational change and business goals. Faced with a choice, they will focus on business goals (appropriately so) and skip the effort of loosening vertical boundaries.

For example, a large firm in a changing industry went through an elaborate strategic planning process using this framework:

Vision:	The future
Mission:	The focus
Goals and measures:	The target
Companywide strategies and competitive advantages:	The foundation
Portfolio strategies:	The business mix
Strategic plans:	The actions

After spending enormous effort completing this process, senior management put together a few quick thoughts about "organizational effectiveness" but made no changes to align the organization with the strategy. To some extent, they assumed that the organization would align itself. The organization ended up with a well-conceived strategy but no infrastructure to sustain it.

By contrast, the following vision and mission statements do show an awareness of the issues critical to making vision happen: "To become a dynamic learning organization where people are enthusiastic partners in attaining organizational objectives" (Delco Chassis—now Delphi Automotive Systems); "We are dedicated to being the world's best at bringing people together and giving them easy access to each other and to the information and services they want and need anytime, anywhere" (AT&T). These visions acknowledge that business results occur through healthy hierarchies.

A simple test of the alignment between strategy and vertical structure is to read your organization's mission statement and ask if it mentions how the organization must act to meet its business objectives. If it doesn't, organizational practices may not be aligned to business goals.

To further discover the logic of alignment, answer these three simple questions:

1. *What are our future goals?* Whatever framework you choose for articulating where your business is headed (vision, mission, strategic intent, aspiration, or foresight), the challenge is to paint an exciting picture of what the business needs to look like in order to succeed—not only today but two or more years out. This picture should include markets served, financial objectives, products delivered, and technology required as well as the unique competitive advantages you might exploit.

2. *What capabilities will we need to meet our goals?*[2] Think both of processes and of the people skills needed to accomplish the goals. For example, to reach financial goals, a firm must be capable not only in broad financial processes such as monitoring and controlling costs, squeezing inventories, and managing receivables, but also in its people—it needs skilled financial analysts, cost accountants, auditors, and systems designers. And all these

skilled people must have such general capabilities as dependability, predictability, speed, responsiveness, and ability to learn.

3. *What organizational initiatives will build the capabilities?* By viewing organizational initiatives in the context of developing ways to achieve business strategies, you can avoid disconnected initiatives and management fads. You can connect the wires. Then, as new initiatives inevitably emerge, the ability to assess and implement them in an ongoing, integrated stream woven around capabilities ensures that the organization will change more effectively over time.

These three questions are tools for drawing an intellectual circuit blueprint of the way activities and business strategies and goals can be wired together.

Develop a Sustained and Visible Management Commitment

In creating a healthy lifestyle, the critical challenge is to translate intention into action. Likewise, firms succeed in creating healthy hierarchies because they translate the concepts of vertical boundarylessness into specific behavior in each and every nook and cranny of the firm. When employees get up to go home, they can specify how their day's work differed because of the healthy hierarchy initiatives. This should be particularly true for senior executives, since it is with them that commitment to action needs to start.

At Zurich Financial Services, CEO Rolf Huppi has committed himself to what he calls "social capital"—the sum of the firm's "experience, knowledge, capability and competency." Social capital is Huppi's version of management commitment to learning. Huppi has given Zurich a clear vision of organization-wide learning, with explicit milestones. He has also supported this vision by creating "practice boards" designed to share knowledge and experiences among Zurich divisions and businesses. People who are knowledgeable about consumer insurance products in one geographical region, for example, get together with practice board members from other regions a few times a year to share their experience. Huppi's practice boards ensure that emerging best ideas are transferred to the rest of the company. He believes that creating such learning (or in his terms, "sharing social capital") will ensure that Zurich Financial accomplishes its global objectives.

Another example comes from the first few years of the GE cultural transformation, which met with initial skepticism among many employees. In one workshop, a twenty-year employee privately remarked, "This culture change stuff is garbage—just one more of those damn things that eat our time for a while and then go away." The employee questioned Jack Welch's commitment to recrafting the GE organization. Welch, however, carried out his commitment, not just through words but through actions. Right from the beginning, he devoted a significant portion of every Corporate Executive Council meeting to the transformation. In essence, he insisted that each of his business leaders report regularly, both to him and to their peers, about change activities and accomplishments. In addition, Welch devoted significant portions of his own time to talking with groups of employees, particularly those in training, about the change and how it was going. He constantly passed on the employees' responses to his business leaders, often through handwritten notes. Finally, three years into the effort, Welch made it clear that he expected his senior team to produce business results while demonstrating the values of the new GE. And he dramatically removed several leaders who were getting results in the old GE style. More than a decade later few people anywhere in the world question Jack Welch's commitment to sustained cultural change.

Senior managers, however, are not the only ones who need to act. Wiring the right components together requires many actions, many of them mini-steps, at every level. In the final analysis, it is the encouragement of mini-steps throughout the organization that makes the most difference. For example:

- Every supervisor can spend a portion of each staff meeting asking for advice on how to work more effectively. This may sound trite, but it works—the resulting dialogue gives a powerful signal that it is all right to voice opinions and suggestions.
- Managers can make frequent informal visits to plants and operations and encourage employees to come forward with ideas for improving work. Managers' walk-arounds can bring them face to face with employees and their problems.

- Managers can hold all-plant, all-department, or all-employee meetings to share information and encourage action.
- Organizations can form process improvement teams to work in areas that affect team members. Executives can personally commit significant time each month to hear and respond to team reports and recommendations.
- Managers can get quick results in work improvement with simple but realistic e-mail suggestion systems. Employees must be assured that management will respond to ideas within hours or days, and will share the savings when a cost-cutting idea is implemented.
- Managers can produce quarterly summaries of new ideas and practices in their groups and use these documents to build awareness among employees and to share ideas with other managers.

Dow Chemical Chairman William S. Stavropoulos has acted on the premise that multiple actions at multiple levels demonstrate management commitment. When Stavropoulos, then president and COO, ended his November 1993 meeting with his top two hundred managers, he knew he had conveyed the essence of Dow's business imperatives. He also knew he had articulated as best he could the set of managerial behaviors required to change the firm's culture and achieve its business goals. But he also knew that unless his audience could translate his ideas into their actions, he would be unsuccessful. As a result, he made "achieving the new culture" a priority by requiring all managers to take a series of specific steps: present the Dow blueprint to their own employees, identify and remove barriers to change in each work unit, and do a 360-degree feedback exercise. These actions made creating a healthy hierarchy as much a management priority as meeting business imperatives. As Stavropoulos put it: "If managers don't invest the people time, it is unlikely they will succeed. Leaders at all levels of the company must devote 20 to 30 percent of their time to people. . . . What will employees think if we don't spend enough time defining accountability and coaching— so they end up needing to constantly double-check things with us before taking action? In short, hell will freeze over before employees believe that we want to change this company."

Take a Cumulative Approach

To shift healthy hierarchy initiatives from marginal to mainstream, you have to treat them as evolutionary rather than revolutionary. Management practices are *revolutionary* when each new technique— quality circles, continuous improvement, TQM, reengineering— comes as a redeemer of the previous practice, now seen as antiquated and inept. Revolutionary management practices easily become fads to be tasted and tested, then rejected and renounced. Moreover, champions of different initiatives may end up competing against each other for management attention.

Management practices are *evolutionary* when new initiatives add value to their predecessors. From this point of view, quality circles helped employees explore the importance of quality and team-work, continuous improvement added a disciplined process, TQM showed the importance of customer focus for quality, reengineer-ing showed the importance of improving work processes to ensure quality, and Six Sigma provided disciplined analytical tools to take quality even further. Evolutionary practices encourage managers to sustain commitment to change.

No one practice makes a healthy hierarchy—that requires the impact of many practices. For example, longtime baseball manager Tony Larussa has devised a "law of accumulation."[3] Basically, he says that little things add up. So focus on them. In baseball, four base hits equal a run, three walks equal a run, three stolen bases equal a run, and three runs can equal a win. The more Larussa can dis-sect his goal of scoring more runs than the other team into sub-goals and focus attention on each of those subgoals, the more little things he can add up, putting them together for success.

Likewise, no one practice will guarantee a healthy hierarchy, but the cumulation of lots of the right subgoals will make it happen.

Develop a Shared Mindset

Nordstrom, a specialty retailer, has received high marks in a dy-namic, aggressive industry. At a time when many retailers were struggling to hold their ground, Nordstrom tripled its number of stores, raised its sales tenfold, and grew from a small Northwest re-gional firm to a national presence.

No one factor explains Nordstrom's success. The stores are easy for customers to navigate. Live piano music sets the tone. And the inventory is exceptional, particularly in shoes—some stores have over 100,000 pairs. However, if you ask customers why they shop at Nordstrom, they probably won't put convenience, inventory, or price at the top of the list. Instead, they'll talk about the commitment and support they get from dedicated employees. Nordstrom employees—often called Nordies—are devoted to customer service and proud of service stories that have become legends, like the one about the employee who graciously gave a customer credit for a returned set of automobile tires even though Nordstrom does not sell tires. Nordies routinely accompany customers throughout a store to put together outfits. They phone around to locate desired merchandise in other Nordstrom stores, and they accept return items unquestioningly.[4]

To make this level of service a reality, Nordstrom created a new form of governance. Store executives ensure employees' commitment to exceptional customer service not by monitoring employee behavior with many supervisors or phantom customers wandering the floor but by supporting a culture in which employee expectations of being able to deliver outstanding service are inviolate.

Traditional firms govern employees through direct observation. Employees do the right thing in the right way mostly because managers are visibly checking on employee behavior. Healthy hierarchy firms govern employee behavior through shared mindsets. You don't need layers of supervision when employees share the firm's values and beliefs and know how to support them.

You can test the degree to which a shared mindset is present in your organization with the following relatively simple but highly revealing six-step exercise:

1. Identify your organization's top team. (Probably the top managers and the next tier or two of direct reports. It will generally consist of from ten to twenty people.)
2. Give each team member three 3x5 cards.
3. Ask each person to write one "top thing" per card in answer to the question: What are the top three things we want our customers to think of when they see our name? (Agreement on this is critical to a shared mindset.)

4. Collect the 3x5 cards and sort them into clusters of common answers. (We have found it important to be strict in the sorting process and to put cards into different piles when their wording differs, even if some of the underlying meaning is similar.)
5. Determine the extent to which there is a shared mindset by counting the percentage of cards that fall in the top three clusters. (Our rule of thumb is that a shared mindset exists when 75 percent of the answers are in the top three clusters.)
6. Discuss the exercise results and what you want customers to know you for.

The mindset exercise may be done with an entire corporation or a business or function within the corporation. We predict that at Nordstrom, the unity measure would probably be well into the 90 percent range. However, after running dozens of groups through the exercise, we have learned that most management teams lack a shared mindset about what they want their company to be known for. At the same time, focusing on a shared mindset for the outside (customers) helps unify the mindset inside (among the team), and once the clusters are shared with the group, the process of creating a shared mindset is relatively straightforward.

For example, in one company, we did this exercise with twenty-two of the top human resource executives. Only 45 percent of the cards ended up in the top three piles. However, after putting all the responses on the table and discussing the customer implications of each response, the team created a shared mindset for the HR function during a one-day workshop.

Tuning the System

Wiring together the components of alignment, commitment through action, cumulation, and shared mindset results in the overall system needed to build a healthy hierarchy. Getting the system to produce music and not just noise, however, requires a great deal of tuning among the four dimensions of information, competence, authority, and rewards.

First, each dimension must be carefully tuned to meet specific operational and business requirements. For example, driving more authority for complex customer decisions out to the field may increase speed, customer satisfaction, and short-term revenues, but if the field commits to products that manufacturing or distribution cannot deliver, then any gains will quickly sink in a sea of contention.

Second, the tuning of each dimension needs to be integrated with the tuning of the others, otherwise the signal will warble and get on everyone's nerves. However, the notion that managers can create a healthy hierarchy by tuning single dimensions is, as we discussed earlier, a myth.

Though we suggest a number of tuning actions here, we don't offer them as set recipes. Businesses are living organisms and thus moving targets. Managers may implement an action only to have the organization throw up its immune defense and prevent the action from working. Alternatively, people may understand an action, assimilate it, and be ready to move on to the next practically in the same breath. This section is just a menu of possibilities to be selected and integrated to fit your unique situation. Also, many other resources can provide more detail on implementing the actions we suggest. Our purpose here is to define the parameters of the actions that will loosen vertical boundaries, rather than to discuss details of day-to-day execution.

Sharing Information

In nearly every employee attitude survey, communication shows up as a problem. Employees generally feel they are not informed enough or are actually misinformed about organizational goals and initiatives. Without information, they know they cannot keep customers in the loop of product changes and development, service procedures, or pricing. They find it difficult to take empowered actions on their own or to feel they have a voice in the firm. This is true even with today's intranets, Web pages, search engines, and ubiquitous information flows. Having lots of information does not necessarily mean you have the right information, that it is digestible, current, or targeted. Even when companies invest millions in "knowledge management," they often fail to get the right information in the right form to the right people at the right time.

The five specific actions listed in the box are the ones we have found useful for sharing information effectively, with or without the assistance of technology.

Actions for Effectively Sharing Information

- Align channel and message.
- Share good and bad news.
- Use both cognitive and emotive news.
- Make messages both complex and simple.
- Use information to encourage change.

Align Channel and Message

Many means, or channels, for sharing information exist. When the channel matches the message, communication is improved. For example, memos, e-mail, and videotapes are all important channels for factual information. However, one-on-one or small-group meetings are much more useful channels for information meant to help employees change behavior. Aligning purpose and medium helps managers share information effectively; misalignment produces communication failures. In one firm, managers held weekly staff "communication meetings" where each person described the week's activity and plans. Useful as the information was, most people resented the meeting time—the same information could have been shared more efficiently through static media.

Figure 3.1 is a visual guide for aligning purpose and channel. The shadowed section indicates whether a channel is most appropriate for sharing factual information or shaping behavior. Thus if the purpose is primarily to share factual information, then bulletins and the like can be used successfully. FedEx, for example, produces daily videos of the previous day's performance to inform employees about work flow. Conversely, if a change in behavior is desired (for example, a new performance assessment process), a memo is *not* the right way to communicate. Such changes require personal contact that makes employees part of the change process.

Each organization needs to decide what formats are best for it—reflecting its own resources and information collection systems—and what frequency makes sense for its people. For example, Honda distributes printed copies of its strategic plan to all employees. Marriott Hotel newsletters have a question-and-answer section from customers about excellent service. Microsoft created

Figure 3.1. Aligning Communication.

How to Communicate	Purposes of Communication	
Channel	*Share Information*	*Shape Behavior*
Face-to-face (one-on-one)		
Symbolic (meeting, rally)		
Interactive media (telephone, voice mail, fax, e-mail)		
Personal static media (letter, memo, report)	*Aligned*	
Impersonal static media (bulletin, flyer, newsletter, video)		

a best-practice database to share ideas across units about innovative work practices. Harry Kraemer of Baxter Healthcare shares weekly information about cash flow with employees and investors in a "letter from the chairman" to keep attention focused on financial results. The World Bank has an information kiosk on its intranet for quick distribution of critical information. Of course, whatever its format, the distribution of information should be open and honest.

It is often worthwhile to create a *communication plan* that identifies a year's worth of activities and shows your commitment to share information. If it identifies what information is to be shared, who it is to be shared with, when it is to be shared, and how it is to be shared, the plan can be a strong support for a healthy hierarchy.

For example, in a company making significant changes in financial reporting, managers employed the following four steps to build a communication plan. First, they identified the message they wanted to share about the new system, concluding that the message had four parts: general background information, benefits, culture change required, and personal concerns and implications. They then identified five audiences for the message: site leaders and project managers, senior managers, all system users, all employees affected by the system, and all external customers affected by the system. Third, they planned to share the message over a twenty-month period broken into seven quarters. And finally, they designated multiple tools for communicating the message.

The sum of their efforts was the chart in Figure 3.2. At first, this chart may seem overwhelming, an overspecification of the communication effort. It proved worthwhile, however—using this plan, the company found that the new financial system met much less resistance than other changes had, that consistent messages about the new system pervaded all parts of the organization, and that the new system was implemented more quickly than had been thought possible.

Share Both Good and Bad News

Some managers focus on either good or bad news. Cheerleaders tell the good news, and let employees be surprised by the bad. Pessimists harp on problems, and employees never hear the good news. Successful sharing of information puts a premium on objectivity.

Figure 3.2. Sample Communication and Training Plan.

Schedule for System Roll-Out

Audience	4Q	1Q	2Q	3Q	4Q	1Q	2Q
	Design		Load and Test		Implement	Parallel Run/Test	
	(8 Months)		(5 Months)		(3 Months)	(4 Months)	
	All Groups			Implementation Group 1			
	(Fixed Schedule)			(Shifts by Implementation Group)			
Group 1 Site leaders, project teams, developers		D	A D	G A BMD L 2 1/2/3 44 44	G	2 A B M D L 1/2/3 4 4 4 4	
Group 2 Senior management		1	1/2/32				
Group 3 All users		P	CD PiPN	PIIPII/P 11122 3	HOKQKE 323343	OFH J 233	
Group 4 All employees		As required C D 1	1'1 1		4	4	
Group 5 External customers		D 1	1			G	A BMD 1/2/3 444 2

Media Type:
A. Videotape
B. Interactive video
C. Talking points
D. Personal approach
E. Voicemail
F. Broadcast
G. Prototype
H. Brochure handed out with paychecks
I. Poster
J. Message printed on paycheck
K. Local (site) news
L. Promotional handouts
M. Documentation and manuals
N. Personal letter from executive
O. All-hands meetings, quarterly results
P. Newsletter
Q. Letter from local GMs

Message to Communicate:
1. General background information
2. Benefits
3. Culture change explanation
4. Personal concerns

For example, at The Limited, executives and store managers receive a weekly report of store sales. This report specifies revenues and profit per store and identifies what clothing products are selling where, supplemented by personal comments from the chairman, Les Wexner. It gives managers and leaders throughout The Limited a common understanding not only of what's happening in the business but of how the chairman is thinking about these developments. It also allows weekly store-to-store performance comparisons, enabling subsequent decisions about what should change for a particular store or region to become more successful.

Use Both Cognitive and Emotive News

Tony Rucci was in many ways the intellectual architect of the Baxter and American Hospital Supply merger in the 1980s and the Baxter Healthcare global strategy in the 1990s.[5] He has a Ph.D. in organizational psychology and his cognitive abilities are widely respected. However, much of his success came when he shared with employees his personal experiences of having a father who worked in the coal mines, whose company abused him and his workmates with bad policies, and who brought some of his troubles into his home. When Rucci talked about policies and values, everyone knew not only his intellectual prowess but his emotional commitment to these policies. This combination gave him enormous credibility. Along the same lines, when Nike Inc. developed a curriculum for its high-potential managers, one of the centerpieces of the program was helping managers learn to tell their personal stories in ways that demonstrated their emotional commitment to the firm.

Many managers hesitate to share the emotional impact of information with their people, perhaps assuming that mature adults handle everything rationally. It is more realistic to assume that everyone in the workplace has emotions and that information, particularly about change, triggers those emotions. Sharing emotional as well as rational messages is important to increasing the permeability of vertical hierarchies.

Make Messages Both Complex and Simple

Information can be shared in both complex and simple ways. When Larry Bossidy became CEO of AlliedSignal in 1991, he talked about "three P's": performance (meeting the numbers), portfolio (getting the right product mix), and people (attracting and motivating the employees). This simple message could be and was communicated to all employees. From 1991 until Bossidy merged AlliedSignal with Honeywell in 1999, each year brought another simple message from Bossidy about key priorities.

During Bossidy's tenure, no one at AlliedSignal believed these simple messages were simple to implement. In fact, they were part of a long turnaround process and they required complex initiatives and actions. But in the midst of that complexity, AlliedSignal executives derived a clear focus from the basic messages. That focus anchored their work and made it easier to relate change to all levels of employees—and create one of the great corporate success stories of the 1990s.

Other senior executives have employed this simple-complex information strategy with powerful results. In the early 1990s, GE's Jack Welch was well known for his transformational theme: speed, simplicity, and self-confidence. Similarly, during the successful integration of Warner Lambert Pharmaceuticals into Pfizer in 2000, president Hank McKinnell emphasized the theme of "the best get better" as a rallying cry for a complex set of strategies to transform two separate companies into one powerhouse.

Use Information to Encourage Change

In times of rapid change, sharing information widely is essential to counter people's natural anxieties and fears of the unknown. Without facts, employees grasp at rumors about what is or is not happening and may become preoccupied with them.

For example, in an insurance firm undergoing a change to account management from geographic management, rumors were rampant: the company would divest businesses, fire managers, and completely transform itself. Because management did not share the real details widely enough, the rumor mill drove employee anxiety beyond reason, and employees resisted implementing the new direction, thinking erroneously that more changes were to come.

In contrast, when one of drugmaker SmithKline Beecham's (now GlaxoSmithKline's) R&D management teams set out to change clinical data operations from a functional to a team organization, it included a number of creative communication mechanisms in its plan. First, it held a series of all-hands meetings to explain the team concept and what it would involve. The human resource manager then conducted a number of "systematic meetings" with employees (without other managers present) to get employee views. Simultaneously, the management team created an interactive database, using Lotus Notes, so that any data operations employee could raise questions, make comments, or voice concerns. That database was then used to stimulate an ongoing virtual dialogue among hundreds of affected employees. In addition, management set up a formal discussion group of representatives from the key functional groups to think through all ramifications of the change in such areas as staffing, job rotation, skill mix, training, and compensation, posting the notes from their meetings on the database. The result of this open communication blitz was fascinating: employees started pressing management to get on with the change, to stop talking about it and make it happen. Management responded by accelerating the schedule and completing the transition in less than nine months instead of the planned year and a half.

In general, then, employees are willing to change and to act in the best interests of the firm, but they rarely get the information they need to do so effectively. The broad dissemination of information is one dimension that can be tuned—that is, legitimated—to various degrees to make vertical boundaries more permeable.

Developing Competencies

As we described in Chapter Two, competencies are the critical skills needed to do jobs effectively. Healthy hierarchies develop these competencies wherever needed, without regard to rank, position, or status. When competencies don't develop at all levels, companies often get into trouble.

The next box lists the five ways we propose for building competence across vertical boundaries.

Actions for Building Competence

- Conduct a competence audit.
- Improve staffing.
- Train and develop.
- Establish career banding.
- Establish a 360-degree feedback process.

Conduct a Competence Audit

Creating healthy hierarchies often requires the development of new skills at many different levels. For example, managers may need to strengthen their ability to stand before employees, discuss ideas openly and candidly, and respond to questions directly; salespeople may need to learn how to do their own credit checks; shop workers may need to learn how to inspect their own work or make their own rework decisions. To identify these changing competency requirements, managers can conduct a competence audit.

Competence audits revolve around two questions:

- *Given the goal of creating a healthy hierarchy, what technical competencies will be required of employees at all levels of the organization?* Technical competencies are the know-how required to do a job. For example, employees in manufacturing might need to know more about marketing and vice versa.
- *Given the goal of creating a healthy hierarchy, what cultural competencies will be required of employees at all levels of the organization?* Cultural competencies guide how employees relate to each other within a level and across levels.

Figure 3.3 is a model for determining a company's *competence gap,* the difference between current technical and cultural competencies and competencies that will be needed in the future, given the changes the company faces. Today, such changes often include such issues as globalization, technological innovation, customer demand, competitive pressure, or government regulation.

When we perform the analysis suggested in Figure 3.3, we generally find that the largest gap is in cultural competencies. For example, while employees in the Saturn division of General Motors required new technical skills (for example, computer skills and abilities to use new materials), their largest competence gap was in how to work together (for example, in cross-functional teams and shared decision making).

Because the real value of the competence audit comes less from the information and more from the dialogue that it generates (as with many change tools), we recommend using an iterative, interactive method for both collecting and assessing the data. A small, cross-hierarchy team might put together a first-cut list of current

Figure 3.3. Model for Competence Audit.

Type of Competence	Skills We Have Currently	Changes Facing Our Business	Skills We Will Need in the Future
Technical			
Cultural			

└─────── Competence Gap ───────┘

competencies, both technical and cultural. That list can then be turned into a questionnaire and either sent to employees or used in discussions with them. Next, the team can work with senior management to agree on key changes facing the organization and speculate about new competencies that will be needed to succeed. This information can be further enriched through focus group discussions with multiple levels of employees and through discussions with customers. Finally, cross-organizational groups can identify and discuss some of the gaps between current competency levels and future needs.

Stan Schrager, when senior vice president for human resources at Chase Manhattan, conducted a variation on this process for Chase's wholesale bank. He focused on identifying the key competencies customers would demand from relationship officers in the coming years and the extent to which the bank's current professional complement would be able to respond. He found that customers would be seeking a much more tailored set of skills, expecting their bankers to be experienced in a particular industry, have in-depth knowledge of financial instruments and markets unique to customer needs, and know the customer company in some detail. As a result, Schrager worked with the managers of the wholesale bank to create a database for matching relationship managers with particular and changing needs of corporate customers. The database also identified across-the-board competency gaps to be filled.

Improve Staffing

Once a competency gap is identified, two choices exist for reducing it: buying (hiring) or building (training and developing) talent. Therefore, staffing decisions must focus on who comes into the organization, who moves up, and who moves out.

Acquiring the right talent is the first and perhaps most critical staffing decision because it determines a firm's long-term skill base. Successful companies follow three principles in hiring:

Spend time screening applicants. In their St. Louis brewery, Miller Brewing Company managers spent over a hundred hours per hire reviewing applications, testing and interviewing applicants, and making sure that the two hundred new hires were the right match. Miller executives believe their St. Louis facility is now staffed with one of the most talented workforces in their industry.

Involve customers in screening. Southwest Airlines asks frequent fliers to interview flight attendant finalists who have passed the Southwest screen for technical skills. Passengers look for attitude, personality, and energy. Anyone traveling on Southwest can probably perceive a service difference.

Bring in new talent. When Stan Gault became chairman of Rubbermaid in 1982, he replaced 160 of the top 161 people. This influx of talent enabled Rubbermaid to redefine its culture and become more innovative. To increase workforce competence, Larry Bossidy at AlliedSignal similarly replaced 90 of the top 120 people in his first fifteen months in office. In contrast, we have worked with a number of senior executives who came into new positions and tried to engineer major transformations without bringing in any new people. In almost all cases, they eventually changed their stance.

Outside talent, however, is not without its price. Clearly, when too many individuals come in from outside, a firm loses continuity.[6] At firms like Rubbermaid, such transformation was probably appropriate. At other firms, continuity may be more important.

In addition to hiring new talent, managers should concentrate on succession planning, developing backup talent within the firm. At Baxter Healthcare, executives spend a significant amount of time reviewing talent. They identify business needs, then suggest career moves for critical employees. As a result, Baxter executives believe they have created management depth to lead the company into the future.

Finally, organizations also need to move people out in a constructive way, as part of the firm's natural evolution. If managers compromise on competence rather than let people go, they contribute to a build-up of incompetence or mismatched competence that usually leads to knee-jerk downsizing later. Better to follow World Bank's example and build a more flexible and responsive organization with mechanisms to help managers and employees separate. The bank has a "performance advisory service," where trained specialists advise managers on dealing with staffing situations; a "job search center" to help employees at all levels find alternative employment; a "career advisory service" to help employees match their skills with career options; and a number of financial alternatives for employees to make exiting the bank an easier process.

Train and Develop

When organizations build competence through training and development, the key to success is providing experience that focuses directly on closing identified gaps. Larry Bossidy, for example, besides bringing new talent into AlliedSignal, also required thousands of managers and employees to go through a series of training courses and projects to learn customer-focused quality skills—competencies he and his team had determined were critical for future success. At the World Bank, also, senior managers have identified a set of critical competencies for their technical development specialists, creating a required core curriculum and a series of tailored seminars. Here are several effective strategies for building competence through training and development:

Define programs around competencies that align with strategy. At Boeing and PPG, training programs are clearly linked to business strategies and company core values. Training programs are not in the catalogue merely because they have been offered in the past, but because they are linked to business goals.

Train in teams. Increasingly, we see companies training whole teams. Teams can apply what they learn to real job issues, so team training leads to action learning. For example, at General Motors, CEO Rick Wagoner has identified speed as a key cultural characteristic ensuring the company's future success. To encourage speed, he has put together what he calls "GoFast" workshops. Managers come to these workshops with real business problems, and then apply a set of key disciplines to them to make things happen fast. For example, participants in a GoFast session who were consolidating separate car and truck engineering groups into a single vehicle engineering group applied principles of speed to this challenge, bringing class insights directly to the job. This action-learning workshop integrated training and application experience, simultaneously reinforcing the training and solving a specific business problem.

Find alternatives to training. The Center for Creative Leadership lists twenty-two "development in place" activities, that is, ways to develop talent without formal training.[7] It's useful to find task force assignments, job rotations, and other opportunities that deliver experiences employees would not otherwise receive.

Include customers. Increasingly, we see firms opening their training to customers and suppliers. At Motorola University, 45 percent of participants are *not* Motorola employees—they're suppliers and customers invited in as a way to build their loyalty while building their competencies. Similarly, GE's Crotonville facility provides as much education to customers and key suppliers as it does to GE employees.

Leverage technology. Technology today allows firms to train many employees at one time and at multiple sites. For example, Price-WaterhouseCoopers trains managers around the world through videoconferences and Web-based training modules.

Increase Competence Through Career Banding

Many traditional companies grade both jobs and people, resulting in a point system by which jobs can be compared and a pay system devised to ensure internal and external equity. In other words, a person is a "level 10" or a "level 25" regardless of working in production, sales, or finance, and a similar pay schedule applies across these different units. Similar classifications can be used to determine who can appropriately fill a job. Such systems were exceedingly useful in newly complex functional organizations, fostering pay equity and providing a rational system for filling jobs and an understood pathway for career advancement with relatively little nepotism or subjectivity.

Today, however, job-grading systems often serve only to reinforce hierarchical inflexibility. In particular, they lead to narrow, rigid definitions that stop jobs from keeping up with fast-changing environments. They interfere with matching competence to job requirements—candidates must fit the specified grade, even though the needed skills may reside at higher or lower grades. They also preclude matching jobs to competencies, and it turns out that most jobs today are better done when the employee shapes the job than when the job piles set duties on the employee. Moreover, job-grading systems tend not to allow for team-based work, where the essence of the task is to orchestrate and mobilize skills from many sources. Finally, job grading reinforces ladder climbing for career advancement and discourages building competence and contribution.

An alternative to job grading is *career banding,* organizing jobs around broad, flexible career categories. Each category allows for a wide range of salaries, based largely on competence and performance. One bank that made the switch started with seven levels of vice presidents, so many that no one cared and the title lost meaning. It shifted to four career bands: executive, manager, contributor, and member. Executives are those who direct bank operations. Managers supervise groups of employees. Contributors perform individual specialty jobs, such as loan officer. Members perform jobs such as teller that interface with customers. Having career options within these broad bands replaces employees' need to move up a single career ladder. Someone who does want to shift career focus can apply to move into another career band. Such a move, however, is based as much on a desire for different work as on a desire for more pay or advancement.

It is hard to get people to work together when they are constantly competing for the next grade up. Career banding lets employees focus more on what needs doing than on how to advance. Banded hierarchies stay healthier because the organization becomes more flexible when employees can be rewarded and reinforced through lateral moves. Banding is particularly useful in downsized firms that haven't enough openings to move high-performers up the hierarchy anyway. People can focus on becoming the best in their career band instead of aiming for vertical advancement up that single ladder.

Of course, when organizations establish too many subcategories within a band, the concept is effectively neutralized. The power of career banding lies in simplicity, having a limited number of career categories within which managers and employees have a wide and flexible range of salaries.

Establish a 360-Degree Feedback Process

The final means of building competence is through multi-rater or *360-degree feedback*. In this process, a manager's supervisor, peers, employees, and even customers answer questions about the extent to which the manager demonstrates certain desired competencies. With this kind of rich all-round feedback, managers can easily identify the areas they need to address for both personal and organizational success. Contrast this with the traditional practice of giving managers formal feedback only from their bosses, feedback that focuses managers on personal compensation and advancement.

Here is a first-step, low-risk version of 360-degree feedback: a week before a subordinate's scheduled appraisal, suggest this: "Come in prepared to tell me one thing I could do differently that would help you do your job better." No hard copy of this feedback goes into your formal HR file, and your boss won't hear about it. But it will let you begin to tap the potential of 360-degree feedback. Also, it's only right for a manager who wants employees to start getting their own 360-degree feedback to go through the process first.

Many organizations have incorporated 360-degree feedback processes into their competence-building activities with great success.[8] They have produced some rules of thumb from their experiences:

- *Make sure everyone knows how the data will be protected.* Everyone involved needs to knows that confidentiality will be preserved throughout data collection, storage, and use. Many firms use third parties to ensure such confidentiality.
- *Define behaviors to be appraised.* Generic requests for feedback ("How is Sally doing?") will elicit generic responses ("Fine").

Specify the behaviors that supervisors, peers, and subordinates are to assess.

- *Involve customers.* At Marriott, the satisfaction forms left on the pillows at night become part of the feedback given employees who served the customer. Customer feedback completes the picture of employee performance.
- *Specify the purpose.* Many firms use 360-degree feedback exclusively for development, and almost never share the information with anyone other than its object. Increasingly, however, firms like General Electric, Boeing, AT&T, and Hewlett-Packard are using 360-degree feedback as a form of performance appraisal. It is crucial to specify how the feedback will be used before it is collected.
- *Use the data.* To get the most from 360-degree feedback, do more than hand it to the individual being scored. Discuss implications, review results for development, and possibly tie results to rewards.
- *Track data over time.* To get the full developmental benefit, track the data over time. For example, at GE Appliances, 360-degree feedback data are tracked annually. Success is measured by trends, not by any one year's data.
- *Keep it simple and automated.* Because 360-degree feedback can be both bulky and time-consuming, it is important to keep it streamlined. Many firms, such as the World Bank, make extensive use of e-mail questionnaires that can be answered in minutes and then tallied with computer programs. Automated reports with summary data and verbatim "qualitative comments" are then provided for each manager.

Boundaries loosen with 360-degree feedback as employees learn to look in all directions for learning, not just to the boss. More important, the competence-building process is vastly accelerated and enriched through multiple sources of input.

Shifting Authority to the Point of Impact: Who Decides What

Authority is the third dimension that requires digital tuning in a healthy hierarchy. Often, this means shifting some responsibility and accountability from the top to the bottom of the organization.

The goal is to place decisions as close to the action as possible—so that people who have the most current read on a situation can act immediately.

The classic example of shifting authority is the once-revolutionary concept of allowing assembly line workers to stop the line to solve the problems they see, rather than catching problems later through inspection and quality checks. It is now well accepted that, with shifted authority, the overall production of perfect units is much higher and its overall cost (without armies of inspectors) much lower.

Other examples of driving authority closer to the action can be seen when salespeople can close deals and negotiate prices without checking in with the home office, when customer service representatives can resolve problems and complete transactions on-line, and when employees can purchase their own materials without getting approvals. In all these cases, not only are decisions speeded up but employee commitment to doing a good job is much increased.

Shifting Authority

Leaders can take four specific actions summarized in this section to tune the authority dimension for fast but effective decisions.

Actions for Shifting Authority

- Challenge current decision-making assumptions.
- Use town meetings to shift authority.
- Shift management roles from controller to coach.
- Remove layers if necessary.

Challenge Current Decision-Making Assumptions

Most organizations are infused with assumptions about who can and cannot make various types of decisions. Some are based on analysis, but many are historical artifacts ("Remember the lathe that got trashed when that operator tried to fix it!") or long-standing images ("That's a senior management decision!"). Yet often, when these assumptions are changed, new ways develop that make the old ones look ridiculous in retrospect. Today, few people raise an eyebrow when they hear that Saturn employees can stop the assembly line at any time if they experience problems, or that Electronic Data Systems (EDS) client managers have the authority to meet client needs even if it means contracting services for the client outside EDS.

To move decisions to the right level, managers need to challenge their hidden assumptions. They can start by asking themselves a series of simple questions.

- Who has the information and skills to make sure this is a high-quality decision? Have these people been involved in the decision?
- If you had to trust one person to make this decision, who would it be? Has this person been involved in the decision?
- Who will be required to implement this decision? Have these people been involved in making the decision?

A shift in authority at GE Medical Systems, manufacturers of medical imaging devices, illustrates the necessary thought process. In the early 1990s, company executives realized their markets were increasingly global. In this environment, their approval process for major sales, requiring a head office committee decision, was unacceptably slow, particularly when different time zones were factored in. In response, they gave increased latitude to field sales personnel to make pricing and delivery decisions on their own, allowing them to apply available information regarding inventories, manufacturing costs and schedules, competitor prices, and more. The only caveat was that the salesperson making the commitments had to ensure that the organization could meet them and to accept being held accountable for the customer's satisfaction.

Driving decisions downward requires continual reexamination and letting go. When a subordinate comes to a manager for a decision, the manager needs to ask, "What makes me the one to make that decision?" If the answer is that the manager has information the subordinate lacks, the next question must be, "What keeps me from sharing that information?" Managers also need to keep asking themselves, "How often have I reversed, or declined to approve, a decision of this kind?" If the answer is never, then the next question should be, "What value am I adding by signing off on this stuff?" And again, "What keeps me from delegating this decision?"

For example, at the World Bank, a study revealed that the resident board of directors examined every loan request but almost never turned one down because senior management had already done a rigorous approval process. As a result, the board shifted its focus to policy decisions and select loans of a politically sensitive nature.

The oil service firm B.J. Hughes illustrates how different things can look when decisions are closer to the point of action. At Hughes, senior managers had realized that the price of centralized decision making was lack of speed (decisions centrally made were slower to implement), questionable accuracy (each new layer of management involved in a decision took that decision further from the point of impact), and lowered commitment (employees passed the buck on decisions, removing themselves from responsibility). To shift the locus of decision making, the salespeople were authorized to make customer-focused decisions at the point of impact—but first, the entire salesforce underwent detailed training in how to make decisions on product mix, meeting customer requirements, and even pricing. After sales personnel became frontline decision makers and cycle time for meeting customer needs dropped significantly, senior managers assumed new roles. No longer responsible for command-and-control activities and making decisions, they focused on coaching and on ensuring that employees had the information and competence to do their work. Essentially, the organization was turned upside down.

Use Town Meetings to Shift Authority

The *town meeting* is a vehicle first used by General Electric as part of its transformational Work-Out. The metaphor comes from the original governance system of colonial New England, where town residents would meet as a total community, in marathon sessions, to debate issues and make decisions about town laws, procedures, and policies.

In a typical GE town meeting, employees come together for dialogue and debate about organizational and business issues, often off-site and away from the pressures of work. Participants have common ground—they report to the same boss, work with a similar customer, or work on the same business process, but they always represent multiple levels of the hierarchy. Prior to the town meeting, participants work in small groups for one to two days to generate ideas for changing or improving the business. These ideas may include relatively simple actions such as removing reports, canceling or focusing meetings, eliminating or streamlining approval processes, or changing policies. Or they may involve more profound and complex changes, such as redesigning a manufacturing process, setting up a new business venture, or changing a customer service routine.

The main town meeting considers these ideas as a boundaryless decision-making forum. That is, the entire community reviews and debates the ideas and comes to a decision. A senior business leader chairs the session, which can include anywhere from 15 to 150 people. The leader's responsibility is to make sure that every idea is either approved or killed (or occasionally sent back to the drawing board) and that everyone understands the decision.

Town meetings drive change in authority patterns by making the decision-making process visible. In effective town meetings, business leaders do not just make decisions in front of an audience, they work through the decision thought process with the group. For example, here is an actual dialogue from a GE town meeting focused on reducing cycle times in a leasing business:

GROUP MEMBER [*Presenting a recommendation*]: Let's eliminate the regional manager's signature on all the paperwork when we have to liquidate an asset coming off lease. . . . We can let the branch manager sign off. It takes an extra thirty minutes for the regional manager to sign all the papers for each unit. It's at least forty hours per month for each regional manager—not to mention the slowdown of our processing, particularly when the regional manager is not immediately available.

BUSINESS LEADER: What value does the regional manager's signature add?

FIRST REGIONAL MANAGER [*Uncomfortable about letting go of the signing authority*]: There are some cost considerations here regarding the price for liquidation. It's got to be a management-controlled decision.

BUSINESS LEADER: Do the regional managers pay any real attention to what they are signing? In other words, do they ever not sign, or change the price, or change anything on the paper?

SECOND REGIONAL MANAGER: It's basically a rubber stamp. We never look at the numbers. We just sign.

FINANCE MANAGER: None of these papers are ever kicked back. The salesperson knows what the numbers are, and our computer systems provide a final check anyway.

BUSINESS LEADER: So there doesn't seem to be any reason for the regional manager to get involved. Let's make the change!

GROUP: [*Loud cheers*].

Note that the dialogue included a safe way for people to challenge the regional manager who did not want to shift authority downward. In many town meetings, the senior business leader is challenged, too—something that would rarely, if ever, happen in the normal course of organizational events.

Town meetings also help shift authority by educating people in their real degrees of freedom. Often, decisions move up the line not because senior people want to make all the decisions but because workers lack the self-confidence to decide things on their own. So they pass the buck up—and up and up. Or even more often, they make no decision, assuming that someone higher up will take care of things.

In town meetings, leaders can challenge employees to grab control of decisions that they should be making. An extreme example of this took place during a town meeting at Tungsram, GE's Hungarian lighting acquisition. After years of state ownership, employees were unused to deciding anything on their own and, in fact, were afraid to do so. At a town meeting chaired by George Varga, the Hungarian-born manager who was GE's first chairman of Tungsram, dozens of ideas were presented for improving product quality and speeding development of a particular lamp. After each and every presentation, Varga said, "You don't need me to decide whether or not to do that. Make your own decision!" After two hours of this, an engineer started out with, "I know I don't need you to make this decision . . . so here's what we're going to do, whether you like it or not." At that point, Varga stood up and applauded—and the authority process of Tungsram made an almost palpable shift.

At GE, Baxter Healthcare, GlaxoSmithKline, the World Bank, and dozens of other organizations, managers have used town meetings as a means of removing vertical boundaries and engaging employees in the creation of a healthier hierarchy. Lessons from these companies suggest that magic seems to happen when

- Participants work on issues that matter both to them and to the company. Passion about the issues helps to promote real change.
- Leaders don't use staff to insulate them from their employees. Leaders' staff members can participate but not serve as filters.
- Decisions are made in real time. Rather than defer decisions for further thought, the leader works with the group to make decisions on the spot.
- The atmosphere (created by a facilitator, warm-up exercises, and so on) allows private concerns to be openly shared and solved. People need to feel safe enough to challenge their bosses, without fear of consequences.
- Assigned champions follow up to make sure that decisions get implemented. This helps ensure that the town meeting truly becomes part of a process for shifting authority and not just a one-time event.
- Senior managers spend significant time at the town meeting. Often, good town meetings last for many hours, with both grueling and exciting debate. The willingness of senior people to devote this kind of time is itself a powerful symbol of change.

Shift Management Roles from Controller to Coach

Most managers are proud to be managers. They see the managerial title and rank as an honor, giving them privilege, respect, and status. And part of that status is the manager's traditional role of being in control and making tough decisions for others. Therefore, as we have discussed, many managers resist the shift to a healthy hierarchy because they fear they may be made redundant or will not know how to play the new role.

To fine-tune the authority dimension, you need to shift this mentality. First of all, managers need to learn what it means to be a coach instead of a controller. It helps to ask them to inductively derive the characteristics of good coaches and then discuss how to apply those attributes to their work. Workshops can help them figure out what manager-coaches do: lay out game plans then let the employees execute the plans; lead by example more than edict and earn respect from action more than title; work with and for employees; and apply discipline as teachers, to help employees learn and improve, rather than as auditors, to catch and punish inadequate behavior.

Second, provide opportunities for managers to learn how to coach. Training modules on facilitation, team building, and group problem solving can teach managers the tools of coaching. Managers can be encouraged to pair up in a *buddy-feedback* system and learn from observing and giving feedback to each other.

Third, make heroes of managers who reach their goals through team and individual coaching. When you recognize and reward those known as good coaches and developers of talent—perhaps with a "coach of the month" award for managers nominated by employees—others will take note.

The controller-to-coach shift was a critical element in the transformation of Consolidated Edison's East River power plant for New York City. For fifty years, East River had been strongly hierarchical, with several layers of decision makers. The system worked well when Con Edison had a public utility's virtual monopoly and its management's main job was to ensure stable, reliable power at rates approved by the regulatory commission. In the 1990s, however, as power generation became a competitive commodity, the plant had to become much more flexible, able to adjust output quickly and reliably—and with far less cost—than in the past.

One of the key requirements was to get equipment repair prioritized, planned, and implemented without close supervision from higher-ups. Plant management set up several fully autonomous mini-units to run sections of the plant—each containing its own operations, maintenance, and technical staff. However, faced with the loss of their familiar roles in the chain of command and without a consolidated understanding of their new roles, the maintenance, operations, and technical services supervisors tended to fall back into old patterns, supervising the details of a task and even doing the work themselves instead of orchestrating their new units. Eventually, the plant manager realized that these supervisors needed help to grasp their new role as coaches, trainers, and on-the-spot problem solvers. He therefore involved the supervisors in task teams and projects, and scheduled seminars for them with a consultant. After a number of months, it started to become clear which supervisors would be able to drop the detail work and make the transition to the new role. The plant manager then began to consider the personnel changes that would be required to move forward with the new organization.

Remove Layers If Necessary

The fourth part of tuning the authority dimension is removing excess layers of decision makers. GE's Jack Welch once noted that layers of management are like sweaters—when you wear a lot of them, you cannot tell if it is cold outside. Removing layers of managers gets the organization closer to reality and helps decision making move faster, tie in with customer needs, and be more responsive to changing situations. Also, removing layers of management and increasing span of control ensures that the remaining managers cannot get too engrossed in details. Unable to watch all their employees closely, they are forced to ensure that employees have the skills to do the work and then let those employees decide how to get things done on their own. Increasing span of control leaves managers almost no choice but to liberate employees to act responsibly.

Removing layers of managers in a way that loosens vertical boundaries, however, is not as easy as taking off sweaters. There are three distinct challenges to be addressed.

Structure. If the organization's structure uses management layers to integrate diverse work tasks or processes, this integration may not happen naturally or easily without the layers. For example, taking out layers of engineering management may require new mechanisms for coordinating product designs with manufacturing and marketing.

People movement. Removing layers has personnel implications. In the short term, the former managers themselves will need to be retrained, replaced, or possibly outplaced or retired. Long term, with fewer managerial positions available for promotion, the organization will need different career paths and compensation and incentive systems.

Governance. A new process of governance needs to be created. At the minimum, management must determine forums for decision making (for example, who will come to staff meetings), create means of performance appraisal, and develop new communication channels.

This kind of thinking is exemplified by the way Sally Richardson adjusted the manager-to-employee ratio in the Medicaid Bureau of the Federal Health Care Financing Administration (HCFA), taking it from 1:5 to 1:12. Before beginning the process, HCFA agreed to create a technical career path that would let former managers move into policy and project roles without losing compensation or promotion opportunities. Richardson then commissioned a "streamlining team" of employees and managers to design a new organization that would meet the delayering criteria, be more flexible and responsive to changing policies, and provide better service to the states and other constituents. The team was asked to consider organizing around processes, around customers, or around strategic goals, and to create an open dialogue about team thinking with the whole organization. In this way, Richardson avoided imposing delayering as painful surgery. Instead, she used it as an opportunity to encourage empowerment and stimulate innovative thinking throughout the bureau.

Matching Rewards with Goals

Since people generally adapt to incentives, reward systems are a significant dimension for loosening vertical boundaries. However, reward systems generally are not well tuned. Managers often *hope* employees will be motivated toward a particular goal even though they get *rewarded* for something else. In a university, deans hope faculty are teaching effectively but often reward research. It should be no surprise, then, that faculty spend more time doing research than teaching. Similarly, in many commercial firms, executives hope managers will exhibit collaboration and teamwork but base rewards on individual targets, causing most managers to concentrate on their own functions. Reward systems are also often out of tune because organizations reward what is easy to measure. One reason deans measure research is that it is easy to quantify. The number of articles a faculty member publishes is indisputable, whereas quality of teaching is a fuzzy quantity, and end-of-semester student evaluations may not be true indicators as an easy grader or amusing but uninformative speaker may well garner rave reviews. Similarly, companies often measure objective outcomes like profitability, performance against plan, and other financial goals. Teamwork and collaboration goals may be desired, but they literally *don't count*—they're inconvenient to measure so no one tries to measure them.

We have found three practices (summarized in the box) particularly useful in tuning the rewards dimension.

Practices for Shifting Rewards

- Base rewards on performance and skill.
- Share rewards up and down the organization.
- Use nonfinancial rewards.

Base Rewards on Performance and Skill

As noted, traditional hierarchies reward people primarily by position. In essence, compensation and perquisites are rewards for past achievement and are not necessarily linked to current job performance. As organizations flatten and more people vie for fewer vertical positions, this reward system becomes dysfunctional. Realizing they cannot advance, people often retire in place or become cynical.

One powerful way of shifting a reward system is to base compensation less on position and much more on performance and skills, using these three components:

- A fixed base salary determined by past contributions, adjusted yearly for cost of living and market equity.

- Skills pay based on demonstrated competence or proficiency in certain areas valued by the organization and relevant to the job category (for example, languages, technical skills, negotiation, analytical abilities, and so on).
- Performance pay based on a combination of firm, unit, and individual performance.

The percentages of these three components will vary depending on the organization, the market, and the position. But the general principle is that base salary should be no more than 60 percent of the total. This forces people to focus on achievement and skill development to boost their pay.

Naturally, to put such a system in place, you need measurement systems that can track performance and proficiency, along with a process for allocation. For example, Canadian mounted police on the border patrol are tested for language skills, and those who are bilingual in French and English receive larger salaries than those who speak only one language. Bilingual officers are also given annual proficiency exams to encourage the upkeep and continued usage of their skill.

Wall Street firms have had these kinds of systems for many years, tying compensation directly to deal or trading performance. Many traders make far more money than their senior managers, giving the best performers an incentive to remain in the game. However, the Wall Street bonus system is prone to abuse, encouraging people to focus on results at any cost. One solution to such abuses is to design measurement systems to include long-term performance, team contribution, customer relationships, and ethical and legal behavior. The balanced scorecard approach that many companies have adopted is an effective way of putting these elements together.[9]

Share Rewards Up and Down the Organization

In the 1980s, a number of firms underwent management buy-outs. The theory was that if the incentives were right, managers would work harder and smarter, making private firms more competitive than public ones. After the Borg Warner management buy-out, managers who stayed on were required to invest from $50,000 to $1 million apiece in the new firm. The intent was to make each manager's personal stake significant and challenging enough to change behavior in the firm. And indeed, unpublished data collected by Sibson Consulting in Princeton, New Jersey, showed that buy-out firms were three times as productive as public firms in the same industry.

Incentives work. When people have much of their net worth committed to their firm, they make different decisions. Rather than fly business class, they fly coach; rather than fly three people to a meeting, they fly one; rather than hold needless face-to-face meetings, they use teleconferencing.

Other corporate initiatives can invest employees in the firm, with the implicit contract that those who stay with the company and perform well will be successful if the company succeeds. PepsiCo's Sharepower program gives all employees shares in the company as part of their compensation. United Parcel Service employees also receive ownership stakes—which paid off handsomely when the firm went public. Sara Lee and Eastman Kodak have instituted programs that encourage (and at times require) managers at different levels to own significant shares of company stock. The rationale is that even without taking a firm private, managers can have financial commitments to its performance. An important concern when Goldman Sachs went public was that employees maintain their commitment to the new firm. This "emotional equity" was achieved by ensuring that almost every professional employee in the publicly traded Goldman Sachs had some financial equity. Nordstrom's high commission based on sales has been seen as an important part of employee commitment to customer service. Nordies know that when they form long-term relationships with customers, those customers will keep buying from them over time, and they will be rewarded.

Stock options can build management commitment, but it is important to verify how far across the board they go. One executive who bragged about an "extended" stock option program was surprised to learn that it reached only 8 percent of the total payroll. In contrast, part of Wal-Mart's success over the years has been a systematic stock option program for all employees, from check-out associates to senior managers. Stock ownership has encouraged employees to satisfy customers and achieve store performance targets and has helped create a relatively stable workforce in an industry characterized by extensive turnover.

Targeted financial bonuses have been helpful at TRINOVA, where special "Chairman Awards" have been allocated to employees who make exceptional contributions to firm performance. First of America has instituted a "gotcha" rewards program: managers can hand out money, stock, and other prizes to employees caught doing something above and beyond.

Use Nonfinancial Rewards

Nonfinancial rewards can be incredibly varied, limited only by an organization's creativity: a parking space allocated to the employee of the month, congratulatory letters from executives to employees (or their families), special dinners and recognition for exceptional performance, press releases praising employees, valued temporary assignments, learning visits to best-practice companies, attendance at professional seminars, or the opportunity for advanced training. Again, however, these rewards loosen vertical boundaries only when they are given for performance, not position.

One of the more creative applications of nonfinancial rewards comes from the professional development committee chaired by Jeana Wirtenberg in AT&T's human resource division. For three years, this committee has accepted self- and other nominations for "role models of HR excellence" anywhere in AT&T. Judged by a panel using criteria based on the HR vision at AT&T, winning employees receive individual or team recognition at an awards dinner—and wide publicity throughout the company and in local newspapers. They also have an opportunity to present their best practices at an annual AT&T-wide HR symposium.

Putting It All Together: How Do You Know It's Working?

This chapter sets out four components that need to be wired together and four dimensions that can be tuned to create more permeable vertical boundaries (summarized in Figure 3.4). To begin putting these ideas together in a change strategy for your organization, we suggest that you make some notes on the following questions and then review them with your colleagues.

1. *To what extent are the four components (alignment, commitment, cumulation, and shared mindset) in place in our organization?* Are they wired together properly? What specific steps should we take to tighten the wiring?

**Figure 3.4. Wiring and Tuning Dimensions
for Creating Healthy Hierarchies.**

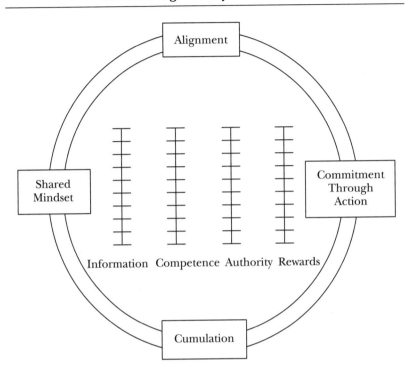

2. *Which of the four dimensions is most out of tune and could use the most work?* What specific steps can we take to tune this dimension in the proper direction?

3. *If we tune one dimension, are there adjustments we need to make in the other three to keep our vertical boundaries in tune?*

Your answers to these three questions will give you the basis for an action-based work program aimed at loosening vertical boundaries and creating a healthy hierarchy. As you proceed, however, you also need to consider how you will know if the actions are working.

AT&T has adopted three measures to assess progress toward a healthier hierarchy. Economic Value Added (EVA) is a measure of financial results. A healthy hierarchy reduces costs through increased productivity. Customer Value Added (CVA) is a measure of customer service scores. A healthy hierarchy increases speed of service and responsiveness. Finally, People Value Added (PVA) is a measure of leadership behavior, diversity, and values. Healthy hierarchies empower people to act.

Here are five broad categories in which you can examine whether actions to increase the permeability of your organization's vertical boundaries are making a difference. The evidence will be both direct and indirect.

- *Check the ratio of employees to managers.* This rough indicator of the span of control will indicate whether layers are being removed.
- *Examine employees' commitment to the business.* Employee commitment may be measured with attitude surveys, but it also shows up in action. Employees should begin to ask more questions about meeting customer goals and improving business performance. Employees should begin to take personal initiative to fix customer problems without waiting for approval. Customers should be sending more unsolicited letters of commendation about employees and their acts of service.
- *Check whether cycle times are reduced.* Increased speed can manifest in a number of areas: response to customer price questions, order-remittance cycles, training program implementation, manufacturing process changes, new plant design, new information system implementation, employee replacement, and financial reports can all take less time than before.
- *Examine employees' self-leadership behaviors.* Healthy hierarchies encourage people to lead themselves, reducing the need for hands-on external leadership. Therefore, when employees act as leaders for themselves, executives should find they have been freed up to spend more time on strategic and customer issues.
- *Check whether a new mindset is in evidence.* When asking employees, suppliers, and customers what the business is known for, managers should begin to get different and more consistent answers.

Part Two

Free Movement Side to Side

Crossing Horizontal Boundaries

First Person: **Daniel Vasella, Chairman and CEO, Novartis AG**

Novartis is a leading global pharmaceutical company created in 1996 by the merger of Sandoz and Ciba-Geigy. Since its creation, Chairman and CEO Daniel Vasella has energetically built up a new structure and implemented an ambitious, growth-oriented strategy designed to accelerate product development and sales. This effort to shape a high-performance organization is a true example of how boundaries can be broken down between functions and geographies, between businesses and their customers.

Trained as a physician, Dan held a number of medical positions in Switzerland before joining Sandoz Pharmaceuticals in 1988. From 1988 to 1996, he held increasingly senior management positions in Sandoz, both in the United States and Switzerland. At the time of the merger with Ciba-Geigy, he was CEO of Sandoz Pharma Ltd. Here are his comments on the ongoing process of creating a boundaryless organization:

At Novartis, three axes are critical to the success of our business: customers and products, geographies, and functions. To be fast and market-oriented, we must overcome the boundaries between these elements. We know that without a common performance mission and common strategies, without simple structures and a common language, common rewards, and common performance measurements, we will not succeed. Shortly after the merger, we therefore worked to align functions and reaffirm the strong need for cooperation. It was not really a new concept, but the way we implemented it definitely changed.

We put special emphasis on the work around the product, for two main reasons. First, a new product averages US$600–800 million of investment from bench to market, taking into account all costs. Therefore, we need to profile products optimally for large markets and minimize fragmentation. The results of our work must be applicable worldwide. In addition, for a product to be relevant to customers and physicians, marketing must be integrated with R&D early in the process. There must be respect and a common language between the researchers and the marketing people. These two groups must act as two halves of the same brain. Production must also be in step with R&D from an early point in the process, so that the product is in its final shape in time for approvals.

These organizational objectives have led us to create an international project team (IPT) for each project, spanning marketing, R&D, and production. The role of the IPT is to unite all critical functions in the most efficient manner, with the goal of producing marketable products in the shortest possible time, at reasonable cost and with impeccable quality. Our output in the recent past demonstrates the value of this approach compared to previous systems. We now have a process of commonality—and excellence—in development, marketing, and sales.

Alone, an organizational function at its best can become a repository of excellence and provide a storehouse of knowledge, quality, and discipline relevant to a specific job to be done—for example, conducting clinical trials. This is very important and we do not want to undermine or disband that pride in functional expertise. However, when you move to a cross-functional working group model, you have to remember that all functions must add value. There must be open communication among people brought together to solve a problem. People must physically be present and they must contribute. Such a model does not lend itself to individuals who are stubborn and egotistical; instead, it values self-assured, open, inquisitive people who see the advancement and successful marketing of their common project as their main purpose.

You would expect working in a boundary-free model to be more complex and time consuming. And it does indeed take more time up front, from problem formulation to solution identification. But the time spent aligning project-team members toward common goals is much more than regained in implementation. Overall, the entire process is faster. And speed is our key to innovation.

We have also articulated a common vision, a common purpose resulting in a common culture based on tangible or quantitative information. You cannot expect people to work together in a team if you offer incentives that reward individual performance only. Therefore, we have instituted a reward system that aligns employees, teams, and shareholders. In addition, we have freshened up the organization by hiring new people from outside.

At the working level, we faced an array of specific problems and challenges. To overcome these in a more efficient way, we developed a process called "Fast Action for Results" (FAR), loosely derived from GE's Work-Out process. Our FAR process identifies issues common to different parts of the organization. In the past, people often talked on a bilateral basis, but problems cannot be solved by addressing only small, separate pieces. FAR, instead, reaches much wider and involves multiple parties in the process with expertise and a clear objective. By understanding all relevant aspects of a problem, getting multiple ideas for its solution and on-the-spot approval from key leaders, people can resolve problems expeditiously and across borders.

We consider FAR a very useful tool for approaching key challenges and issues we are facing. And we never imposed it. FAR has evolved organically. As it became clear that it works, people began using it more and more widely.

When we were considering the size of the FAR initiative, we pondered whether to take a broad-scale approach, with activities across the whole company, or to start small and let it progress at its own pace. We chose a middle road, encouraging and resourcing— but not mandating—a broad-scale rollout. Though this approach meant FAR took longer to settle in as a company practice, it also gave it more staying power. A deep cultural change takes time, but that's fine. We wanted to be sure we were moving in the right direction and knew where we wanted to end up.

I said before that there must be a common aspiration in what we want to achieve. There must be a common platform and a common understanding. There also needs to be a leader bringing the various players together. The cross-functional approach demonstrates the difference between dividing the pie and figuring out how to make the pie bigger.

Where are the barriers to cross-functional communication? Where have things gone more slowly and where has there been resistance?

Problems can arise when people feel that sharing ideas means they lose ownership, that something is being taken away from them. The sense of territory is inherent in human nature. The counter-measure against this fear is organizational trust, which is best reflected in areas where people have learned to work as a team in a fact-based fashion. In such a process, the team shares success and recognition. So it's not a question of removing all boundaries—it's about making people feel familiar and more at ease so that they get better results.

Critical insights strengthen competitive advantage. We are also applying an integrated approach with doctors and patients. For a recent product launch, we invited a group of physicians, consultants, and patients together to act as a project team and discuss how to proceed. We believe it's vital to bring customers into this setting. This hooks us directly into their needs and provides us with firsthand insights into the sensitivities of the market.

For a new respiratory drug, I went to such a meeting and asked the physicians how they would use the drug, which patients they would give it to, and what they thought the price should be. They were extremely helpful. It is invaluable to listen to customers because they provide you not only with answers and information but with critical insights that strengthen your competitive advantage.

We've found that sharing knowledge reduces boundaries. Technology has definitely helped us speed things up, providing instant communication across hierarchies and geographies. For example, our people at the Genomics Institute of the Novartis Foundation (GNF) regularly communicate with researchers at Scripps Research Institute and at our other sites around the world. We have purposely funded a knowledge link to accelerate the transfer of ideas across the company and to encourage GNF to serve as an incubator of innovation within Novartis. The science and knowledge sites are now technologically linked.

Technology also plays a role in knowledge management—we have identified internal experts for specific topics and offer broad access to internal know-how resources. When you share knowledge, you have fewer boundaries. Chat rooms with patients and newsletters for patient support groups are other informal ways to communicate and to share ideas.

After the merger there was a big overall shift in our company. We even chose a new name. We were able to break down quite a few of the existing organizational boundaries. We focused on what we wanted to be, not on what we were. People who did not want to play the new game left.

In the end, business is a marathon, not a hundred-yard sprint. It's a question of endurance and perseverance. We needed to identify the most critical business processes to reach our objectives. This is where we started, but we also realized that we can't stop there. We needed integration among the various players—R&D, physicians, marketing. Otherwise, all we would do is pass along activities sequentially to the next person, like on an assembly line, with no coordination or sharing. Quality would suffer.

Now we need to work on our core value drivers. In many respects, we are doing better than industry average. We have reduced time, been first to market, and thereby cut costs. In those areas, we are doing quite a good job. But now we need to look at how we work in the marketplace and upgrade our performance there. Individual countries need aspirations beyond their own territory, so we must instill a true sense of globalism. They need to be willing to listen, to share and to learn, to exchange and incorporate best practices from each other. Our next step is, therefore, to find a standard way of approaching excellence. We are moving forward on that.

Some say standards kill creativity. But if you want to be an outstanding, creative swordfighter, you have first to master the basics. The same applies for innovation. You must master the basic tools before you can innovate. This mastery provides freedom for more ambitious creativity, not constraint. To convey a common vision and clear objectives, you must communicate at all levels consistently over a period of time. This will keep you on a course that will take you where you want to go.

Chapter Four

Beyond Turf and Territory

Vertical boundaries form the floors and ceilings of an organization's house; horizontal boundaries form the room walls—the dividing lines between divisions, units, and functions. Whereas vertical boundaries shape definitions of status and career progression, horizontal boundaries define functional specialties such as marketing, sales, or engineering. The boundaries that distinguish people within a function—for example, hourly from salaried employees, union from nonunion, permanent from temporary—are also horizontal dividers, with each group having its own rules and regulations, ways of tracking time, access to buildings or files, and so on. In short, horizontal boundaries are the way people divide up the territory within the firm.

Just as organizations need to maintain some vertical boundaries, they also need some degree of horizontal task delineation. A house with no load-bearing walls has no structure and will collapse. However, houses can afford more open space than they often get, more modular walls, more light flowing from room to room, and much more traffic throughout. So this chapter examines how you can make your horizontal boundaries more adjustable and permeable so that your entire organization can operate with greater speed, flexibility, integration, and innovation.

Boxes, Boxes, Boxes

Horizontal boundaries are almost as ingrained in human affairs as vertical, particularly since they, too, arise from the natural order of social life. While vertical boundaries derived from parent-child authority relationships, horizontal boundaries emerged from task differentiation in primitive societies, as work began to be distributed among categories of clan and family members, sometimes based on skills and sometimes based on social definitions. Thus, for example, young children would gather herbs or berries; older boys and men would specialize in hunting; older girls and women would prepare food and provide medical treatment. These were the original specialties that helped to make social organization possible by splitting up diverse tasks among groups of people.

Today's organizations likewise arrange themselves around specialties—engineering, manufacturing, marketing and sales, human resources, administration, and so on. Some may have upwards of twenty such departments, each forming a mini-organization with its own agenda, resources, and vertical structure. These groups of hierarchical specialty units are often called silo or stovepipe organizations, because they form sets of stacks on the organization chart.

The modern history of the silo structure can be traced to two developments. First, as Adam Smith described in 1776 in his classic *Wealth of Nations,* economists recognized that organizations gained tremendous productivity when each worker did a single task and then passed the product to another worker.[1] Smith described a number of settings where this system was more efficient than having each person handle the full range of tasks required to produce a product. He saw that fragmenting a large process allowed employees to learn to do a single task well and also conserved the time individual workers required to change tools, locations, and frame of mind to move from task to task.

The second development that spurred horizontal task specialization, particularly in manufacturing, was technology. The moving assembly line, created in large scale by Henry Ford as a key to increasing productivity, brought the work to the workers rather than the other way around. Combined with task specialization, it meant that huge efficiencies could be gained by dividing the workforce into welders, polishers, inspectors, and so on.

Eventually the mentality of task specialization spread beyond the manufacturing floor. As technology spurred large-scale mass production, a whole series of support functions—purchasing, engineering, maintenance, quality control, inventory management, training—emerged to keep the production machine going. Then the product needed to be shipped, warehoused, distributed, marketed, and sold, and each of these tasks was given over to specialists who could provide focus and expertise. Finally, as these functions proliferated, additional functions were needed at the corporate level to tie tasks together, ensure cross-functional equity, and provide overall control. This led to the rise of further specialties such as finance, personnel, legal, audit, tax, and more.

To further complicate things, leaders such as Alfred Sloan Jr. of GM grouped functions into parallel divisions, each producing a different product or category of products (for example, the Chevrolet Division or the Cadillac Division). Thus was born the modern vertical/horizontal corporation with its array of divisions, each with its stacked functions, all reporting upward to a centralized executive group.

This model proliferated wildly after World War II. Manufacturing organizations added droves of workers and departments to the horizontal spread and armies of managers to the vertical layers. Like out-of-control cell division, each new growth surge added a new field office, a new product division, a new department. The 1950s and 1960s saw the rise of gigantic corporations employing tens of thousands of people with hundreds of departments and divisions.

In the 1970s and 1980s, knowledge specialization pushed the cells to divide yet again. Departments of chemists, for example, split into departments of biochemists, geochemists, thermonuclear chemists, and so on. Engineers became process engineers, electrical engineers, chemical engineers, and more, each specialty with its own knowledge base and its own administrative structure. Even manufacturing jobs subdivided as workers confronted new, highly complex machines or computers. Thus, for example, tool and die makers, who once could run assorted lathes, grinding machines, drills, and presses, now had to specialize in particular computer-controlled machine tools that required months of rigorous training. Similarly, corporate finance people began to divide themselves into cost accountants, budget analysts, tax experts, and more.

Today, more horizontal lines and degrees of specialization mark our educational systems and work structures than ever before. The cell division appears never ending, and the rapid pace of change makes the proliferation geometrically harder to stop.

Further driving the process is everyone's natural desire to relate to people with shared interests. Whenever people form functional groups, members bond in ways that solidify the group and its unique identity. It's hard to bond to hundreds or thousands of people at a time, so smaller groups in an organization make it easier for people to get to know and accept those they work with most closely. However, such groupings also tend to validate people's penchant for stereotyping the outside world, dividing the universe into camps of "us" and "them." We easily support those in "our" group and easily find fault with those in other groups, whether of race, belief, or corporate function. This tendency is sibling and clan rivalry writ large.

Signs of horizontal bonding abound in most organizations: the marketing people all go out for drinks together, the secretaries have their own table in the cafeteria, the chemists have their own jokes. Some of these horizontal boundaries are useful, but some prevent necessary cross-fertilization of ideas and information.

Haywire Horizontal Boundaries

As long as size, role clarity, specialization, and control led to success, the horizontal division of labor worked well. The new success factors of speed, flexibility, integration, and innovation, however, make horizontal boundaries as problematic as vertical boundaries. Mazes of functional boxes inevitably create delay, indecision, uncoordinated action, and least-common-denominator products and services.

These days there are more variables than most companies can predict, and control of those variables is temporary at best. In response, companies must create permeability not only up and down the hierarchy but also across the horizontal spans. Failure to do so can lead to the five typical dysfunctions shown in the box, which we call haywire horizontal boundaries.

Warning Signs of Haywire Horizontal Boundaries

- Slow, sequential cycle times
- Protected turf
- Suboptimization of organizational goals
- The enemy-within syndrome
- Customers doing their own integration

Slow, Sequential Cycle Times

When several departments or divisions must each act one by one to create a new product or respond to a customer, cycle times can seem to take forever. For example, in all too many traditional manufacturing firms, research and development people design a new product and then turn the design over to engineering to create prototypes. Because engineering may not fully understand or trust R&D, it redoes the design before finalizing the engineering specifications. It then passes the job to manufacturing, which does another redesign to make it easier to assemble and sends the proposed product to marketing. But marketing can't sell the product because it's not what customers require. This process of "throwing ideas over the wall" not only takes endless time and untold resources but often fails. Sociologist and consultant Bruce Phillips found that the sequential development process of the big three U.S. carmakers in the early 1980s added literally years to Detroit's efforts to bring new cars to market and meant new cars were based on customer requirements as much as six years out of date.[2] Japanese manufacturers—designing and producing models in half the time—moved smoothly into Detroit's market.

When work flows from function to function, the assumption is that each specialty adds some unique value. Each function is also assumed to operate in its own way, so collaboration is not possible. Furthermore, each function must wait until those up the line have done their thing, so each receiving function can build on the sending function's contributions. Meanwhile, weeks go by and the customer waits.

When horizontal boundaries become permeable, a different logic emerges, allowing functions to work in parallel. It is often surprising how many work processes that once seemed obviously sequential can be done simultaneously.

For example, at SmithKline Beecham (now GlaxoSmithKline), as throughout the pharmaceutical industry, drug development is a long, expensive process. Reductions in R&D cycle time provide significant patient and financial benefits. Yet for many years, SmithKline Beecham regarded large portions of the process, particularly the handling of clinical trial data, as necessarily sequential. Based on this assumption, the clinical operations unit consisted of numerous specialty functions: clinicians who set up trial parameters, statisticians who created data analysis protocols, operations people who arranged clinical sites, systems people who arranged collection of data, data-entry specialists who coded data into computer systems, clinical quality specialists who checked data accuracy, biometrics experts who analyzed data, and regulatory specialists who put data into formats acceptable for FDA submission. Each specialty operated semiautonomously, taking work from one group and passing it on to the next, and all too often the company ended up with problems that required significant backtracking or even a whole new cycle. As a result, it took an average of eight months to get a drug from clinical trial to FDA submission, with many projects running significantly longer.

To shorten the cycle time, SmithKline Beecham challenged the sequential logic. For example, it replaced the multitude of functional clinical operations departments with what it termed DARTs— Data Analysis and Reporting Teams. Each DART contained all the specialties needed to support the clinical operations cycle for a new drug from beginning to end. DART members were charged with the goal of working together, in parallel, to take as much cycle time as possible out of the process. In very short order, the teams began to find collaborative opportunities. For example, by designing the research protocol around FDA submission requirements from the beginning, they eliminated weeks of reformatting and additional data collection. By creating more standardized data collection methods, they eliminated data-entry time and errors. Using these ideas and many more, it took the DARTs less than a year to reduce the average cycle time significantly—even though the number of projects dramatically increased.

Protected Turf

Once horizontal boundaries solidify, each department guards its power and resources. Any change in process is seen as attacking the status quo rather than aiding the organization, and people end up spending more time protecting turf than securing or satisfying customers. For example, when NASA brought together several scientific, educational, engineering, and satellite production departments under one executive to promote interdisciplinary collaboration on common scientific problems, the first week's hottest issue of debate was not how to pull together the research programs but who would control the scheduling of conference rooms.

Turf disputes are classic signs of rigid horizontal boundaries. The logic of specialization makes them seem inevitable. A group assigned a particular task—and assessed and rewarded for the performance of that task—has a vested interest in maintaining control over it. Giving up any part of the task may raise questions about whether the group is needed. Giving up any degree of control over the task by letting others participate may prevent the group from meeting its standards. So the rational thing to do is to protect its turf, to maintain the resources and authority necessary to perform its particular specialty.

Today, this view is myopic. It ignores the overall purpose the group is supposed to serve. Loosening horizontal boundaries restores the broader perspective. Turf issues decrease and reconfigurations of the overall process gain acceptability.

To return to Consolidated Edison's Waterside plant, years of tradition made functional boundaries particularly solid. Plagued by slow response to equipment maintenance orders, the plant held a workshop with a team of managers and union people to address the problem. The team mapped out the overall process and found that a major bottleneck was the maintenance planning function, which prioritized requests, laid out the repair sequence, and identified the tools and equipment needed for each job. The planning function saw its role as ensuring safe maintenance procedures, but by doing every job—big or small—with the same level of detail and without input from plant operators and mechanics, it was creating a huge backlog.

Mechanics and operators had been complaining about these precise problems for years. The planning function had always responded that its procedures made sure all equipment deficiencies were identified correctly and no repair shortcuts would compromise safety. During the workshop, all sides saw the entire process for the first time, and the need for collaboration was clear. From this perspective, they all accepted a number of experimental steps: joint planning of jobs by operators, mechanics, and planners; accelerated handling of small, standard jobs; and an agreed turnaround time for planning larger jobs. Owing to these and other steps, the maintenance backlog almost disappeared in six months, and a more productive, less turf-oriented relationship grew up among maintenance, operations, and planning units.

Suboptimization of Organizational Goals

A third warning sign of haywire horizontal boundaries occurs when functional specialists put localized goals ahead of the organization's goals so as to optimize their own achievements and rewards. For example, in one organization, engineering researchers registered several dozen patents each year and took great pride in this accomplishment. Unfortunately, their patents rarely if ever led to commercial products, nor did the group do much to improve existing products or processes. From the engineers' perspective, they were achieving functional goals, but those goals had superseded the company's goals of producing products and solving problems. The engineers had suboptimized themselves as resources, forgetting the old saying, "Never confuse the end of the ditch with the horizon."

Even when shifting from functional to organizational goals seems obviously desirable, it is often a wrenching change. For example, when Gary Weber became vice president of technology for PPG's Glass Group, the group's Harmarville Research Center had been through a 40 percent layoff and was struggling to adjust to the reduced staff. At the same time, the center was asked to adapt to a major shift of business strategies—from introducing value-added products to reducing costs through manufacturing process improvement. This additional change met with resistance and skepticism. Weber held town meetings to air people's concerns and communicate the need to change. It soon became clear that many people were firmly locked into long-standing goals that did not match what the company needed. Only after continued dialogue and debate, coupled with some reorganization of responsibilities and cooperation of local management, did Harmarville manage to turn so that its staff all aimed at the same horizon.

The Enemy-Within Syndrome

A fourth warning sign of horizontal calcification is internal strife. Whether over major or trivial issues, these conflicts divide the staff and sap their energy. They often generate the enemy-within syndrome, as groups identify each other as bad guys and see plots everywhere. Departments feud over resources, prerogative, and power. We know of several organizations that have canceled important projects because of interdepartmental conflict over design or marketing concepts, despite customer demand for the product. And we have seen more than one group intentionally sabotage another to gain power or territory for itself. By way of illustration, one of us recently consulted with a major airline seeking to improve baggage-handling services in one of its hub airports. It turned out that the airline had two separate teams of people working at the airport, each with its own territory. The station manager and staff handled luggage check-in and ticketing, while the ground crew team handled loading luggage onto planes, transferring bags between planes, and unloading arriving planes. Although the station departure people had lots of ideas for improving the baggage-handling process and were even willing to help between flights, the ground crew managers and staff did not want any of their help or input. Similarly, when the station manager was asked for his recommendation about how to improve customer satisfaction, he responded, "Get the customers to carry their own bags! Don't let those [ground crew] people touch them."

The enemy-within syndrome is one of the most debilitating organizational problems; it is like a cancer in the organizational body. Turf wars and squabbles are nearly always highly charged because they originate at a gut level that is not subject to management redirection. That is why John Etling, former president of GeneralCologne Re, distributed "no turf" buttons to his senior management team when he was trying to implement a major customer-focused quality effort. (The buttons showed a bright green chunk of lawn with a red diagonal line through it.) His view was that the only way to deal with internal battles was to call attention to them—but with a sense of humor. This is certainly a better alternative than viewing the organizational world as full of enemies. If all the bullets are spent on infighting, there may be none left for the competitors beyond the walls.

Customers Doing Their Own Integration

As a firm's task specialization increases, customers commonly end up handling the integration of products and services, which is the fifth warning sign of haywire horizontal boundaries. In such situations, no one is accountable for overall customer satisfaction. Imagine shopping at a haberdashery with five departments—suits, shirts, ties, socks, and shoes—that don't work together. To buy a complete outfit, you not only have to deal with five salespeople, you also have to match up the colors and patterns for yourself.

For twenty years, IBM sold computers in much the same way— with rigidly separate divisions specializing in mainframes, minis, and microcomputers or focused on information systems, payroll systems, and so on. IBM customers had to figure out how to blend the various products. The insurance industry also works largely on the nonintegrated model. Customers often receive calls from two or three salespeople at a time, with one selling life insurance while another sells automobile or home or business insurance.

Integration, as noted earlier, is one of the new success factors because it allows organizations to be more responsive to customers and to react more quickly. That's why banks are scrambling to offer one-stop service for all financial needs; computer vendors are putting together packages of hardware, software, and training systems; and media and telecommunications firms are setting up fully integrated home systems for television, data, news, movies, and interactive communications all on one cable line.

Fidelity Investments has worked hard to cross horizontal boundaries so retail customers do not have to integrate products on their own. For many years, as Fidelity grew its business, each product line operated as an independent, entrepreneurial entity—seeking out its own customers and serving them in its own ways. Though this fueled tremendous growth, it also forced individual investors to do their own integration of Fidelity's many products. Customers had to construct their own portfolio strategies and deal with a vast array of service representatives and contact points—all the while being further solicited for business by other Fidelity groups.

In 1992, Roger Servison, then head of Fidelity's retail marketing company, realized customers were becoming overwhelmed and frustrated. Moreover, many lacked the skills and sophistication to develop an integrated investment strategy. He began meeting with his peers, who ran the various parts of the retail business, and his own product managers, who drove the markets of various mutual funds. Together, they formulated a vision for a more integrated retail business and started dozens of projects aimed both at making it easier to do business with Fidelity and at helping customers develop an integrated investment strategy. One project, for example, standardized the customer applications for different products, reducing their number from over three hundred to three. Another project pulled together a database that delivered integrated sets of performance reports and investment information for customers. Still other projects created tools for investors developing their own portfolio strategies.

The net result was a significant increase in customer satisfaction ratings and a 2 percent improvement in overall market share after almost ten years of market share stability. Clearly, when Fidelity made its horizontal boundaries more permeable, customers saw the difference.

Centralization Versus Decentralization: The Swinging Pendulum

When the warning signs of haywire horizontal boundaries appear, most organizations react by changing the organization chart. They apply structural solutions to behavioral or process challenges, attacking specific symptoms rather than the underlying dynamics of the symptoms. Like the little Dutch boy with his finger in the dike, executives who take the structural route usually find there are not enough fingers to plug all the holes.

Consider the following typical scenario: poor communications, turf battles, and the like are compromising customer responsiveness and draining resources, and top management decides the organization is too widely dispersed, too functionalized, and too expensive. They reorganize to eliminate redundancies and weed out unproductive people and departments. Or perhaps the firm fails to get a new product designed and into the market on time. Again, management decides that the culprit is the variety of committees and units that had to act—and again, the typical response is to rein in horizontal spread through centralization of resources and decision making. People are shifted around or laid off, resources reassigned, field offices consolidated, and so on. Predictably, these moves lower costs, reduce redundancies, and perhaps even increase productivity—in the short term.

However, after a short breathing space, the firm begins to feel out of touch with the marketplace. Too many of its resources are now at the head office, and not enough expertise is close to the customer. Employees in the field—and customers—begin to see the firm as slow and unresponsive. The various lines of business complain the centralized functions respond too sluggishly, interfering with the lines' efforts to innovate, to produce product, and to serve customers.

The firm has resolved some resource problems, but it has sacrificed speed and flexibility. Gradually, the swarm of specialized units begins to reappear. Responsiveness and speed go up but so do costs, sometimes astoundingly. Customers like the speed but find themselves once again doing their own integration of products. (If only Norman Rockwell were alive to capture the scene: picture that special moment when three or four representatives from the same company, who have never met, are introduced to one another by a customer in the customer's waiting room.) The organization reverts to a decentralized structure and decision making. The original problems resurface, and a few years later the organization regroups a third time.

The centralization/decentralization debate has dominated management literature for more than forty years. In theory, the dilemma goes to the heart of how an organization can control and integrate its different disciplines while allowing them to maintain independent integrity and functionality. In reality, however, the debate has become a faddish game, in which organizations swing back and forth like pendulums. More than one consulting firm has earned a fine living by recommending that a decentralized organization centralize and then, a few years later, coming back to recommend decentralization. Each solution appears rational—until the (predictable) problems arise.

The matrix organization is often implemented as a solution to the dilemma. Theoretically, a matrix organization is both centralized and decentralized, and employees are given some combination of functional, product, and geographic accountability. For example, at any one time, an employee may be responsible for a function (say, engineering), a product line (say, laundry detergent), and a geography (say, Asia-Pacific).

The matrix is ingenious in theory but confusing in practice. Russell Ackoff accurately describes the problems with the matrix organization:

> In matrix organizations, employees have two bosses. One is the head of the input (support or staff) unit of which they are a part; the other is the head of the output (line) unit to which they are

assigned. [These two bosses] jointly determine [an employee's] chances for promotion and his salary increase, and they determine performance goals with him. . . . This property of the design produces what might be called "organizational schizophrenia." When an employee's bosses do not agree or have different value systems, the employee does not know how to behave. This can be very stressful. The decision regarding to whom to pay attention is usually made politically rather than in the best interests of the organization.[3]

In short, the concept of the matrix is flawed. In addition to the inherent schizophrenia Ackoff describes, it blurs accountability for results, allowing an employee to choose between conflicting priorities and to blame the priority not chosen for problems and delays. As a Conference Board report notes, "General managers have long complained about their inability to hold one person accountable for business successes and (especially) failures."[4] In addition, the matrix organization often becomes cumbersome and costly. When many people feel compelled to contribute to decisions, decision making is slow, and travel, meeting, and communication costs high.

In the 1980s and 1990s, Digital Equipment Corporation was perhaps the best-known example of a matrix organization. Under founder Kenneth Olsen, DEC's matrix promoted high levels of involvement and collaboration in decision making, but it also allowed functions to stonewall, making agreement on major programs and strategic directions very difficult. DEC was unable to move fast enough to keep up with its industry. Every decision required a committee and intense consultation back and forth between product groups, functions, and geographies. Enormous costs were added as each group built its own support structure rather than share with others. Even after abandoning the matrix under CEO Robert Palmer in the mid-1990s, DEC was unable to learn how to operate quickly and nimbly, and as a result was forced to sell itself to Compaq in 1998 and essentially go out of business.

Reframing the Question: From Structure to Process

We believe that "Should we centralize or decentralize?" is the wrong question—so the answer will never be right. Instead of looking for structural solutions to what is fundamentally a process challenge, organizations should be asking how to permeate horizontal boundaries and improve speed, flexibility, integration, and innovation.

To reframe the question, management must first view the organization not as a set of functional boxes but as a set of *shared resources and competencies* that collectively define the organization's range of activities. Only then can management address the more fundamental question: *How does the organization create processes to ensure that all its shared resources and competencies—arrayed across the horizontal spectrum—create value for customers?*

Framing the issue this way shifts the focus from a mechanical model to an organic one—from organizing, influencing, and bringing together a collection of separate functions to transforming inputs into outputs through series of processes and subprocesses to which people with different skills and disciplines contribute. Management must shape these processes efficiently, in a way that maximizes customer satisfaction and builds capability across the firm.

In his work on organizational design, Jay Galbraith, a professor at the Institute of Management Development in Geneva, coined the term the "front/back organization."[5] In an organization's "back room" are many shared resources and competencies. They may be arrayed by function, product, or geography—it doesn't matter. In the "front room" are customers who have unique and special demands. Finding *processes* to move these resources from the back room to the front room when needed, in the needed configuration, is the true challenge. This kind of front/back movement—done quickly, flexibly, creatively, and tailored to each customer—is what boundaryless horizontal behavior is all about.

Loosening horizontal boundaries, then, calls for integration, not decentralization; process, not function; and teamwork, not individual effort. When the organization is viewed integratively as composed of shared resources, it puts an end to the centralize/decentralize debate's structural questions about power, authority, and priority. Shared resources are not about which horizontal function has power but how the organization uses processes to mobilize resources, solve problems, and meet customer needs. In other words, process is more important than function. Process deals with how value is added to goods and services and activities. It is not about how much attention is paid to a functional leader.

Making It Happen:
Principles for Creating Horizontal Harmony

In our view, there are five key organizational principles (listed in the box) to keep in mind as you work to develop permeable horizontal boundaries and integrate shared resources.

Principles for Creating Horizontal Harmony

- Keep the focus on the customer.
- Show one face to the customer.
- Form and re-form teams to serve the customer.
- Maintain a competence pool.
- Share learnings across customer teams.

Keep the Focus on the Customer

The boundaryless horizontal organization begins and ends with customers. Its entire focus is to anticipate and serve changing customer needs. Moreover, it works to see itself from the customer's point of view. The boundaryless horizontal organization is effective when all employees understand and feel the needs of the customer and all internal processes aim to form and strengthen external customer relationships.

Show One Face to the Customer

Once the focus is on the customer, the task is to make it easy for the customer to access resources, products, and services across the horizontal spectrum. This requires organizations to provide customers with a single, simple, consistent point of access. For example, a large computer firm with multiple product lines recently realized that it was not unlikely for representatives of up to six of those product lines to be meeting with one customer. At worst, none of them knew about the others—and even when they were aware of one another, they inevitably presented a confusing array of possibilities for interacting with their firm.

This does not mean that only one company representative should interact with each customer. On the contrary, mobilizing horizontal resources may allow many more skills and talents to serve the customer. However, to truly satisfy that customer, either one person or one process-point must have the prime account-ability for making sure that the customer gets everything needed.

In some cases, a specific individual becomes the customer manager. This job involves being thoroughly schooled in how the customer operates and giving advice about what the customer needs before the need arises. The customer manager also corrals the resources of the firm to serve those customer needs as fluidly and responsively as possible. In other cases, the single face the customer sees might be a process-point—an 800 number or a personalized page on the organization's Web site. Particularly in large-scale retail operations, it is impossible for a single person to tend to each customer's needs. However, it is possible to have a consistent point that customers can easily reach and that provides staff with access to information about all the customers and their needs. A good example is Fidelity's 800-number service. No matter which service representative answers a call, the same information about the customer is available, and a consistent way of talking with the customer is used.

Form and Re-form Teams to Serve the Customer

Once the organization has focused on customer needs and provided one face for customer contact, actual customer service is provided by fluid teams composed of the competencies and resources the customer requires to meet current and perhaps future needs. These teams draw upon the appropriate resources wherever they may reside in the organization. In that sense, the teams are ad hoc, temporary, or even virtual, although they may be semipermanent for large or complex customers. Each team is dynamic: as additional customer needs are identified, additional resources and competencies are added, and the team is re-formed again.

Furthermore, these teams are not necessarily part of an organizational structure. They handle processes across functions more than responsibilities within functions. Team leadership roles are shared, depending on the needs of the customer. The teams may include individuals from multiple functions within the corporation and, through alliances and subcontracts, even individuals who work in other firms. Finally, the teams are measured by their ability to use resources from inside the firm to add value for customers outside the firm.

Maintain a Competence Pool

To staff fluid and dynamic customer teams, successful organizations maintain a pool of competent people with the skills to meet customer requirements. These people may be arrayed by function (manufacturing, sales, or whatever), or by product or geography. But they derive their legitimacy from becoming part of a customer team. Those who are never needed on a customer team are soon spotted as irrelevant; they're apt to wind up out the door in short order.

One implication of the competence pool principle is that function leaders must constantly assess and refresh the competence of people in their disciplines and match that competence with existing and emerging customer needs. For example, at the World Bank, sector managers provide career development guidance for technical specialists on country development projects, because they must ensure that these specialists maintain cutting-edge skills in their disciplines. The bank can then match people with certain skills to projects that require them.

Similarly, HR competency systems have become increasingly common over the past ten years. These systems allow organizations to manage individuals according to the knowledge and behaviors that enable them to do the job of the present as well as the future in a technically excellent way. Firms that have identified those competencies have moved away from formal training and experience as a key source of selection data. Instead, they match people to jobs or assignments according to proven ability to achieve results, as indicated by assessment of the relevant competencies. Companies using competencies can also train staff and create systems to ensure that the right skills and abilities exist over time.

Share Learnings Across Customer Teams

The final principle for loosening horizontal boundaries is to create a learning process. As multidisciplinary teams work across boundaries to serve customers, they gain tremendous insights into those customers, into team members' specialties, and into processes for working together. Those insights must be captured and shared, or the boundaryless horizontal process becomes expensive and inefficient, requiring constant relearning of the same lessons. To avoid losing critical information and competencies, the organization must establish mechanisms for sharing best practices. To cite the World Bank again, its technical sector teams all contribute to, and have access to, Internet-based knowledge management sites that capture best practices, tools, and resources. These learnings are reinforced through periodic "education weeks" where specialists from different parts of the world get together to share knowledge. One of the key roles of sector leadership is to facilitate and manage these mechanisms.

The Service Model of Horizontal Harmony

The boundaryless horizontal organization is already a feature of most service firms. And the principles we have been discussing are among those that have guided professional service firms for decades.

For example, one of the large public accounting firms begins its work with a focus on customers (principle 1). Customer needs are identified through surveys, focus groups, and constant interaction with the customers. Dedicated customer managers (principle 2) lead the accounting effort for major clients. These customer managers are generally senior partners who know the customers' business well enough to give advice whether the client asks for it or not. They usually stay with large accounts long enough to ensure continuity, and they form multiple relationships within the accounts to ensure stability.

Customer managers have the responsibility to pull together resources to meet clients' financial reporting needs (principle 3). These resources form a customer team dedicated to both the constant and transient needs of the customer. Many team members come from the resource pool of the accounting firm. Some may be aligned with a particular function (information systems or manufacturing, for example), some may be aligned with products (particular auditing requirements), and some may be aligned with geographies (requirements in different global markets). The team formed by the customer manager may also include experts from outside the accounting firm if client issues require special expertise. Membership on the team is not permanent, of course, because client needs constantly change. However, the team's primary challenge is always to create processes for shifting inner resources and competencies out to the customers.

Inside the accounting firm, employees work in what may seem like traditional roles related to functions, product lines, or geography. However, all realize they are really shared resources that may be mobilized for a team at any time (principle 4). Employees unable to translate their expertise to customer value are identified and replaced. Finally, each team in the firm shares best practices with other teams, so that all clients benefit from the knowledge and ideas gleaned from particular clients (principle 5).

Law, advertising, and consulting firms follow the boundaryless horizontal model when they assign a senior partner as the "relationship manager" for an account. This person's job is to diagnose and anticipate account needs and to assemble resources from inside and outside the firm to ensure that those needs are met quickly and effectively. Movie studios use the boundaryless model when the producer pulls together a temporary team of writers, directors, cast members, editors, and other resources to produce a film. Some team members come from the producer's organization, most come as subcontractors, united around a particular project. Construction and engineering firms also organize around large clients to ensure that these clients' needs are met over time.

Horizontal Harmony in Other Organizations

Companies other than service organizations are rapidly emerging as users of horizontal organizational logic. Consider the following examples:

Zurich Financial Services. Zurich Financial Services is one of the oldest and most stable firms in the financial service industry. Through the 1980s and 1990s, it acquired businesses in the United Kingdom (Eagle Star) and in the United States (Farmers and Scudder). As competition in the financial services industry heated up in the late 1990s, it created "practice boards" to spread knowledge and expertise across its multiple businesses and multiple geographies.

These practice boards were focused on common customer interests, regardless of the geography in which the customer worked. For example, one practice board focused on consumers, and began to drive innovation in insurance products for consumers anywhere in the world. The practice boards then identified areas where experiments were either going on or could go on, so that new products for consumers could be tested in any one geographical region. Members of the practice boards, who are consumer experts in different regions, meet monthly or quarterly to share their experiences and ideas. The practice boards allow Zurich to leverage knowledge, expertise, and innovation—so that once a new product is manufactured and tested, multiple distribution channels are immediately available.

Baxter Healthcare. A leader in the hospital supply business, Baxter offers over twenty thousand products to hospitals around the world. It assigned specific employees to form long-term relationships with hospitals, beginning with traditional market research, surveys, and focus groups to find out what customers wanted. The relationship became more intimate when Baxter gave many of its hospital customers computers and software to connect them on-line to Baxter's distribution network. However, true customer intimacy came when Baxter representatives offered hospitals the full range of Baxter resources. Customers could attend Baxter training programs and participate in performance appraisals for Baxter employees, while Baxter employees gave hospitals expert assistance in creating their own effective teams. As Baxter developed over time, it sold some of its businesses to other companies. Cardinal Health acquired a major portion of what was originally Baxter Healthcare. Frank LaFasto, who is now at Cardinal Health as a vice president of human resources, continues to spend at least 30 percent of his time with customers, facilitating team building and problem-solving sessions. Through these contacts, Cardinal Health has formed strong partnerships with preferred accounts.

Both of these examples illustrate the five basic principles of a boundaryless horizontal organization—and the important shifts that can occur when resources are deployed to serve customers. Again, the key is not to focus on structural means of bringing disciplines together. Rather, structures shift when flexible processes mobilize the resources of the firm to meet customer needs.

Creating Horizontal Harmony: Overcoming the Immune Response

No new form or process emerges without bruises, and correcting haywire horizontal boundaries is no exception. In many organizations, people find great comfort in their functional identities. They relate most closely to their functional counterparts, assess their careers and achievements against functional goals, and maintain high degrees of loyalty to their functional leaders. In short, their functions are their homes, the places where they speak a common language and where they feel most comfortable.

This comfort has enormous emotional and psychological power, and many professionals and functional experts view attempts at change as threats or attacks. Listening to the customer might mean abandoning the functional "right" way; working with other disciplines might mean learning new languages or ways of thinking; and working in changing teams might mean losing that sense of home, becoming disconcertingly rootless. No matter how sensible looser horizontal boundaries might be, people's existing emotional attachments may spark strong anxiety or resistance.

To overcome this resistance and fight through inevitable immune responses, leaders can take the four preparatory steps listed in the box before moving on to the actions described in Chapter Five.

Preparatory Steps for Overcoming Resistance to Horizontal Change

- Create new mental models.
- Encourage and teach teamwork.
- Define measures of shared resources success.
- Restructure quickly.

Create New Mental Models

Mental models can form the greatest barrier to the success of a horizontal boundary transformation. Old models are almost impossible to give up without new ones to replace them. People in closed functional boxes need to know what things will look like when their boxes open up or even disappear. What will be different? The two methods for creating new mental models that we have found helpful are these: send employees to visit companies that employ boundaryless horizontal behavior and create a boundaryless model on a small scale in your own organization.

For example, early in 1994, World Bank executives realized that the bank's human resource function needed to be better aligned with its operations organization, HR's prime client. One aspect of this alignment was to create flexible HR teams that could mobilize a variety of disciplines to meet changing needs of operations managers and staff. Since the basic HR approach had been unchanged for years, the proposed shift met with both skepticism and confusion, and few really understood what it meant. To view a tangible model, teams of HR and client personnel visited organizations with teams similar to those proposed for the World Bank, including Chase Manhattan Bank (now JP Morgan-Chase), Northern Telecom (now Nortel Networks), and Hewlett-Packard. These visits and subsequent discussions helped management refine its thinking and generated enough support to allow the bank to move ahead.

At Carrier Corporation, then-CEO William Frago wanted to create a boundaryless process for sharing product systems expertise. Because this was likely to involve dismantling and reallocating a number of large divisional and functional units and changing the mindset of many valuable professionals, Frago decided to begin overcoming resistance by starting small. He asked one vice president (formerly head of a large division) to pull together a very small team of engineers and purchasing, quality, and financial people to create a common technology platform, across the worldwide Carrier organization, for room air conditioners.

At first, the vice president and many of his peers were in shock—how could you be a senior executive without being in charge of an entire product system and having hundreds of people reporting to you? Both a vertical and a horizontal boundary mindset prevented them from recognizing that the larger issue was to contribute to the company by improving its processes. But this VP eventually saved the company millions of dollars by standardizing technology components through international cooperation among divisions. Once a new mental model of product systems leadership, focused around contribution to results and development of cross-disciplinary processes, was operating in one area of the company, Frago was able to expand it over the next year to include the offerings of all Carrier's product systems.

Encourage and Teach Teamwork

Boundaryless horizontal organizations require exquisite, flexible teamwork. Because teams will change as business needs change, organizational members must be able to join and lead teams quickly to solve particular problems. This is especially true in corporations forming business units in Eastern Europe, China, India, and other emerging markets—where change is especially rapid and flexibility means survival.

The best way to encourage and teach teamwork is to put people on real teams that work on real business problems and to use those teams as learning vehicles. This was the approach that Matthias Bellmann took when he was head of Management Learning at Siemens in the late 1990s. As a worldwide provider of everything from mobile phones to gas turbines to information services, the company depended heavily on the collaboration of managers from different units who might be serving common customers, markets, or geographies. Yet its traditional organization and incentive system had never encouraged such collaboration. To teach managers how to engage in cross-unit initiatives, Bellmann, in collaboration with consultant Robert Schaffer, made cross-unit "business impact projects" the centerpiece of a development process involving thousands of managers. Each project team consisted of managers from different product areas, functions, and geographies; each one had to show measurable results on a real business problem in about four months. For example, a team in Latin America worked on a plan to increase sales of services (as opposed to equipment). To achieve the goal, the team needed to experiment with ways of overcoming traditional rivalries among businesses and country operations. By focusing on both the business goal and the collaborative agenda, the team was able to land new contracts in Columbia and Brazil—and learn how to work across horizontal boundaries.[6]

Define Measures of Shared Resources Success

As a third preparatory step, executives can set the stage for horizontal boundarylessness by setting desired measures that can only be achieved through a process of sharing resources. We have found these three measures particularly useful:

- *Higher customer satisfaction:* assessed by collecting data from surveys, focus groups, targeted interviews, or other customer focused information.
- *Lower cost of services:* assessed through productivity measures or budget reductions.
- *Reduced cycle time:* assessed through speed of responses and greater productivity.

Measures of success must be established at the beginning of an effort. In essence, they serve as goals, stakes driven into the ground that people can reach only by loosening horizontal boundaries.

Restructure Quickly

In some situations, you may need to restructure or consolidate before you can devise processes for weaving together horizontal resources. When multiple units do essentially the same work, the similar activities must be pulled under the same umbrella—either to generate some immediate savings or at least to identify processes employed and competencies that exist—before you start figuring out how best to transform the activities.

A key success factor in such consolidations is to move fast. In most downsizing efforts, rapid, bold decisions invite employees to focus on the future. The time from announcement to actual practice should be as short as possible, even if many details and processes cannot be worked out beforehand. Likewise, in moving toward a model of shared horizontal resources, it is better to implement changes quickly so that employees always know their status within the organization.

When Northern Telecom (now Nortel) decided to implement a boundaryless horizontal human resource organization, it created a shared HR service center—revising functions and reducing personnel from approximately 750 to 390. That step put it in a position to leverage certain processes across the organization. To carry out the consolidation, the company employed a large-scale conference process. First, to develop a vision for the new HR service group, forty people representing many HR roles and HR internal customers sequestered themselves for three days, using teleconferencing and memos to keep all other employees apprised of their progress. With a vision established, another large group met two weeks later in a second conference to design the new organization to fit the vision. Then everyone wanted to know who was to be included in the new organization. Just one month after the process started, they were all told what was going to happen to their individual jobs. People could then get on with the process of implementing the new vision or of finding new jobs (with Northern Telecom's help). In less than three months, the new structure was up and running, teams were designing new horizontal processes, and approximately three hundred people who needed new jobs had been placed inside and outside Northern Telecom.[7]

Getting Started:
How Haywire Are Your Horizontal Boundaries?

At this point, we suggest that you reflect for a few moments on the nature of your current horizontal boundaries. Questionnaire #3 can help you assess the extent to which such boundaries may be haywire and the extent to which your organization already has processes to share resources. Part 1 of the questionnaire asks you to map your organizational functions according to importance to key customers and degree of collaboration with other functions. Part 2 asks you to identify warning signs in your organization. Part 3 asks you to identify the degree of horizontal harmony in your organization.

Questionnaire #3

Stepping Up to the Line: How Congruent Are Your Organization's Horizontal Boundaries?

PART 1: MAP RELATIONSHIPS

Instructions: In the space below, identify ten or more functional disciplines or specialties that exist as different units in your organization.

Now use the following table to note the ways in which these units contribute to key customers and collaborate with each other. This will produce an informal map of the horizontal groups in your organization.

Organizational Unit	Professional Disciplines in the Unit	Extent of Collaboration with Other Functions (High, Medium, Low)	Contributions to Customers	Effectiveness of the Function as Viewed by the Customer (High, Medium, Low)

PART 2: IDENTIFY WARNING SIGNS

Instructions: Assess your organization on the following warning signs of haywire horizontal boundaries. Use the scale next to each statement to indicate the extent to which the statement characterizes your organization's behavior, circling a number from 1 (not true at all) to 5 (very true). Also, make a note of an example that supports your assessment.

	Not true at all				Very true
1. Organizational processes tend to be slow and sequential instead of fast and parallel.	1	2	3	4	5
2. Functional groups are more concerned with protecting their turf than with serving the customer.	1	2	3	4	5
3. Functional groups and disciplines place greater priority on meeting their own functional goals than on contributing to overall organizational achievements.	1	2	3	4	5

(continued)

Questionnaire #3 *(continued)*

	Not true at all				Very true
4. Functional groups and disciplines regard each other with suspicion, blame each other for problems, and operate as though the enemy is within the organization.	1	2	3	4	5
5. The customer needs to integrate our products and services.	1	2	3	4	5
6. Our organization tends to swing back and forth between centralization and decentralization every few years.	1	2	3	4	5

PART 3: ASSESS HORIZONTAL HARMONY

Instructions: Identify the extent to which your organization applies the five principles for creating horizontal harmony. Use the scale next to each statement to indicate the extent to which the statement characterizes your organization's behavior, circling a number from 1 (not true at all) to 5 (very true).

	Not true at all				Very true
1. The focus of attention is always on the customer.	1	2	3	4	5
2. The customer has a single point of contact with our organization.	1	2	3	4	5
3. We form and re-form teams to serve the customer.	1	2	3	4	5
4. We have an extensive pool of competence that we can draw upon for customer teams—and we keep that pool refreshed.	1	2	3	4	5
5. We have active and robust processes for sharing learnings across customer teams and across functions.	1	2	3	4	5

Questionnaire Follow-Up

Ask a group of peers from different disciplines and functions within your organization to review this questionnaire. Then discuss everyone's responses to see if you and your peers have a shared view of your organization's horizontal health. The resulting information will give you a more solid foundation on which to construct an action program, using the ideas in Chapter Five.

Chapter Five

Integrating Resources to Serve the Customer

To create boundaryless horizontal organizations, companies must see themselves as sets of shared resources and competencies mobilized in different ways at different times to meet customer needs. The challenge is to make sure this mobilization occurs quickly and effortlessly.

Think back to the musical analogy in Chapter Two. Customer needs change so fast that an organization must improvise like a jazz band rather than play classical music from a score. This chapter provides five *improv vehicles* (listed in the box)—specific tools for loosening horizontal boundaries so employees can improvise effectively. Again, not all these vehicles may fit your situation at this time. The ones that do fit may not be of equal importance. Together, however, they will help you frame an action strategy to create and maintain harmony on the horizontal level.

Improv Vehicles for Permeating Horizontal Boundaries

- Orient work around core processes.
- Tackle processes through targeted teams.
- Turn vertical dimensions (information, competence, authority and rewards) sideways.
- Create shared services for support processes.
- Develop organizational learning capability.

Orient Work Around Core Processes

Core processes transform materials and know-how (inputs) into products and services that meet customer needs (outputs). Therefore, orienting work around core processes is the first improv vehicle that you can use to make horizontal boundaries permeable. This orientation shifts the emphasis from engineering work or systems work, which tend to be internally focused, to cross-functional process work, which by definition is externally customer focused. Orienting work around core processes in the four ways described here also supplies the foundation on which all the remaining improv vehicles will build.

Orienting Work Around Core Processes

- Define core processes.
- Set customer-focused stretch objectives for each process.
- Assign process leaders.
- Remove process barriers and streamline process flows.

Define Core Processes

Processes cut across an organization and represent the flow and transformation of information, decisions, materials, or resources to serve customers. Many firms use processes like these:

- *Commercialization of technology:* Turning ideas into products and services.
- *Order fulfillment:* Receiving customer requests and supplying goods or services.
- *Purchasing:* Ordering and acquiring supplies.
- *Service:* Addressing and satisfying customer complaints and needs for information and training.

Firms also have processes that focus on internal customers. For example, the development of employee competence is a process serving all units of the organization, as are internal communication, employee payment processing, and many others. In general, however, these are not core but support processes—necessary to keep the organization going but not directly focused on meeting customer needs. It turns out that support processes can often be managed in different ways from core processes—for example, through shared service groups, outsourcing, or automation.

Every organization has its own definition of core processes. For example, the World Bank's operating regions, which work with developing countries to reduce poverty, define some of their core processes as country assistance strategies, economic and sector analytical work, project development and approval, and portfolio (or project) supervision. Fidelity Investments focuses on processes for customer acquisition, service, and retention and for investment management.

To define your company's core processes, ask: Who are our key customers? What are the flows from input to output that add value to these customers? What are the main products or outputs that our customers look to us to provide? What steps are necessary to produce these outputs?

Set Customer-Focused Stretch Objectives for Each Process

It's best to evaluate each identified core process against external customer measures—internal measures can be misleading. For example, one manufacturer of large transformers routinely scored 95 percent on "parts shipped on time" when it defined *shipped* as "left company property." But shipped transformers often moved only to a flatbed rail car on a railroad-owned siding adjacent to the plant—where they sat for weeks while company employees worked on them and customers fumed. A new customer-focused process measure provided a better indictor of timeliness: "products received by the customer on time." Under this measure, the score fell to about 75 percent.

Typical customer-focused process measures are reduced cycle time, decreased costs through logistical integration, and increased responsiveness through fewer steps in meeting customer needs. To develop measures like these, go to your best source of data—your customers. Ask them how *they* assess your effectiveness and what it would take to provide everything they can imagine getting from your product or service. Then look at your organization—are you measuring indicators that match your customers' expectations? Or are you following the airlines' example? Most airline passengers have experienced the joy of sitting on a plane that rolled away from the gate exactly on time only to stop on the tarmac a few feet away, whereupon the stewardess announces that the destination airport is closed or the plane has a problem and that they are not going anywhere for quite a while. They are victims of the definition of *on-time departure* that says, "left the gate within fifteen minutes of schedule." Although passengers would much prefer to do their waiting in the terminal, the industry's performance measures do not recognize that expectation. Like the transformers on the railroad siding, the passengers have been shipped "on time."

Putting the right measures in place, of course, is only the starting point. Setting ambitious goals for process improvements is equally critical. Without such goals, people think about maintaining the numbers rather than changing them. Stretch goals force fresh thinking about the processes themselves. For example, the president of a major drug company recently told his R&D organization to reduce the cycle time from "first human test" to "FDA approval" from ten years to four. Before he set this seemingly impossible goal, R&D managers were working very hard to streamline the process, but they were not questioning the process itself. Facing up to a six-year improvement goal, they began to consider a host of new ideas for constructing a "drug development factory," for using information technology in new ways, and for outsourcing portions of the process. Although it is too early to see results, the change in managers' thinking alone has been palpable.

Assign Process Leaders

The next step is to assign clear accountability to process leaders to see that the goals are met. A process leader is equivalent to the lead in a jazz band, who not only plays an instrument but gets the other players to jam together. The lead also arranges for a place to play, makes sure the music gets started, and often sets the beat.

Similarly, process leaders shepherd the flow of information, materials, or resources across boundaries, while often playing a functional role at the same time. For example, Hewlett-Packard identified order fulfillment as one of the firm's top three *"hoshin,"* or priorities.

Someone was then placed in charge of ensuring that this process was managed and improved throughout the corporation. This manager reported to the executive committee and had the ability to work across all product, functional, and geographic boundaries to make sure the order-fulfillment process worked effectively.

Remove Process Barriers and Streamline Process Flows

Since identifying processes is only valuable insofar as it leads to tangible improvement from the customers' perspective, one of the jobs of the process leader is to remove barriers and streamline and reconfigure process flows so others can meet the stretch goals.

A number of tools exist for improving process flows. For example, town meetings of process participants, as described in Chapter Three, can find quick hits, process barriers easily agreed on for removal. GE Capital used a town meeting to take weeks out of its internal process for purchasing office materials, computer supplies, and contractor services. Participants represented GE Capital businesses that used the purchasing process and GE Capital's corporate purchasing and payment processing functions. In two days, these people discovered that virtually all purchases, whether for $20 or $20,000, were subject to the same process; that almost all purchases required five or six approvals; and that all purchases required extensive paperwork (in green, pink, and yellow copies) even though the same information existed in an electronic database. Participants quickly agreed on changes in approvals, eliminated the paperwork copies, and created an "express" process (requiring no approvals) for purchases under $2,500. They then appointed a process leader to coordinate more extensive changes. Figure 5.1 shows how radically the overall process was simplified after several more town meetings.

Other tools to adjust process flows come from the methodologies of quality control and reengineering—for example, process mapping, flowcharting, root-cause analysis, Pareto charts, and statistical process control.[1] The key to using these tools is to combine them with the steps outlined earlier, that is, a measurable, customer-focused stretch goal, a cross-functional team, and a process leader to pull it all together. Otherwise, they're about as useful in reshaping the organization as so many hammers—it doesn't matter who or what gets pounded with them, the results are unlikely to be constructive.

Figure 5.1. GE Capital Purchasing Process Map.

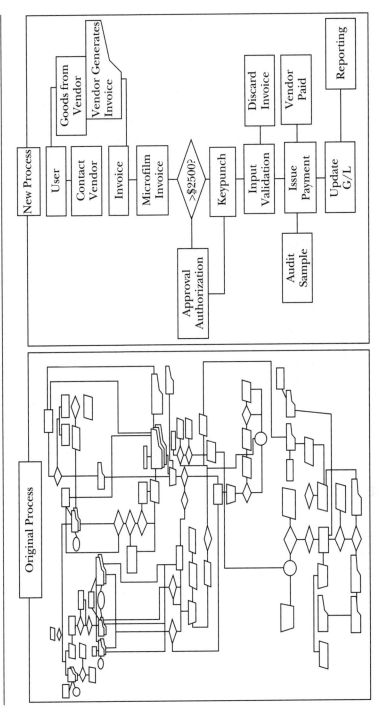

An overall improvement effort undertaken by what was then J.P. Morgan & Company exemplifies the effective use of a number of process streamlining tools. In 1993, Morgan was trying to boost some of its key cash and securities processing businesses by installing electronic communications tools in customer sites—thus giving customers direct access to and control over transfers, funds flows, and information. Morgan was selling the service, but it was piling up customer satisfaction problems right from the start by taking as much as six weeks to complete an installation.

To resolve these problems, Morgan management pulled together a client access implementation reengineering (CAIR) team. Led by a product manager, the team included representatives from technical services, systems, client administration, product development, and client relations. The team created a "responsibility matrix" (Exhibit 5.1) that specified who was responsible and who else was involved for each process step. The team also developed a process map of the installation needed for an upcoming client. (The team's map is shown in Exhibit 5.2.) Team members then brainstormed ways of slashing the time required. Ideas included pre-filled forms (so customers could check off information rather than write it in), customized training modules for customers based on their own usage patterns, a program on diskette to download technical specifications from the customer environment, and simulation of the customer environment at Morgan so that system bugs could be worked out before installation.

After these innovations, a model installation was completed successfully in a record seven days. Equally important, the installation received a high satisfaction score from the customer. In the following months, the CAIR team identified further innovations and eventually created an ongoing process for doing every installation, no matter how big, in less than two weeks. Thus the Morgan team reoriented one part of the firm's business around a core process, successfully applying the first vehicle for creating the boundaryless horizontal organization.

Tackle Processes Through Targeted Teams

Once an organization focuses on processes instead of units, teaming becomes a critical improv vehicle for bringing together the right resources to manage and refine these processes. Though

Exhibit 5.1. J.P. Morgan & Co. Responsibility Matrix.

Task	Key Players								
	IC	TL	SLS	SM	CSR	CTS	LEG	CST	CSH
1. Sell Access									
• Negotiate with client									
• Complete contract									
• Complete licensing agreement									
• Establish accounts									
• Set up billing procedures									
• Agree on the schedule with client									
2. Assemble Implementation Team									
• Designate team leader									
• Select team									
• Conduct launch meeting									
• Assign responsibilities									
• Clarify expectations									
3. Analyze Client Business									
• Send technical survey to client									
• Collect in-house "intelligence" about client									
• Determine client H/W requirements									
• Determine client user profile									
4. Prepare Client Training									
• Determine training requirements									
• Review training curriculum with client									
• Compile training material									
5. Configure and Test System									
• Set up hub									
• Set up CWS									
• Set up Host									
• Set up BWS									
• Test system									
6. Install CWS and Test System									
• Confirm client visit									
• Install CWS software/hardware									
• Test CWS software									
7. Train Client									
• Provide overview and introduction to system									
• Train security administrator									
• Train systems administration									
• Train for instructions									
8. Follow-up with Client									
• Send implemen									

NOTE: Coding for key players' levels of involvement: R = responsible for completing the task; P = participant in the task; I = needs to be informed when task is completed; A = needs to approve task.

Exhibit 5.2. J.P. Morgan & Co. Implementation Process Map.

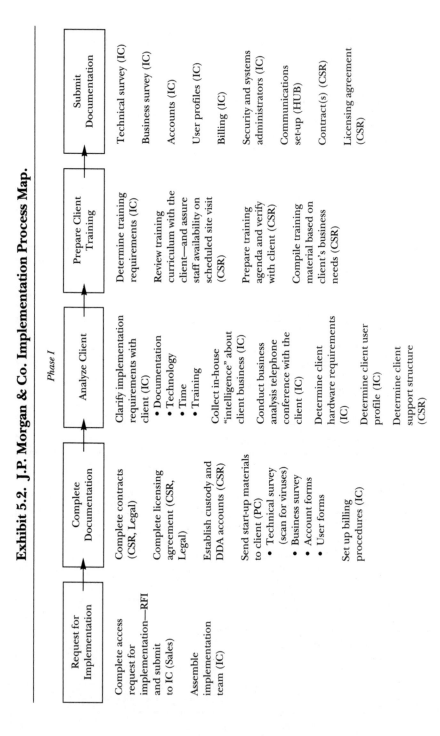

Phase I

Request for Implementation	Complete Documentation	Analyze Client	Prepare Client Training	Submit Documentation
Complete access request for implementation—RFI and submit to IC (Sales)	Complete contracts (CSR, Legal)	Clarify implementation requirements with client (IC) • Documentation • Technology • Time • Training	Determine training requirements (IC)	Technical survey (IC)
Assemble implementation team (IC)	Complete licensing agreement (CSR, Legal)	Collect in-house "intelligence" about client business (IC)	Review training curriculum with the client—and assure staff availability on scheduled site visit (CSR)	Business survey (IC)
	Establish custody and DDA accounts (CSR)	Conduct business analysis telephone conference with the client (IC)		Accounts (IC)
	Send start-up materials to client (PC) • Technical survey (scan for viruses) • Business survey • Account forms • User forms	Determine client hardware requirements (IC)	Prepare training agenda and verify with client (CSR)	User profiles (IC) Billing (IC)
	Set up billing procedures (IC)	Determine client user profile (IC)	Compile training material based on client's business needs (CSR)	Security and systems administrators (IC)
		Determine client support structure (CSR)		Communications set-up (HUB)
				Contract(s) (CSR)
				Licensing agreement (CSR)

Phase II

Configure System (In-house) → **Test System (In-house)** → **Install and Test System (On-site)** → **Train Client** → **Follow-up With Client**

Configure System (In-house)	Test System (In-house)	Install and Test System (On-site)	Train Client	Follow-up With Client
Disseminate documentation to Hub Admin, CTS and BIC (IC)	Test System end-to-end (CTS)	Confirm client visit, training schedule and set-up (CTS)	Provide overview and introduction (CTS)	Send implementation survey to the client and follow up (IC)
Set up Hub (HUB)	Scan CWS software ("Unzipped") for viruses	Install CWS software (CTS)	Train on security administration (CTS)	Track volumes (CSR)
Set up CWS (CTS)	Prepare CWS software	Scan client PC(s) for viruses	Train on systems administration (CTS)	Track straight-through rates (CSR)
Set up Host(s) (BIC)	Create and store CWS back up (CTS)	Test CWS Software (CTS)	Train on instructions and reporting based on client's business needs	Ensure revenue is being collected (CSR)
Set up BWS (BIC)			Train client on support structure/contacts (CTS)	Send overall access survey to client and follow up (IC)
				Relay client feedback to Product Development (CTS)
				File implementation report (CTS)

some processes can be managed by soloists playing virtuoso music by themselves, most require a carefully chosen ensemble to blend different instruments together.

The concept of teaming is not new, but it is often misunderstood. In the popular business press, teams have often been billed as the answer to every problem—one more magic bullet. The reality, however, is much more complex. Yes, teams are in many ways the lifeblood of organizations with permeable horizontal boundaries. As they bring skills together to accomplish processes, they increase employee commitment, productivity, and feelings of ownership, and they also increase a firm's range of ideas and create a beneficial social ambiance.

But teams are not appropriate for every kind of work; nor are all teams the same. For example, consultants Jon Katzenbach and Doug Smith make a useful distinction between *working groups* and *teams*.[2] Working groups have a common leader and may meet to share information and make common decisions, but each member is individually accountable for achieving results. Groups do not do real, hash-it-out work together. Team members, in contrast, have shared goals and shared accountability. They produce something together and no one member can meet team goals unless the others do so. In addition to shared goals, we would add that effective teams share the following features:

- A horizontal process that includes a number of different disciplines, functions, or skills.
- An agreed-upon way of working that cuts across the boundaries.
- A set of measures and rewards for success.

We have seen numerous companies invest heavily in team-building activities, team facilitation, team psychometric testing, and more, with the well-intentioned aim of improving team functioning. Yet in many cases, the so-called teams did not have shared goals or collective outputs that depended on joint work. Rather, they were collections of people with assorted organizational relationships.

Many senior management teams are working groups. Members run their semiautonomous businesses or product lines in parallel. There's no horizontal process that cuts across the entire organization, and no collective work product. The final financial results, the goals, are merely aggregated numbers, totaled up from each individual unit.

Moreover, senior management is often most effective as a working group. Part of the success of GE Capital as a financial services conglomerate stemmed from former CEO Gary Wendt's insistence that his business leaders did not always need to operate as a team. Instead, he wanted them to be individually accountable for delivering the numbers for their own businesses, even if that meant occasionally competing with another GE Capital business. Integration across businesses was expected to come from sharing best practices and competitive information, particularly through quarterly executive council meetings. In this way, Wendt kept his business leaders totally focused on their own operations. Within their own businesses, however, most of these leaders did foster horizontal teams around core processes. For example, GE Capital Aviation Services (GECAS), one of the world's largest aircraft leasers, organized around regional "deal teams"—marketing people and underwriters, along with financial, legal, operations, and service people, and others as needed—bringing together resources from the functional organization for a particular customer or deal and then re-forming these resources for the next deal.

To assess the effectiveness of cross-functional teams in your own organization, you can use the Team Effectiveness Checklist (Exhibit 5.3). This checklist contains a number of self-diagnostic questions that test whether your team is really a team and the extent to which your team has the ingredients in place to make it work successfully. We suggest that you answer the questions and discuss the scores in collaboration with other team members.

When using teams as an improv vehicle to cross horizontal boundaries, it's necessary to consider the type of team needed. Organizational theorist J. D. Thompson noted many years ago that teams come in three basic types, each appropriate to different kinds of cross-functional situations.[3] Selecting the right type is as critical as deciding whether to have a team or not.

Thompson's three types are pooled, sequential interdependent, and reciprocal teams. It is critical to use the right type of team if horizontal boundaries are to be loosened rather than solidified. Table 5.1 will help in targeting the right type of team to a situation.

Exhibit 5.3. Team Effectiveness Checklist.

Instructions: Answer each question by placing the appropriate number of points in the space provided: 5 = to a great extent; 3 = sometimes; 1 = hardly at all.

Part 1. Teams need to be organized around horizontal processes that include different disciplines, functions, or skills.

___ 1. To what extent is there one key process that provides the focus for our team?

___ 2. To what extent does our team represent all of the functions or disciplines that contribute to this process?

___ 3. To what extent is our team composed of the skills needed to maintain and improve this process?

___ 4. To what extent does our team have the ability to add or delete competencies?

Part 2. Teams need to have a shared view of what is to be accomplished, a goal toward which all team members contribute.

___ 5. To what extent is there a specific goal (or goals) that our team needs to accomplish?

___ 6. To what extent do our goals align with and contribute to the overall business goals and objectives?

___ 7. To what extent are our team goals clear and defined in simple terms, so that all team members understand what the team is trying to do?

___ 8. To what extent are our team goals shared among all users of the team's output?

Part 3. Teams need to have agreed-upon ways of working that cut across boundaries.

___ 9. To what extent has our team defined how it will solve problems, make decisions, and handle conflict in the team?

___ 10. To what extent does our team have a process for dealing with poor performance or discipline issues within the team?

___ 11. To what extent does our team dedicate time to assessing team members' ability to work as a team?

___ 12. To what extent is our team clear about roles, about who does what to accomplish team goals?

___ 13. To what extent do all members of our team feel empowered to voice their opinions so that the team makes better and more informed decisions than individuals acting alone?

Part 4. Teams need shared measures of success and ways of rewarding achievement.

___ 14. To what extent are our team's goals measurable and operational?

___ 15. To what extent do all members of our team feel personal responsibility for team results?

___ 16. To what extent do team members share in the rewards earned by our team?

___   **Total score**

Scoring: Interpret your score as follows:

- *65 or more.* Your team is most likely a true team and is functioning reasonably well. You might want to focus on the few key scores that were lowest or the category that received the lowest scores and do some fine-tuning.
- *45 to 65.* There are probably some significant weaknesses in the way your team is functioning. Look to see if the weaknesses are across the board or if there are targeted categories that need immediate attention.
- *Below 45.* You should examine whether your team is really a team and whether team members understand what it means to be a team. The material in the next section on types of teams might be particularly helpful.

The following examples illustrate how targeted teams work in practice.

Pooled teams. In pooled teams, individual team members have no direct connection with each other. They do, however, have a common goal (which distinguishes them from working groups), and the team outcome is determined essentially by adding up team members' quotas or outputs. USAA Insurance is an example of the pooled team approach to customer service among the new breed of 800-number insurance agencies. These agencies have gained rapid market share by consolidating claims services—previously provided by local agents and several head office support functions—into teams or representatives available through an 800 number.

At USAA, each customer who calls in is assigned to a team and to a person on that team. Subsequent calls from the customer go to that primary person, who answers questions and can process an entire

Table 5.1. Targeted Teams: How to Choose the Right Type.

	Pooled	Sequential Interdependent	Reciprocal
Definition	Individual work added together to achieve a common goal	Individual work tied together in sequence to achieve a common goal	Collective work to achieve a common goal
Criteria for using	When the same processes can be performed simultaneously by multiple team members	When a process can be divided into sequential tasks or subprocesses	When the process is constantly changing or needs to be uniquely applied for each situation or customer; when there is a need for creating something new
Horizontal boundary issues	Need for common training, materials, and procedures All members need to carry their own weight How to manage variation in output	How to manage hand-offs Can some tasks be performed in parallel? How can the process be speeded up?	How to replicate and learn from different applications How to assign and manage roles and responsibilities
Examples	Piecework Bowling team	Assembly line Relay race	New product development Hospital operating room Basketball team

claim, thus maintaining a feeling of personal service. If the primary person is unavailable, however, another team member can handle the call because each transaction with the customer is dutifully recorded in the database so that any team member can review the case and be up to date on that customer. In other words, each team member is responsible for a group of customers. The team and the technology provide backup. The net result is that the customer always gets personal attention, and USAA finds that even without on-site agents, customer satisfaction is as high as industry norms.[4]

The sales process also lends itself to a pooled team approach because it allows each member to use a personal approach to achieving the sale. By contrast, sequential interdependent teams can be disastrous for customer service or sales, as customers get frustrated when handed off from function to function.

Sequential interdependent teams. The members of a sequential interdependent team depend on each other in a chain. One person's output becomes the next person's input, as in an assembly line. People work alone, but toward a common goal. Because people depend on each other for input, the critical issue is the management of the interfaces. At Eastman Kodak, a sequential interdependent team approach was used to reinvigorate the Black & White Film Division. Manager Stephen Frangos found his division weighted down with old technology, older equipment, rather traditional functional processes, poor performance, and bad morale.

To revitalize the division, Frangos formed a number of sequential interdependent teams organized around key manufacturing and business processes. They were given increased responsibility for managing their end-to-end processes, for making decisions that affected their operations, and for reengineering their work flows. They then spent time setting work norms, defining process and business goals, agreeing on hand-off procedures, and improving work processes. As a by-product, the teams also became social forums for employees to share concerns and celebrate successes. The division not only turned around its financial performance but transformed its culture. Employees became reenergized. They felt more commitment to their job and work.[5]

Reciprocal teams. The members of reciprocal teams have a common goal but not a routinized work flow. Instead, they work collectively together. Reciprocal teams are found in hospital operating rooms, where people work in a highly synchronized and unified manner to save a patient even though each situation is unique. New product development teams and problem-solving task forces are also usually best organized as reciprocal teams.

Harley-Davidson used a reciprocal team approach to sustain a companywide turnaround. Harley's market share dropped from over 60 percent to 25 percent in the late 1970s, and managers took over the ownership of the firm in 1982. Over the next decade, the Harley motorcycle became a symbol of freedom, an emblem of a lifestyle shared by customers of all ages and social ranks. But Richard Teerlink, then president and CEO of Harley-Davidson Inc., knew that to bring Harley to a new stage of success in the 1990s, much more creativity and innovation would be needed. He wanted to create an organization that avoided internal politics and boundaries, sharpened its focus on innovative products that gave added value to customers, and empowered employees. With these goals in mind, he and his top managers created a team-based organization to replace the traditional hierarchical structure.

The new Harley organization was envisioned as three overlapping circles: create demand, produce product, and provide support. The "create demand" team integrated all activities related to customers: market research, customer service, distribution, and customer contact. The "produce product" team focused on engineering, manufacturing, and assembling the product. The "provide support" team consisted of the staff support functions—finance, human resources, and so on.

Because these teams were reciprocal, they were not hierarchically focused. Each team voted on its leader, set goals as a team, and operated collectively to achieve goals for its area of operation. It also shared accountability and rewards for performance within its domain.

At the intersection of the three overlapping circles was the Long Range Strategy Group, which included Teerlink and Jeff Bleustein, then president and COO of Harley-Davidson Motor Company. Each circle team also nominated two members to serve on the committee. Thus the concept of reciprocal teamwork was the dominant logic in the new Harley organization—an organization that helped Harley ride beyond its performance in the early part of the decade.

Turn Vertical Dimensions Sideways

Once the organization is oriented around processes and has targeted teams to manage and improve these processes, the same four dimensions that needed tuning in the vertical dimension—information, competence, authority, and rewards—come into play again. To enhance the effectiveness of the process and team approach, they must be tuned sideways—across functions, disciplines, and product groups—amplifying the music played by the teams. Reconceiving these dimensions so they expand and reverberate across horizontal boundaries is the third improv vehicle that can help create horizontal boundarylessness.

These are specific tools and techniques for moving these four dimensions across different types of process teams and structures:

Tools and Techniques for Moving Four Dimensions Sideways

- *Information:* Use common databases across functions; conduct cross-functional meetings; publish cross-functional intranet postings, newsletters, videos, and other communications; co-locate related functions.
- *Competence:* Use cross-functional rotation planning; transfer best practices and create common culture at a corporate university.
- *Authority:* Encourage team decision processes; use working team huddles; set up cross-functional steering committees.
- *Rewards:* For pooled teams, use individual rewards; for sequential interdependent teams, combine individual and team rewards; for reciprocal teams, use team objectives, team measures (including 360-degree feedback), and team rewards.

Moving Information Sideways

We've found four primary ways to move information sideways, across horizontal boundaries. First, information may be shared across functions by creating common databases and e-mail distribution lists.

Second, information can be shared in cross-functional meetings. Motorola holds an annual conference, attended by executives from almost every functional and business group, for sharing the best from quality teams across the company. The conference is also a motivator and a reward for the teams.

Third, traditional written and videotaped information sharing still work. These are among the ways that AT&T disseminates results of its annual award process for best practices in human resources.

Finally, simply putting people together is a powerful tool for encouraging horizontal information exchange. When NASA wanted to study the global water cycle and its effect on climate variations, one of the first steps was to transfer a number of scientists, educators, and flight engineers to an interdisciplinary center where they would rub shoulders with each other.

Moving Competence Sideways

The two primary vehicles for moving competence across horizontal boundaries are rotation planning and cross-functional training.

Rotation planning is, of course, the intentional movement of people from one function, process, or product group to another. The goal is to increase personal competence by broadening each individual's experience and to increase overall organizational competence as groups learn from the rotated employees. For example, Unilever moves employees across product lines and around the world to ensure that competencies flow across functions.

Cross-functional training, in which people from different disciplines and product groups train together, produces two types of learning. On one hand, people informally exchange ideas and techniques; on the other, the common experience encourages a common organizational culture and language. Motorola and its famous university are perhaps the best example of using training and development experiences to engender cross-functional competence. For example, when the company wanted to expand operations in China, Motorola University was its forum for building ability to compete there. Managers from product lines that would market in China, managers who had experience entering international markets, and managers who had functional expertise on competing in China were brought together to share experiences, ideas, and approaches.

Moving Authority Sideways

Authority or decision making can be moved across horizontal boundaries in a number of ways.

The first vehicle is to enhance team decision making by giving teams authority to make decisions about their work processes and by agreeing upon consultation routines. For example, each of Harley-Davidson's three circle teams can make decisions about processes within its circle. However, if the decision affects another circle, the first circle must systematically touch base with those who would be affected before enacting the decision.

Another tool for encouraging horizontal decision making is called the *huddle*. Originally developed by Wal-Mart, the huddle brings people together from different functions or from different process steps, usually on a regular basis, for very quick and disciplined on-the-spot decision making. At the World Bank, a team of HR generalists and HR specialists who support two operating regions huddles for thirty minutes each morning to share client information and make immediate decisions about policy positions, client support, and individual cases. Once a week, the huddle expands to include the support team that processes transactions. These expanded huddles make immediate decisions about streamlining or eliminating various transaction processes that have raised questions during the week.

A third vehicle for enhancing horizontal decision making is the cross-functional steering committee. In Motorola's communications sector, this committee consists of the leaders from engineering, manufacturing, finance, marketing, quality, and so on, and it makes critical decisions about new product development projects. Whenever new product development teams arrive at an important decision point (what material to use for a part, which vendor to use, whether to change a technical design, how to position a product in the line, how to price a product, and the like), the project lead calls together the steering committee. The committee's job is to make a decision that is owned by all functions across the horizontal spectrum.

Moving Rewards Sideways

As teams become more cross-functional, reward systems must change correspondingly—each type of team requires a different strategy for motivational rewards. Because people in pooled teams work individually, individual measures and rewards or commission systems make sense. People who go beyond expectations can be rewarded, while good workers will not be penalized when a team member dodges a share of the load.

The reward system for sequentially interdependent teams probably needs to be a combination of individual and team incentives. People need incentives both for doing their own work effectively and for managing the hand-offs and interfaces that make a difference to the achievement of the collective team goal. At the same time, sequentially interdependent teams often perform well in the context of gain-sharing plans that include an entire plant or work site. In this case, the incentives to work together may outweigh the loss of individual incentive, particularly if the collective plan provides *line of sight,* meaning that individuals can see how they contribute to the team's objectives and how they benefit when the team succeeds.

Reciprocal teams are the most highly cross-functional and require reward systems to match. When it is impossible to measure how much each individual contributed, then team-based rewards for achievement are needed so that each team member receives bonuses, recognition, trips, and the like equally.

Create Shared Services for Support Processes

A number of support processes normally bolster and facilitate the core processes.[6] Usually resident in staff functions such as personnel, legal, and finance, these support processes often unintentionally armor-plate horizontal boundaries because they are oriented toward control rather than service or because the demand for them is greater than the resources they can make available at an effective cost.

Shared services—the consolidation of staff service functions—provides the fourth improv vehicle for loosening horizontal boundaries. In divisionalized companies, each operating unit has dedicated support units, and overall service often improves when these separate activities combine horizontally. For example, at Honeywell International and Amoco Corporation, shared services include law, finance, information systems, human resources, real estate, and security.

In many companies, the same teams or individuals that manage core processes also provide various support processes—which deflect their energy from their core processes. For example, a new product development team manager might also be responsible for handling employment verification for team members, signing off on or filling out forms for changes in employment status, and hiring part-time workers. In a shared services environment, these activities are unbundled, or separated out, from the core processes.

When support processes are both *shared* and *services,* people can concentrate on their core process responsibilities. This can produce tremendous productivity gains. As long as the emphasis is on service instead of corporate control and functional turf, those core processes receive far better support.

Despite the surface resemblance, shared services is not an alternate form of centralization. It is the opposite of centralization because, as one manager of a shared services unit summed it up, "the user is the chooser of the services offered." Corporate does not control who uses what services. It is a *pull* system and not a *push* system. The distinction is critical and leads to a number of other differences, summarized in Table 5.2.

You can begin the shared services process by looking for common or similar services provided by multiple support units. Clearly, the large corporation that found it had three separate payroll systems

Table 5.2. Differences Between Centralized and Shared Services.

Centralized Services	Shared Services
• Control the field.	• Are controlled by process users.
• Retain power at the top of the hierarchy.	• Disperse power and influence.
• Push activities to the field.	• Allow process users to pull resources from corporate.

feeding separate and differently formatted information into the corporate accounting system uncovered a major opportunity. The company that found it had over twenty different "training registration and tracking" services but no overall data about training utilization had discovered a less dramatic but still highly useful one.

After identifying such opportunities, ask: Could pulling together these processes give us greater speed, flexibility, integration, and innovation at less cost? If a number of support processes pass this test, the next issue is to determine the appropriate type of shared services to use.

Two Types Of Shared Services

Organizational support processes fall into two types—transaction based and transformation based—which require different modes of delivery. Two primary criteria define the appropriate delivery mode: how often the support process is used across the organization and what expertise is required to provide the support. The matrix in Figure 5.2 shows the relationship between these two criteria, whether a shared services approach is recommended at all, and if so, which one is recommended.

Transaction-Based Activities Performed in Service Centers

Transaction-based activities are largely routine administrative tasks with standardized service requirements that can be common across numerous business locations. They are also usually high-volume activities. For a human resource group, for example, they include administering benefits policies, adjusting individual compensation and processing the payroll, keeping vacation records, tracking training, organizing corporate charitable campaigns, managing relocation activities, handling travel reimbursements, responding to job applicants, and providing employment verification.

These information-intense and routine services lend themselves to remote but well-trained administrative personnel or even automated channels such as 800 numbers, voice mail, e-mail, voice recognition systems, and videoconferencing—especially when transaction frequency is high. In such cases, the shared service function can easily be located in a single physical area, a *service center.*

Figure 5.2. Selecting a Shared Services Approach.

		Low	High
Frequency or Volume of Process Across the Organization	High	Create service centers (high-tech)	Create centers of expertise—in-house or outsourced (high-touch)
	Low	Allow each unit to manage on its own	Outsource or contract service outside

Technical and Organizational
Expertise Required

When Nortel created such a service center for HR information inquiries (part of the consolidation described in Chapter Four), for instance, it went from seventy people across seven locations to fewer than forty people in one location, saving over $1 million per year with an initial investment of only $500,000. Nortel also discovered that about 30 percent of all incoming inquiries could be managed satisfactorily without face-to-face intervention.

As companies have streamlined the management of transaction-based services since the mid-1990s, they have gone through several stages. First, a number of companies, including Nortel, IBM, Marriott, and Sharp created service centers where all HR transactions were centralized, standardized, and automated. Employees could use a toll-free number to manage all HR transactions. This service center approach quickly became the standard for companies seeking efficiency in administrative services. More recently, companies have discovered that the next phase of opportunity is employee self-sufficiency. When the standard transactions are automated in a Web environment, employees themselves can gather information on options and manage their own HR transactions. This work often involves enterprise-wide information systems such as Peoplesoft, SAP, or Oracle that integrate a large amount of employee-related data.

These systems become even more powerful when the information is framed into an employee portal so employees can access that data and actively use it. While a few companies have created their own employee portals, the most common approach is to outsource the process to an outside firm. Exult, for example, is under contract with Zurich DP, Bank of America, and others to channel data from existing enterprise-wide employee data systems into an employee portal. These companies' employees can use enterprise-wide data systems to adjust their administrative profiles. Line managers can also access select components of employee profiles so they can make more informed employee decisions. Thus a British Petroleum engineer in the mid-East can now log on in the morning and learn the five things that need to be done to relocate back to the United Kingdom. The system would point out that four of those transactions can be completed by the engineer, but a manager must help execute the fifth. The engineer would be responsible for getting those five things done before the relocation home occurs. Similarly, a manager in Europe might log on in the morning and find out that three employees are due for performance appraisals within the next few weeks. This manager can use the system to retrieve comprehensive data on employee performance over the last year, and then complete an on-line performance appraisal.

Of course, when a simple support process is rarely called for, building a service center is probably undesirable. Each business unit or core process team may prefer to handle such transactions on its own. For example, in an organization that rarely uses temporary clerical support, making such support a service center function would probably be seen as bureaucratic and meddlesome rather than helpful.

Transformation-Based Activities Performed in Centers of Expertise

Transformation-based activities are nonroutine and nonadministrative, involving unique situations and person-to-person contact, deep knowledge, and individual expertise. For example, transformation-based activities in an HR context include staffing, career planning and development, compensation analysis, communication (PR and media), employee and union relations, and organizational development. Other expertise-based services in an organization might include tax accounting, security planning, real-estate strategy and planning, and systems development.

Sharing transformation-based services requires a high-touch rather than high-tech approach. The specific vehicle is a *center of expertise*. Staffed by experts in the appropriate support processes, the center can advise the whole company, providing an in-house consulting function. A center of expertise is most appropriate when cost and workload preclude putting a full-time expert in each business location or unit, but the combined volume across the organization will support a staff of one or more.

PPG, for instance, established ten Centers of Human Resource Expertise to support its strategic business units, none of which could afford to maintain the centers' level and range of expertise on its own. Center names were chosen to be understandable to customers: Productivity/Employee Satisfaction, Measurement, External Factors, Leadership, Work Processes/Operating Methods, Safety and Environment, Workforce Skills, Organization Structure, and Business Strategy. At each center, one or two experts offered advice and counsel on specific business problems and worked on projects for the strategic business units.

Generic expertise (applicable anywhere) can be addressed differently from organizational expertise (requiring deep knowledge of a specific company). Setting up a pension plan, administering it, and managing the funds are highly specialized skills, but they are generic. They can be applied in almost any kind of setting. However, providing good staffing advice requires organizational as well as technical expertise. The expert should have in-depth knowledge of what a business unit is trying to achieve, the skills it needs, and the pool of talent available.

Most often, both types of expertise are desirable. When there is a high volume of support process work that requires only generic expertise, however, an outsourced center is worth exploring. For example, Continental Bank (now BankAmerica) outsourced its systems development and maintenance activities after determining that the skills required were sufficiently generic to be done by an IBM subsidiary.[7] Many other organizations have outsourced such services as security, language training, food preparation, travel management, and insurance. When expert support requires considerable organizational knowledge, then the center of expertise is usually more effectively kept in-house.

Finally, centers of expertise should be created only if the frequency of support in either generic or organizational expertise warrants it. Failing that, organizations should contract out the services as needed, or use consultants. For example, the retail side of Fidelity Investments periodically requires strategic development of internal communications approaches and materials. To bring both technical skill and organizational knowledge to bear on this part-time need, Fidelity works with the same communications consultant each time, on a long-term retainer, but doesn't try to keep the expertise in-house.

Shared Services in Action: An Evolutionary Approach

Starting in the late 1980s, Albert F. Ritardi, then vice president of corporate administrative services at AlliedSignal, began a multiyear transformation of the services unit from a traditional functional staff group to a series of shared services. His three-phase process illustrates what it takes to use shared services as a vehicle for permeating horizontal boundaries.

When Ritardi first took over Corporate Administrative Services, it had a corporate staff of several hundred who managed pension services, administration, HR information systems, aviation services, travel, real estate and facilities, transportation and distribution, payroll processing, and security. Some functions supported headquarters staff while others covered the entire corporation. All, however, were performed along traditional lines—through establishment of policy and procedures, monitoring of those procedures, and hands-on implementation of day-to-day tasks. Costs were high and service mentality low. In fact, most of the staff felt the key to doing their jobs better was to get the operating people to cooperate better.

Given the potpourri of functions, Ritardi's first phase was what he called "census reduction and traditional problem solving." In essence, he took the existing functions and tried to make them work better and less expensively. He consolidated some units and tightened up certain policies and procedures (vendor contracts, for example) to gain immediate cost reductions.

In the process, Ritardi realized that the services fell into two categories—centers of scale (our service centers) and centers of expertise—and that he needed to treat the two categories differently. Centers of scale could reduce costs through consolidation, standardization, process changes, and technology. Therefore, he made activities such as payroll check processing, travel services, transportation and distribution systems, and HR processes such as corporate benefits administration into centers of scale. Meanwhile, centers of expertise could improve service through leveraging advice across the company and getting business units to pay (charge-back) for center services. Ritardi applied this approach to real-estate and property tax consultation, facilities management, benefits consultation, and the development of HR systems applications, among other services.

After two years, Ritardi had reduced the unit's overall headcount by 40 percent and saved the corporation $12 million. However, by this time, he understood that the support processes in the unit represented only a fraction of the support processes performed in the corporation. AlliedSignal was a conglomerate with three semiautonomous sectors: aerospace, automotive, and engineered materials. And in each sector, many of the same support processes that Ritardi's organization managed for corporate staff were being duplicated for sector personnel. For example, he found that Corporate Administrative Services managed only 30 percent of the company's total pension services, only 10 percent of the payroll, and only 20 percent of the security services. Each sector even had its own corporate jets.

Armed with this information, in 1991 Ritardi began a second phase: "consolidation and performance improvement." With the support of AlliedSignal's new chairman, Larry Bossidy, Ritardi set out to bring duplicate support processes together as shared services. Focusing on processes, he and his people identified which part of the corporation handled each key process best. Then, where it made sense, he orchestrated a consolidation of the process at this location. For example, the aerospace sector turned out to have the most advanced payroll processing system. Rather than create a new corporate payroll processing function, AlliedSignal made the aerospace sector the owner of the payroll process for the entire corporation, receiving a fee from the other sectors and from headquarters for the service. Then everyone else shut down their payroll processing organizations.

In many cases, Ritardi's unit became the owner of the process, either because it had the best way of doing it or because the process required a consistent corporate perspective or would be a distraction to a business unit. In a few other cases, responsibility was shared between the corporate center and the sectors. For example, the corporate center of expertise for security oversaw the creation of an outsourced master contract and established guidelines for each business, but many businesses argued that their local needs required process management closer to the situation, so they kept control of the performance of the service.

During the consolidation, Ritardi also focused on performance improvement. Particularly as scale increased, more technology and process improvements were possible. For example, 800-number national customer service response and help lines were established for processes such as savings plan administration, pension delivery, and HR systems and staffing. The overall result was another $12 million of real-cost savings as well as significant customer service improvement.

By the end of 1993, however, Ritardi realized that despite all the consolidations and cost savings, true improvement of the processes had only just begun. Customer service was still not a high enough priority. Thus, he began a third phase of transformation: "reengineering for customer service." In this phase, each center of scale and center of expertise rigorously reworked its support processes, and took out another $18 million of costs.

This work was accelerated when AlliedSignal institutionalized shared services by creating the Global Business Services organization in early 1994. This operation includes a financial business services group, a human resource business services group, an administrative business services group, and a data center/network services group. These four groups share their own support organization, which provides applications development, reengineering help, communications and customer service help, and the like. They also receive input and guidance from a shared services "board of directors" consisting of sector presidents and the senior corporate officers responsible for the finance and human resource processes of the corporation.

When AlliedSignal acquired Honeywell in late 1999 (changing its name to Honeywell International), Global Business Services was a driver of the savings available in the new partnership, and the integration of Honeywell's staff services into Global Business Services was one of two major structural changes that followed the merger. This integration was key to achieving global consistency in operations and procedures. Global Business Services documented savings of over $100 million during the first year of the integration.[8]

Develop Organizational Learning Capability

Developing organizational learning capability is the sound system that connects the organization's various ensembles together.[9] Without it, each new ensemble will be starting from scratch—with no knowledge of its various predecessors' musical ability, no experience to build upon, no riffs and patterns to serve as starting points.

In our definition, *learning capability* is the organization's collective ability to learn from experience and to pass those lessons across boundaries and time. Failing that, the organization will tend to keep recreating solutions rather than building on what it's already accomplished. People will spend too much time figuring out what to do by watching internal colleagues (who are also trying to figure things out) when they should be focusing on the customer.

Our definition also distinguishes between *learning* and *learning capability*. We mean to broaden the scope of learning to an evolutionary process that includes both first-order and second-order learning. This distinction originates in the work of Chris Argyris and Donald Schön of Harvard University.[10] *First-order learning* involves improving the organization's capacity to achieve specific, known objectives; *second-order learning* reevaluates the nature of the objectives and the values and beliefs underlying them. For example, creating a new product involves first-order learning; redesigning the process by which new products are created requires second-order learning.

Generate and Generalize Ideas with Impact

Idea generation without idea generalization is not true learning capability. Many managers try new marketing, manufacturing, and organizational arrangements. Often an individual initiative works, but if it is not generalized to other situations, locations, or customers, then true organizational learning has not occurred.

Similarly, ideas without impact do not create true learning capability. A firm that devotes its training budget to ensuring that managers know how to follow procedures, fill out forms, and create accountabilities is not creating ideas with impact. Any old idea will not do. Organizations with learning capability distinguish between ideas that maintain boundaries and the status quo and ideas that push boundaries and stimulate real change. Thus if an idea has true impact, generalizing it will create value far beyond a one-time application. But if the idea has no impact, then no amount of generalization will make a difference.

Motorola has effectively used learning capability as a key to competitive success. Starting in the mid-1980s with the advent of its Organizational Effectiveness Process (OEP),[11] Motorola made learning capability an explicit vehicle for crossing horizontal boundaries and adding value. The process was launched at the April 1983 annual meeting, when chairman Robert Galvin announced that despite record earnings, Motorola was becoming slow, ponderous, and bureaucratic. He called for its "renewal" without specifying what that meant or how it was to be achieved. That, he said, was up to the officers to figure out. As it turned out, what they created was a powerful iterative learning capability that continues to drive Motorola's success more than a decade later.

Galvin and his team shaped the OEP effort around a framework that outlined issues every officer and business unit should work on. The framework included thoughts about business strategy, structure, management process, and performance goals. Each business unit was to translate this framework into a series of projects—experiments that would give the officers tangible experience in organizational renewal and serve as sparks to ignite specific ideas with impact. Some early projects involved accelerating the product development process for mobile radio products, creating worldwide product responsibilities for the semiconductor sector, and creating new venture teams to explore untapped markets in the communications sector.

To make sure the ideas were generalized beyond a single business unit, each general manager was required to write a yearly paper reporting on experiments and what was learned from them. This process is still used and the papers are still discussed by the senior policy committee and in other management forums. In addition, Motorola uses the annual meeting to review progress, and it produces videotapes and other training programs to spread the word whenever an innovation seems to have application elsewhere.

The result of this generalization process has been the rapid spread of ideas. For example, an experimental new product development process from the Mobile Division in Fort Worth, Texas, soon became commonplace throughout the company. In short, despite ups and downs in the technology markets, Motorola's durability over time has been due not only to its creativity but to its intentional development of learning capability.

Complex firms often find it difficult to ensure that enough employees benefit from new learning opportunities. For example, when a consulting firm landed a contract to develop leaders for Zurich Diversified Products, it initially figured on delivering the program to about four hundred people in a year. However, the goal was to get 5–7 percent of the firm's sixty thousand employees involved with the program within twelve months. Thirteen modules focused on topics such as speed, talent, knowledge sharing, and accountability were created out of the four-day face-to-face program. A brief video reviewed the core principles and lessons of each module. These principles were further segmented into a set of self-paced workbooks. The workbooks included tools that could also be distributed either on a CD-ROM or over the company's intranet. While four hundred people did indeed attend a classroom-based workshop, every attendee left with the videotapes and workbooks to be shared as needed. In addition, HR professionals throughout the company were trained as trainers—so that they could present the appropriate video and workbook to help build expertise whenever their clients or managers experienced any of the thirteen problems.

Finally, the program material was disseminated widely on CDs and on the intranet. Employees who face challenges in any of the module areas now have a self-paced learning program that has been tried and tested across the company to use in their own situations.

In our experience, building learning capability is one of the most powerful ways to ensure long-term competitiveness and success. The box lists three specific steps to develop this capability.

> *Steps for Developing Learning Capability*
>
> - Build a commitment to learning.
> - Understand and foster an organizational learning style.
> - Encourage an idea generalization culture.

Build a Commitment to Learning

People must be taught why learning is critical, and this requires a strong organizational effort. The need for learning can be framed intellectually (to develop competence, capacity for change, ability to compete, and so on) or affectively (for self-improvement), but learning must be backed by executive commitment. If it is just a "nice to do" activity, it will fall by the wayside in the face of other priorities. Commitment to learning can be fostered through such activities as these:

Make learning a visible and central element of the strategic intent. For example, Harley-Davidson made "intellectual curiosity" one of its five core values. It expects all employees to challenge the status quo and look for ways to improve. In former chairman Richard Teerlink's words: "All employees must be willing to question why things are being done they way they are. Open-minded review of every aspect of an organization is essential for success."

Invest in learning. The time and money invested in training programs to create learning strategies, learning activities, and sharing best practices are powerful signals about commitment to learning.

Measure, benchmark, and track learning. Process measures can build learning commitment. For example, when employees track cycle time on processes such as payables, inventory turnaround, and order-to-remittance, they are also tracking their ability to respond—a measure that can encourage the learning of improvements. Similarly, benchmarking external competitors on the same process oftentimes yields useful comparisons that produce learning opportunities.

Create symbols of learning. Awards and events to reward performance encourage the dissemination of ideas throughout an organization.

Understand and Foster an Organizational Learning Style

In addition to creating a commitment to learning, organizations also need to learn how to learn. To gain a better understanding of this, two of us, aided by a colleague, collected data from over 380 businesses around the world.[12] We identified four learning styles, each with implications for developing learning capability.

Learning through continuous improvement. Managers in organizations geared to continuous improvement generate ideas through a constant determination to improve on what has been done. They work to master each step in the process, using suggestion systems, task forces, reengineering design teams, flowcharting, and the like. But these continuous improvement learners tend to have more bureaucratic cultures and a lower capacity for change than other learning types. Thirty-four percent of respondents identified this method as their dominant style.

Learning through competence acquisition. Some organizations demonstrate commitment to learning by acquiring competence (new talent or ideas) from either inside or outside—rotating people into new divisions or buying companies or individuals with certain skills. Firms in this category tend to have a narrower range of new ideas than other learning types, although they are more competitive. When the competencies acquired are about how to produce change, organizations respond by being more competitive. Twenty-five percent of respondents identified this learning method as their dominant style.

Learning through experimentation. Other businesses focus on trying out new ideas right away. They tend to be the first in their industries to market a new product or try new manufacturing tactics. GM's Saturn plant, for example, experiments with new organizational arrangements and manufacturing technologies. These companies are usually willing to try new ideas that haven't been fully tested. They act quickly, knowing that the risks may be high. Our research indicated that such firms faced a higher probability of having difficulty in finding enough alternatives before acting and of not having complete cognitive maps before acting. However, overall, the experimenters have the highest capacity for change. Twenty-one percent of respondents identified this method as their company's dominant learning style.

Learning through boundary spanning. A final group of companies generates ideas by learning what other companies do. Benchmarking best practices is commonplace. For example, Samsung, Motorola, Whirlpool, and Boeing sent hundreds of employees to Japan in the late 1980s and early 1990s to learn Japanese manufacturing technologies. GE formed a consortium with Toshiba, United Packaging, and other noncompetitors to share best practices. However, our research showed that this kind of company often generated too many alternatives (learning possibilities), resulting in difficulty coordinating, sharing, and implementing the new concepts. Boundary spanners also had the lowest overall capacity for change, perhaps because their managers tend to look outside for ideas but do not always make change happen inside the firm. Fifteen percent of respondents identified this method as their dominant learning type.

Understanding these learning styles and knowing which may work best for an organization's strategy, culture, and context can help leaders find more innovative, creative ways to generate and generalize ideas. But learning styles, like personality types, are seldom pure; businesses can and should adopt multiple learning styles. We suggest you talk with your colleagues about which learning style predominates in your organization and whether you feel this style is sufficiently robust. Then identify at least one other style that would be worth fostering to expand your learning range and also identify steps to encourage that style. For example, if your organization tends to focus on continuous improvement, try setting up a best-practices field trip to another company and expose people to learning through boundary spanning.

Encourage an Idea Generalization Culture

A public commitment to learning and an understanding of organizational learning style will flourish only in a supportive culture. Figure 5.3 depicts a management architecture that encourages the growth of such a culture through the design of six domains.

1. *Develop a shared mindset.* When managers build a culture focused on learning capability, they acknowledge the value of learning and explicitly encourage individuals to share ideas across boundaries. Here are several measures that help build commitment to learning into the shared mindset of the company:

Figure 5.3. Creating a Learning Culture.

1. Shared Mindset (Organizational Culture) To what extent does our culture promote learning?			
2. Competence	3. Consequence	4. Governance	5. Capacity for Change
To what extent do we have individual, team, and organizational competencies that facilitate learning?	To what extent does our performance management system encourage learning?	To what extent do our organizational structures and communication processes facilitate learning?	To what extent do our work processes and systems encourage learning?
6. Leadership To what extent do leaders throughout our organization demonstrate a commitment to learning?			

- Welcome inquiry and analysis of all decisions.
- Refrain from punishing failures that are the result of overreaching.
- Encourage a norm of reciprocity (two-way feedback).
- Build dialogue into decision-making processes.
- Avoid a one-best-way mentality that discourages individuals from learning from each other.

The mindset for learning is a critical dimension. Learning can occur along a continuum from superficial to substantial, and substantial learning involves reshaping the fundamental values and culture not only of employees but of the organization as a system. A commitment to learning also recognizes that regular small failures foster learning, whereas constant successes restrict ideas and cause complacency and risk aversion. Small failures improve long-term performance by increasing risk tolerance and problem recognition and encouraging deeper information processing. Leaders need to avoid punishing people for failures (unless they fall into a persistent and avoidable pattern of failure); instead, they must milk failures for learning.

2.   *Build organizational competence.* As discussed, competence relates to the ways in which managers encourage the development of knowledge, skills, and ability. In the context of creating a culture that supports learning, here are some of the specific actions that leaders can take:

- Rotate assignments across divisions systematically.
- Hire knowledgeable outsiders into key positions.
- Hire and promote people with a demonstrated capacity to learn.
- Outplace nonlearners—and tell people the reason for it.
- Build training programs and require ongoing education experiences to share best practices.
- Use postmortems to learn from experience: What did you learn? What will you do differently as a result?

These actions will affect who is moved into, up, and through the organization and how individuals are trained within the organization to develop competencies. They will build learning capability systematically to replace habits of random learning.

3.   *Clarify consequences.* Perhaps the most powerful shaper of a learning culture is the development of clear consequences for learning or not learning. As we discussed earlier, people tend to do what they are rewarded for and to avoid what they are punished for. Desirable consequences for learning enhance a learning culture. Here are some things you can do to attach positive consequences to learning:

- Evaluate learning actions and outcomes during performance appraisals.
- Ask multiple stakeholders to appraise performance (with a 360-degree review, for example).
- Reward employees when they learn from postmortems of mistakes.
- Give special recognition awards to managers who anticipate competency needs and learning strategies.

- Encourage and reward experimentation.
- Tie bonus and incentive systems to learning.
- Hold people accountable for results—without punishing experimental initiatives that fail along the way.

4. *Shape governance processes.* Governance processes are organizational structures, decision-making processes, and communication strategies. Here are some specific actions that shape these process so as to encourage learning.

- Build a fluid organizational structure that is flexible and adaptive.
- Develop and use ad hoc cross-functional teams.
- Establish centers of excellence and rotate jobs in and out to transfer know-how.
- Support routine, fluid, and informal interaction with suppliers and other outsiders.
- Create a campaign to show how ongoing learning is different from but linked to training and education.
- Publish learning dysfunctions openly—not picking on individuals but publicizing behaviors and habits that the organization defines as learning dysfunctions.
- Encourage external benchmarking and communication.
- Share information and successes.

All these activities urge managers to share ideas across boundaries rather than to stockpile them.

5. *Build capacity for change.* Recent technological developments have had a profound impact on the creation of a learning culture. There are now two clear steps to the process. The first is to generate ideas with impact. This is done by locating centers of excellence—places where new ideas are being applied and measurable performance improvements are being achieved. The second is to generalize those ideas across organizational boundaries. The generalization occurs more fluidly through technology. When knowledge is recorded in organizational databases, other employees, anywhere in the world, can access and use that knowledge. For example, McKinsey, Accenture, and other large consulting firms have developed comprehensive knowledge-sharing databases. A partner who needs to prepare a

client proposal about the creation of a customer-focused organization can go into a database, find five or ten partners with similar experiences in other regions, and build on their materials—and if necessary ask them for advice. This makes the knowledge of an entire firm available to any individual partner anywhere in the world. Generalization is therefore leveraged through technology.

Employees' view of organizational change processes is another key influence on the culture of learning. Here are some things you can do to encourage the development of a change orientation:

- Reject business that locks the company or unit into nongrowth patterns.
- Build flexible and current information systems.
- Establish a physical setting that encourages flexibility.
- Create ties with idea sources such as universities.

6.   *Build leadership for learning.* The ultimate test of organizational learning capability is the extent to which leaders can teach others to learn. Here are some ways to build leaders who can create learning capability:

- Teach leaders to coach.
- Teach leaders to facilitate.
- Select leaders who teach.

As leaders become more comfortable with these activities, they will model the learning culture, and they will foster the movement of ideas from one unit to another.

Putting It All Together: Harmony on the Horizontal

This chapter reviews five improv vehicles for loosening horizontal boundaries. With these vehicles, leaders can bring together resources shared in an organization, focus them on customer needs, and create an ongoing process of change and learning—without getting mired in the horizontal boundary issues of territory and turf.

Fluor Daniel, an international construction and engineering firm, demonstrates how these improv vehicles can be used together. The dominant feature of the Fluor Daniel organization is its approximately thirty (the number is variable) operating companies—called "enterprise units"—organized around the core construction process of the firm and representing the interface between Fluor Daniel and its clients. Managers of enterprise units coordinate and control projects for their group of clients. Then, for each major project—say, a pulp and paper mill in New Zealand, a petrochemical plant in the Philippines, or a power plant in Indonesia—a project manager pulls together the resources necessary to accomplish the project, many of them from a resource pool of technical, operational, and administrative competencies.

Learning capability is a critical issue for Fluor Daniel because what happens with one customer provides a competitive advantage with other customers, *if the company can leverage learning*. For example, from their experience in the Philippines, Fluor Daniel executives learned a great deal about working in political and cultural environments very different from those in the United States. These lessons were invaluable to Fluor Daniel when the firm entered Indonesia. It did not have to relearn all the lessons of creating a new business in a new setting because it was able to generalize learning from past experiences that contributed to a successful entry into the Indonesian market.

Fluor Daniel generates ideas by encouraging project managers to solve customer problems creatively, collaborating with both the customers and other project managers. It then generalizes those ideas by building linkages between project managers. The corporate role is not just to set direction and policy but explicitly to share best practices. Corporate managers have the opportunity and obligation to observe innovative client solutions and transfer the insights to other managers.

Other policies at Fluor Daniel also encourage the generalization of ideas. Employees move from one project to another not only to provide technical expertise but to share innovative ideas. Training and development courses apply internal best-practice cases so that managers share insights and innovations. Organizational communications talk about employees who have shared ideas and improved competitiveness. Client managers share questions, and answers are shared through electronic media so that learning across clients occurs.

As Fluor Daniel, Motorola, J.P. Morgan, Honeywell International, and the other organizations described in this chapter illustrate, permeating horizontal boundaries is not a one-time activity. Creating fluidity across disciplines and functions is an ongoing process. It requires constant attention, experimentation, tuning, and learning. Sometimes, as in a jazz ensemble, the music doesn't work the first time out—it has discordant notes or missing instruments or uneven rhythms. Sometimes the musicians do not even get along. But if there is a willingness to keep playing, to try new arrangements, then the beat will go on.

To keep the horizontal harmony going, we suggest that you think through the five improv vehicles described in this chapter and use them to construct an explicit strategy and work program for making your horizontal boundaries more permeable. These questions will help stimulate your thinking and start a dialogue with your colleagues:

- Which improv vehicles might be most helpful to your organization in loosening horizontal boundaries?
- What progress have you already made in implementing or testing improv vehicles? That is, how much have you already oriented around processes? Do you already use targeted teams? Do you have shared service organizations for support processes?
- Where in your organization might it be possible to test ideas from this chapter? Is there a unit, division, or location that can become a learning model for other parts of the organization?

Part Three

Free Movement Along the Value Chain

Crossing External Boundaries

First Person: Jim Madden, President, CEO, and Chairman of the Board, Exult

Exult is a California-based HR outsourcing firm. Since late 1998, Jim Madden has taken the company from a private start-up with two employees to a public firm with over 1,300 people, serving clients such as BP Amoco, Unisys, and Bank of America. Prior to joining Exult, Jim was president of MCI's outsourcing unit and, before that, a leader in Booz-Allen & Hamilton's IT and process reengineering practice.

Exult's experience proves that large global corporations can successfully and cost-efficiently manage key business processes by creating a permeable boundary with a business partner. Exult also manages a series of relationships with business partners who seamlessly provide services to Exult's clients. So Jim has gone through the process of creating permeable external boundaries with both customers and suppliers. Following are his comments on what it takes to lead and sustain this kind of boundaryless organization:

At Exult, we have to work with two categories of boundaries—the internal boundaries within a company that influence how it manages its HR function, and the external boundaries between a company and potential business partners and suppliers. External outsourcing relationships can't succeed unless the internal boundaries can adapt to them. So while Exult is an external provider, we have to pay attention to how our clients work internally.

Human resources is one of the most fragmented areas in any company. Even in a centralized corporation, HR usually has lots of autonomy in the divisions and units. It is hard to enforce standards, common practices, and harmonization of policies. Yet Exult must do this to provide a single point of accountability for operational and administrative HR activities. For example, before we can administer benefits for a client, we need to work on internal standardization. This is an ongoing challenge.

When you look at Exult from outside, you will see a "virtual" company. One quarter to one third of the services we deliver are provided by other firms, our partners. For example, we are not in the recruiting or benefits administration business. But our outsourcing contracts, of which we have five long-term relationships to date, include these services, which need to be provided seamlessly. To do this, we currently have hundreds of subcontractors—an improvement over a year ago when we had thousands of them. And as we continue to rationalize our services and suppliers, I would guess that a year from now the number will be less than two hundred.

This of course is an ongoing process. Our clients rely on us to pick the right partners, some of whom can provide services to more than one of our clients. In other cases, the same supplier is not appropriate for different clients. But overall, we are constantly looking to balance having partners who can provide effective, seamless service with consolidation of relationships so that we can have critical mass and cost-effectiveness. In a perfect world, we want to have relatively few suppliers.

HR outsourcing is a very new phenomenon and still not widely understood. It's analogous to the development of IT outsourcing in the early 1990s. At that time, IT outsourcing was not a recognized industry except for hiring temporary programmers. But then Kodak and Xerox signed milestone contracts to outsource major parts of their IT functions. Suddenly the analysts woke up and realized that fragmented business processes, if brought together, represented billions of dollars of outsourcing potential. And that's when the IT outsourcing industry took off. So today, if you are a CIO, at least once a year you have to justify why you have *not* outsourced.

We see the same thing happening over the next few years not only in human resources but in other functional areas as well—finance, accounting, procurement, customer management. To further this thinking, we suggest that senior executives look at three categories of questions:

- *Time:* How quickly do you need to take this function to the highest level of productivity in the business? Can someone else get you there faster and keep you there?
- *People:* How important is it for you to manage this function yourself—or do you want to put your very best managers and leaders on front line or strategic functions?
- *Money:* Do you want to put your money into something someone else has already built? If a provider has built this already, why should you spend money on it?

In the IT area, if I am trying to make a "build or buy" decision in regard to a data center today, I would be hard-pressed to justify building my own data center. If we fast-forward five years from now, I think the same will be true in all support functions.

At the same time, senior executives have some legitimate concerns about outsourcing business processes. For one, it is important not to downplay the soft side issues of cultural fit. If I were a senior executive, I would give this a high ranking. Does the partner I am considering have values similar to mine? At Exult, for example, one of our values is that we won't force you into a one-size-fits-all mode. You can customize your HR processes. In fact, about 20 percent of our services are tailored. There are other outsourcing firms that are more militaristic. Their value proposition is to run the operations in a certain defined way, save you money, and not provide a lot of care and feeding. I'm not saying that one value is better than another, just that the values of the client and the partner need to be in alignment. So if you're thinking, "I want every last nickel in savings, and I don't care how you do it," go one way, and if you want more flexibility and higher service, go to Exult.

A second concern that some managers will have is that they will pay a premium to fund an outsourcer's profit margins. And rather than do that, they would rather focus on getting to the outsourcer's level of efficiency and presumably saving the money. But I think this is flawed logic. Even the largest global corporations will never be able to get to the same level of scale, and thus efficiency, as an outside provider who can bring together volume from more than one global client. Second, any corporation that goes down this path toward efficiency will have to make investments that we have already made. So they are not factoring in the cost of capital, nor are they considering the ongoing required investment. It is not a one-time event.

If you're thinking about keeping support in-house, internal "shared services" will help improve productivity—it will lower costs and get some efficiency. Essentially, you're creating an outsourcing company within a company. But shared services units eventually reach a wall because they can no longer improve efficiency simply by adding scale—they need to invest more capital. But to justify raising more capital, they have to become commercial—which brings them into the outsourcing business. And at that point, it might make more sense to turn over the operation to an outsourcer who can add scale and invest more easily.

The third fear that many senior executives have about outsourcing is loss of control. "If I give you this process, I really have to trust you." Some of this is grounded in reality and some is just a perception. With outsourcing partnerships, key executives still have to retain the strategic management of the process while the partner provides the operational, technological, and administrative capability. The client has to retain most of the major policy and business decision making.

To make an outsourcing relationship work, the relationship needs to be owned by someone who is accountable for business results, not a "manager of alliances." For example, in our relationships with BP Amoco and Bank of America, the senior HR executives are our clients. We are a natural extension of their departments.

I do see a role for a "manager of alliances and sourcing," but it's a staff and support role. Such a person can help in the transition to outsourcing—to explore and vet potential partners, help negotiate the deal, and structure the relationship. Then, once the relationship is in place, such a manager should periodically audit the partner's performance against the terms of the agreement. But this is not a day-to-day management job.

Another factor in making outsourcing work is that the educational and buy-in process has to go beyond just the head of HR and the CEO. All the key general managers—and thousands of employees—are affected. So when a company moves to an outsourced relationship, it represents a huge change management initiative. The shift to outsourcing is a systemwide change in an organization, not just a transition for the immediate client.

One last point to make is that over the past few years, I have learned a great deal not only about providing outsourced business processes but also about managing a company that itself depends heavily on outsourced partners. This has been a major challenge as well because we also have a natural tendency to want to own everything ourselves. It is difficult to let go and build trusting, permeable relationships across our own external boundaries. So I have had to constantly push my own management team to be true to our model and vision. And this has not been without some pain and ruffled feathers. But the lesson for me is that if I am not consistent with the vision of a virtual company, then it will be nibbled away at the edges.

Chapter Six

Toward Partnership with Customers and Suppliers

Like castles surrounded by walls and moats, many organizations have artificial boundaries between themselves and the outside world. Though not made of stone and water, these boundaries are just as difficult to surmount. And they are just as obsolete. The new success factors of speed, flexibility, integration, and innovation are making boundaries between organizations less and less useful. In fact, hiding behind such boundaries today can be more dangerous than venturing outside.

This is not to say that you should forget all external boundaries and form partnerships, alliances, joint ventures, and collaborations with everyone. That would be chaotic and counterproductive. And it would negate the external boundaries' positive effects: a focus on a manageable (bounded) set of business competencies and priorities, and a sense of identity with others who share a common purpose. However, by making specific external boundaries more permeable, you can dramatically increase speed, flexibility, integration, and innovation. In addition, the more that strategy, technology, management practices, resources, and values flow back and forth naturally, the less necessity there is for crisis-generated breaches of the outer wall. By concentrating on the *value chain* and the process by which organizations link together to create products and services that have more value combined than separate, you can help find a reasonable level of permeability.

Note that while vertical and horizontal boundaries are the floors, ceilings, and internal walls of the organizational house, external boundaries describe not just the outside walls but the community in which the house stands. The objective of loosening internal boundaries is to create a more effective individual organization, one that is more capable of dealing with customers, suppliers, and other external entities. The objective of loosening external boundaries is not only to improve an organization but to make stronger interactive groups of organizations in a value chain. Nonetheless, it is individual firms that must take the actions that improve the chain.

The Value Chain: The Traditional View

All companies form links in chains of entities that produce and distribute products or services to end users. Many companies are in the middle of a value chain, receiving materials, components, and services from suppliers or vendors and selling products or services to customer companies. Along the way, other external entities such as government regulators, investor groups, investment analysts, and even competitors influence the work.

The overall purpose of this chain of relationships is to maximize profit by producing higher value than the competition. That higher value is defined by more desirable features, lower cost, higher quality, and shorter time to market. Consider the automobile industry, especially in the West—most car models require at least ten thousand parts, up to 75 percent of them manufactured by independent suppliers.[1] In addition, dealerships—the customers of most automobile companies—are also independent businesses. Finally, environmental groups, government regulators, and others influence the process all along the chain.

Since early in the twentieth century, most companies, especially in North America, have viewed their value chains from an independent, legalistic perspective. Cooperative arrangements beyond the bare minimum have not only been met with suspicion but have been discouraged or even forbidden by antitrust laws and regulations. As a result, each organization in the chain has been encouraged to see itself as an independent entity, maximizing its own profitability at the expense of its customers and suppliers. Consultants John Carlisle and Robert Parker describe the traditional relationship between members of a value chain as a "sophisticated form of haggling in hopes of making their own piece of the transaction pie larger than the one received by the other party."[2]

This every-company-for-itself attitude leads to five types of value chain boundaries, all of which destroy competitiveness by reducing speed, flexibility, integration, and innovation.

Strategies and plans are developed independently. Organizations traditionally establish their own market targets, resource allocations, and so on without consulting other members of the value chain. Often, this results in some links of the chain being out of sync with other links. For example, when an automobile company keeps design changes secret even from suppliers until the last moment, suppliers find it virtually impossible to meet requirements—especially when they're already geared up to produce the original design.

Information sharing and joint problem solving are limited. Companies with a traditional perspective tend to conceal such information as real cost of materials, profit margins, and all manner of problems viewed as dirty linen. The tendency is to try to solve such problems independently, without letting others in the chain know a problem exists. This result is often a suboptimal or untimely solution or, when a problem is not resolved, an unpleasant surprise for other members of the value chain.

To illustrate: when a tool and die shop ran into trouble with tolerances in a line of precision machinery, management hid the problem, trying to solve it internally. After two weeks of unsuccessful industrial engineering studies and experiments, management told its customer the order would not be shipped on schedule. This event spread severe disruption through downstream production schedules. Finally, in desperation, management brought a materials supplier in, who quickly discovered that a different grade and composition of metal would solve the problem.

Accounting, measurement, and reward systems are separate and unsynchronized. Traditionally, each entity has its own measures, rewards, and ways of accounting for performance. It is not uncommon, for example, for a customer to emphasize and reward quality while the producer emphasizes and rewards volume, productivity, or cost management. In one industrial business, productivity investments were funded at the expense of quality programs. The producer's margins improved, but a key customer soon canceled all contracts until quality performance was upgraded, making the productivity gains moot.

Sales forces push products on their terms. When each member of a value chain aims to maximize its own profitability, salespeople push product, urging customers to take more units at times and prices best suited to the seller. They devote little time to listening to the customer, determining specific needs and requirements, and working collaboratively on the best use of products. Often, the customer ends up with piles of products it can't use and doesn't need.

In a large decentralized bank, for example, different computer vendors had introduced a variety of technologies and systems, each designed to meet a specific need. However, none of the vendors helped bank managers think about overall architecture, communications strategy, or common standards. The result was a frustrating jumble and an eventual decision to spend millions of dollars building new systems from scratch.

Resources are utilized inefficiently. Value chains always include tremendous pools of resources, expertise, and technical and operational knowledge concerning all facets of the business. Yet in the traditional mode, each entity sticks with its own resources; it can't tap into the resources of others. For example, in the late 1980s, a large bank financed a number of leveraged buy-outs and then watched the borrowers flounder. Only after the loans went into default, compromising its own balance sheet, did the bank provide the financial and management expertise the borrowers lacked.

The Search for an Alternative Model

Today, given the pitfalls of traditional value chain boundaries, many companies are looking outside themselves to their entire web of institutional relationships. They want to figure out how to strengthen the web, not just their own strand. In a 1991 Dataquest and Arthur Young survey of 700 start-up and fast-growth companies, nearly 90 percent reported forming strategic alliances.[3] Similarly, alliance expert Robert Lynch reports that the health care industry alone tends to spawn over 550 alliances each year.[4] Other industries, such as pharmaceuticals, electronics, and retail, also generate large numbers of formal and informal cross-company relationships, and a best-practices study of highly successful companies, commissioned by General Electric in 1990, concluded that a focus on customer-supplier partnerships was one of the keys to future competitive success.

The concept is far from new. In fact, the growth of many of today's industries was fueled by cooperative arrangements between firms that were too small or that lacked sufficient skills to mount major ventures on their own. The shipping industry developed through alliances of shipbuilders, insurance underwriters, manufacturers, and trading companies. The electric power industry developed through consortiums of inventors, investors, power generating companies, and equipment manufacturers. (That is why the world headquarters for GE Lighting is to be found in Cleveland's NELA Park—NELA is an acronym for National Electric Lighting Association.)[5]

Today, however, the number of strategic alliances, partnerships, and joint ventures is multiplying at a rate far greater than ever before—a trend Peter Drucker predicted in 1982, saying that "the multinational of tomorrow will be comprised of autonomous partners, linked in a confederation rather than through common ownership."[6] As product life-cycles shrink, global competition heats up and everything moves faster, and companies are realizing that they cannot keep up by working alone. They need to join forces to drive technologies, expand distribution, enter new markets, ensure sources of supply, and match end-user expectations.

At the same time, successful companies are abandoning traditional methods of hostile competition. The costs are too great and the risks too high. Instead, these companies are finding ways of cooperatively integrating with suppliers and customers. As consultants Richard Normann and Rafael Ramirez noted in a 1993 *Harvard Business Review* article: "Increasingly the strategic focus of successful companies is not the company or even the industry but the *value-creating system* itself, within which different economic actors—suppliers, business partners, allies, customers—work together to *co-produce* value. Their key strategic task is the *reconfiguration* of roles and relationships among this constellation of actors in order to mobilize the creation of value in new forms."[7]

Moving the Value Chain from East to West

Adding to the pressure is the fact that many competitors in Asia do not operate in the traditional mode. As University of Massachusetts professor Michael Best notes: "The primary goal of industrial policy in Japan is to promote . . . the entrepreneurial firm, consultative buyer-vendor relations, and inter-firm associations."[8] East Asian companies, as members of *keiretsu*, engage in extensive cooperative arrangements, joint ventures, and even government-sponsored linkages with other members of a value chain—described to us by one Japanese manager as "a river with many branches that flow together." Their cooperative efforts often produce better products faster and with less cost than do the independent ways of working of traditional Western companies.

MIT researchers James Womack, Daniel Jones, and Daniel Roos, in their groundbreaking study of the Japanese automobile industry, describe how "each *keiretsu* consists of perhaps twenty major companies, one in each industrial sector. . . . There is no holding company at the top of the organization. Nor are the companies legally united. Rather, they're held together by cross-locking equity structures—each company owns a portion of every other company's equity in a circular pattern—and a sense of reciprocal obligation. . . . Among the key companies in every group are a bank, an insurance company and a trading company. Each of these has substantial cash resources that can be made available to the members of the group."[9]

Some Western organizations have tried to emulate Eastern arrangements between producers and suppliers, for example by pushing the just-in-time (JIT) inventory concept. Unfortunately, the initial promise was diminished by suppliers who lacked an overall view of the value chain. The result, as Best described, was that JIT became "an instrument for parent firms to shift the costs of holding inventory to supplier firms."[10] When some links could not handle the extra cost or the reduced margins, they collapsed—weakening the chain. This is an example of what MIT professor Peter Senge calls "shifting the burden," which produces a temporary improvement in one location that only masks a more fundamental weakening of the entire system.[11]

GM suppliers felt the pinch of cost shifting during the José Ignacio Lopez purchasing regime—especially when GM purchasing people tore up existing contracts and simply demanded lower prices. Suppliers of struggling retailers run into the same problem. For example, Kmart in the mid-1990s undertook what the *New York Times* called "an all-out offensive to force its manufacturers to carry the burden of its current problems on their books." The *Times* reported that Kmart asked toy manufacturers "to carry goods they ship to it on their books as inventory. . . . 'They are asking the manufacturers to take steps they can't possibly agree to,' said Sean McGowan, an analyst at Gerard Klauer Mattison & Company. . . . Not only would agreeing to such payment terms force toy makers to do the same for their other customers, Mr. McGowan said, it would also squeeze the toy makers."[12]

Recent advances in information technology have improved communication across the value chain, allowing firms to share up-to-date demand forecasts and sales figures with suppliers. At its best, such technology improves efficiency throughout the chain, as when Dell suppliers monitor both customer orders and component consumption rates in real time.[13] Unfortunately, though, shifting the burden continues to be all too common. Costs, quality requirements, inventories, and administrative procedures are increasingly pushed back along the value chain without a full understanding of the implications. Rather than collaborate with other members of the value chain on systemic solutions, many companies continue to go it alone—developing their own productivity programs, competitive awards, and quick fixes for symptoms. When they do think of themselves as links in a value chain, their aim is to force other links to conform to what they think is needed.

In short, even though many organizations know they need a new approach to the value chain, and the technology to support a new approach has developed over the last decade, these organizations often focus more on the mechanics of interorganizational relationships than on the underlying assumptions. To loosen external boundaries and release the power of the value chain, companies must internalize a new set of assumptions for customer-supplier relationships.

Refocusing the Lens: A Rising Tide Raises All Boats

In our view, successful companies in this decade and beyond will be those that take a systemic, boundaryless view of their participation in the value chain. They must acquire an entirely new mind-set, learning to see themselves as parts of an integrated system much like a vertically integrated company with multiple owners.

From this perspective, companies can see that a rising tide raises all boats, that success will come from improving the overall profitability and continuing vitality of the value chain as a whole, rather than just their own bottom lines and organizational health.

Carlisle and Parker describe the boundaryless view of the value chain in this way: "If customer and supplier firms can recognize their common ground in a shared interest in capturing the customer sale which actually nourishes them both, it should be possible for them to work creatively and effectively together to capture that sale for 'their' product."[14] This recognition becomes critical when companies face new competitors whose strategies for winning are based on customer service, quality, cycle time, and constant innovation rather than low cost and technical excellence alone.

The company that loosens its external boundaries will follow the new cooperative and systemic organizational model that is contrasted to the old model in Table 6.1.

Business and Operational Planning Are Coordinated

In the successful value chain, all members collaborate in both strategic and operational business planning. The goal is not only better product development and production planning but common or coordinated administrative and operational procedures such as billing, customer service, purchasing, shipping, and inventory. One member might even take on certain administrative functions for several others, resulting in huge opportunities for chainwide cost reduction.

Here's an illustration of the gains offered by a collaborative approach—and the risks of going it alone. In the summer of 1990, a manufacturer of premium road and racing bicycles redesigned its product line with an eye toward the fitness market. Guided by significant consumer input, the company created a prototype bike that was lighter but stronger than existing products so users could ride longer with less fatigue. Excited by the new product, the salesforce aggressively signed up dealers and took orders for delivery during the spring 1991 selling season. Once company managers saw they had a winner, they geared up for manufacturing and assembly. Unfortunately, the key parts suppliers had been left out of the design

**Table 6.1. Changing Value Chain Assumptions
for Boundaryless Organizations.**

Old Model (Each Organization Aims to Maximize Its Own Profit)	New Model (Each Organization Aims to Maximize Total Value Chain Success)
1. Strategies and plans are developed independently.	1. Business and operational plans are coordinated.
2. Information sharing and joint problem solving are limited.	2. Information is widely shared and problems are solved jointly.
3. Accounting, measurement, and reward systems are separate and unsynchronized.	3. Accounting, measurement, and reward systems are consistent.
4. Salesforce pushes products on salespeople's terms.	4. Selling is a consultative process.
5. Resources are inefficiently utilized.	5. Resources are shared.

process. It turned out that several suppliers critical to the braking systems could not produce the required parts in time for the spring delivery dates. The only alternative was to go to other suppliers whose costs were higher and whose product required extra assembly at the bike company. The new bike debuted successfully, but produced no profit margin to speak of. With that lesson in mind, managers made sure the following year's bike was designed with vendor collaboration from the beginning. This approach resulted in much higher margins for both the bicycle company and its suppliers.

Information Is Widely Shared and Problems Are Solved Jointly

Participants in a boundaryless value chain share information much more freely than they did as solo players. A production problem anywhere in the chain is everyone's concern, calling out the best resources from throughout the system.

For example, GE Appliances has worked for several years to achieve faster and more flexible and responsive manufacturing with improved quality. A key component of the effort is close and strategic collaboration with key parts suppliers. If suppliers can respond faster to changes in production schedules and product designs and manage parts inventories more effectively, then GE Appliances can produce major appliances faster and tailor production more quickly to customer requirements.

To achieve these ends, GE Appliances wanted to develop close information systems linkages to coordinate production, inventory, sales, specification, and scheduling data with suppliers, making them an integrated part of the process and not just an input. Four key suppliers were selected to pilot the information systems link. Initially, they found the data insufficiently detailed and difficult to interpret. Based on this feedback, GE Appliances supplemented the data link with a monthly package of specific analyses and recommendations for action. The approach was then expanded to the twenty-five largest suppliers. Now, GE Appliance engineers work continually with suppliers to improve quality and accelerate the flow of materials through the production process.[15]

Early systems for managing inventory and production across organizational boundaries were cumbersome and proprietary, but the Internet allows organizations to share richer data throughout the value chain with significantly less investment. As a result, management and decision-making systems have changed to leverage these systems' potential. For example, when Wal-Mart's inventory and sales data show changes in sales of Pampers, one person can currently approve changes to production and shipping schedules at Procter & Gamble (the manufacturer) and at 3M (which produces the tape for closing the diapers).[16]

Accounting, Measurement, and Reward Systems Are Consistent

A key requirement for a boundaryless supplier-customer relationship is a common scorekeeping and incentive system so that everyone in the value chain works off the same numbers and aims toward the same set of goals. Successful value chains have joint methods of determining costs, margins, and investments, and have performance goals for each organizational unit derived from those methods. A matching reward system motivates people to achieve the systemwide objectives.

For example, when a manufacturer of auto parts reviewed its sales goals with its leading nationwide distributor, it discovered a subtle but significant disparity in priorities. The manufacturer wanted to emphasize margin goals, but the distributor had created a sales incentive program based on volume—regardless of margin. As a result, sales of low-margin products were far ahead of plan, while sales of higher-priced products lagged and were subject to constant price change requests. A joint manufacturer-distributor team then developed sales goals for specific product categories, and sales incentives offering one level of rewards for total sales volume and higher payouts for sales of high-margin product categories.

Selling Is a Consultative Process

In the boundaryless world, successful companies have new sales priorities. Instead of pushing product, salespeople advise customers and help them crystallize supply requirements and find optimal ways to meet those requirements and best utilize purchased products. In short, salespeople create a pull for product, because as William Frago, former CEO of Carrier Corporation, points out, "You can get much more movement by pulling on a chain than by pushing on it." At the same time, salespeople become conduits into their own companies for customer feedback about desired operational and product delivery improvements and product development and enhancement ideas.

In the Minneapolis branch of IBM, the notion of consultative selling helped shift sales behavior patterns, with striking results. In one case, a potential customer was having trouble determining whether to purchase a new manufacturing system. The IBM rep helped the customer form an interfunctional team to establish criteria for selecting the system. That assistance not only made the sale more timely and efficient, it also ensured that the customer bought what was needed and not what the salesperson wanted to push.

Resources Are Shared

Finally, a systemic view allows twenty-first-century companies to deploy resources and expertise more efficiently throughout the value chain. For example, the developers of a state-of-the-art distribution system in one company might work as consultants to upgrade distribution in other parts of the value chain. This helps companies focus increasingly on their own core competencies, outsourcing support functions such as information systems, human resources, accounting, and even management expertise.

A number of companies now provide training for their customers or suppliers, illustrating how resources in one part of a value chain can benefit other parts. Whirlpool offers customers and dealers extensive management, sales, and technical service training. The Federal Aviation Administration (FAA) trains pilots in FAA standards and guidelines. Greyhound's airline service division provides training for its customers in safety and flight services. And Marriott International develops specialized training in customer service approaches that it offers to selected customers.[17]

As the Internet has enabled information to be shared with more parties, economists have begun to speak of industry *ecosystems.* Rather than negotiating with upstream and downstream value chain partners, companies can now interact with expanded markets of suppliers and customers. Auctions and e-marketplaces now drive efficiencies across industries. Traditional competitors often join one another in purchasing blocs to achieve economies of scale. Even companies in entirely unrelated industries now share information to help control costs: General Mills collaborates with twenty other companies to ensure that trucks travel as close to full as possible.[18] Companies looking to remain competitive are discovering that they must search for efficiencies that cut across organizational boundaries.

Barriers to Boundaryless Customer-Supplier Relationships

While the new, boundaryless view of customer and supplier relationships may sound logical and attractive, getting there is not so easy. We see six substantial barriers that undermine radical change efforts. Before diving headlong into the waters of cross-company collaboration, it is important to be aware of these barriers (shown in the box), to be able to recognize them, and to develop strategies for swimming around them.

Customer-Supplier Relationship Barriers

- Legal and regulatory tradition
- Competitive confusion
- Lack of trust
- Difficulty in letting go of control
- Slowness in learning new managerial skills
- Complexity

Legal and Regulatory Tradition

The first barrier to boundaryless external relationships is the long-standing tradition that threatens legal or antitrust action unless companies in related industries remain totally independent. Thus U.S. commercial law encourages company autonomy and often views collaboration as collusion or restraint of trade.

Though boundaryless relationships clearly must be pursued within the framework of current laws, it is worth observing that respected MIT economist Lester Thurow, in a discussion of U.S. competitiveness vis-à-vis the Japanese, suggests that perhaps the antitrust structure has outlived its usefulness.[19] Consider this example: early in 1993, in the midst of highly speculative and preliminary explorations by TCI, Time Warner, and Microsoft of how cable television, software, hardware, and telecommunications companies might work together, Representative Edward Markey of Massachusetts, chairman of the House Subcommittee on Telecommunications and Finance, sent a letter to federal regulators warning that the proposed alliance could "close the market to competitive entrance."[20] Such an alliance might eventually need to be scrutinized. But in our view, it was far too early to be ringing the monopolistic alarm bell. If, in the early days of important explorations, executives feel that every cross-company meeting or preliminary discussion will be subject to regulatory scrutiny, then they may shy away from potentially productive alliances, not wanting to lose time, resources, and goodwill through battles with government regulators.

The point is that the regulatory environment, while changing slowly (witness the U.S. government's encouragement of an industrywide partnership to build electric cars), is still skeptical or even hostile toward intercompany collaboration. Not all boundaryless arrangements will be viewed as having pure motives, and some may require costly lobbying or time-consuming justifications to dissuade regulatory bodies from seeing restraint of trade.

Competitive Confusion

A second barrier to boundaryless relationships between suppliers and customers is that they have the potential to force companies to stick to one value chain or at least to worry about who is an ally and who is not. For example, a parts producer that forges a highly collaborative relationship with one automaker might be precluded from similar relationships with competing carmakers. Therefore, the potential payoff from the strategic relationship must outweigh the potential loss of business from other sources and the risk of relying on a concentrated customer base.

This is the dilemma that many Wal-Mart suppliers have faced in recent years. Having connected themselves directly to Wal-Mart's data stream, they can now manage inventory, order processing, and payments at far-reduced costs. However, when these suppliers think about transferring these same business practices to Kmart, Home Depot, and similar companies, their first consideration is that Wal-Mart might reduce their share of business if they form a similar alliance with a Wal-Mart rival.

Competitive confusion also arises when business rivals find themselves competing in some arenas but pursuing joint ventures and cooperative arrangements in others. These dual roles are an increasing source of confusion in the computer and telecommunications industry. TCI and AOL-Time Warner compete with each other and with Bell companies to offer data and phone services, but they form alliances with phone companies for other projects. "You very much have to accept that you are going to compete against a company in some places and cooperate in others," the *Wall Street Journal* quotes one communications executive as saying.[21]

A similar competitive confusion crops up in large corporations with multiple business units. For example, GE Motors is a major supplier of small motors to Maytag and provides technical and process improvement training to this value chain partner—even though

Maytag is an arch rival of GE Appliances in the dishwasher and refrigerator markets. For companies that want to establish boundaryless relationships with customers and suppliers, identifying these potentially contradictory relationships and weighing the trade-offs is a major but essential task.

The Trust Barrier

Most traditional companies have long histories of internal conflict between functions or departments. Between companies, the chasms caused by lack of trust can be much deeper. Yet the boundaryless world requires a great deal of cross-company interdependence if the overall value chain is to succeed. That interdependence is based on trust.

Japanese suppliers and customers tend to rely much more on trust and cooperation than do comparable units in the Western production chain. We have watched this Western trust barrier in action in numerous work sessions between suppliers and their customers. In almost all these sessions, one party makes demands based on individual interest rather than joint, value chain interest. If the supplier and customer do not have enough trust to conduct a healthy dialogue about the demands, resulting problems raise the trust barrier further. For example, in discussions between an insurance company and a pension customer, the customer requested a number of ad hoc reports and customized processing procedures. The insurance representatives, trying to please the customer, agreed to everything, despite the problems their company would face in meeting the requests. Later, insurance personnel referred to the customer as "unrealistically demanding." The customer, in turn, was continually frustrated by the difficulty of getting reports that had been agreed to.

Alliance consultant Robert P. Lynch observes that extreme lack of trust between alliance partners can produce these very ugly results:[22]

- The "Fake": competitive companies pretend to be interested in an alliance only to get information about the potential partner.

- The "Steal": companies take competitive technology and information after an alliance breaks up.

- The "Squeeze": financial constraints force one alliance partner to turn over data or technology to the other.

- The "Float": alliance partners get cold feet and leave the joint venture in limbo.

- The "Bleed-Through": one partner takes processes produced in the partnership and applies them to a joint venture with a competitor.

The overall message is that while boundaryless relationships depend on trust between organizations, such trust does not exist a priori. It must be nurtured and encouraged, so that lack of it does not poison relationships and weaken the entire value chain.

The Control Barrier

Most Western companies are used to having total control over their destinies (or the illusion of control). In the boundaryless world, executives must become comfortable with *control sharing*—collaborative, collegial, consultative arrangements with a range of business partners. When external boundaries are loosened, no member of the value chain can dictate arbitrary terms and conditions to others. With limited numbers of strategic partners, companies cannot afford to force a one-sided agenda that might weaken the chain by causing a partner to walk out or collapse. Instead, each partner is responsible for setting its needs in the context of a web of relationships and for working to meet those needs in ways that strengthen the entire web.

One small manufacturer of high-quality, custom-rolled aluminum has made substantial gains by overcoming issues of control with key suppliers and customers. In the early 1990s, this company successfully increased rolling mill productivity by 20 percent through focused reductions of horizontal barriers between such groups as production control, maintenance, and quality assurance. But the productivity boost—equivalent to an extra shift's worth of output—compounded a larger issue that had plagued the company throughout its long history: it was unable to deliver all orders on time. Over the years, it had learned to accept an 80 percent on-time delivery rate as normal. With the extra productivity, however, this customer service level became unacceptable, leading both to customer dissatisfaction and to increasing inventories.

To break its dismal delivery tradition, the company tried an experiment: it would have a model week. During that model week, managers and employees would do everything possible to achieve 100 percent on-time delivery. Sales would not promise product that could not be delivered; production control would plan schedules more than a week in advance; manufacturing would think through new ways of loading the annealing furnaces. After several weeks of preparation, the model week began. And to much general amazement, 100 percent on-time delivery was achieved. Then it was sustained, not just for one week but for two. Then reality hit.

Just when management and staff were feeling that they could control their own destiny, they discovered that a critical, single-source supplier had sent a batch of material with unacceptable defects in the metal structure. With customer-satisfaction time ticking urgently away, managers and staff realized they had no real control over on-time delivery. No matter what they did in-house, they were at the mercy of their suppliers. They could achieve control only by breaking through the boundaries between themselves and their suppliers.

To surmount these boundaries, a company team asked the source of the defective material to join in working sessions aimed at achieving a consistent level of on-time delivery above 95 percent. These sessions uncovered the fact that the structural variations were traceable to an earlier supplier in the value chain, who was providing the raw materials for the aluminum alloy. The session participants then determined that certain material formulations produced different properties in the alloy and that these properties had an effect all the way through the end-use customers' manufacturing processes. That realization led the company to approach on-time delivery in a whole new way. Instead of trying to control its own piece of the value chain process, it focused on creating a collaboration with suppliers and customers that would control the process from beginning to end. The result was a sustained on-time delivery rate that has stayed above 95 percent for several years.

The Skill Barrier

The fifth barrier to boundaryless relationships between members of the value chain is organizations' need to develop a new set of managerial skills. For many years, traditional managers achieved results by using the levers of authority, reward, and punishment and of control of resources. To a large extent, these same methods have been applied to customer and supplier relationships as well. Prices, specifications, timing of deliveries, support services, and so on were all a result of often-rancorous negotiations, ultimately backed up by threats of doing business elsewhere or raising prices.

In the boundaryless relationship with customers and suppliers, these tactics are counterproductive. The same behavioral shifts that support new vertical and horizontal collaborations with employees and colleagues apply to developing external organizational agreements as well. As Peter Drucker put it, the new shape of the corporation "will totally change what is demanded of management. The critical skill in the new multi-national—for most businessmen a brand new one—will be that of coordinating units that cannot be commanded but which have to work together."[23]

Managers must spend their time at the interface between links in the value chain, managing relationships there rather than negotiating terms and conditions. In this role, managers need superb listening skills, a variety of problem-solving techniques, and an ability to build consensus.

To illustrate: a large automotive supply company has three different marketing groups that deal with Detroit, one for each major product line. All three product lines produce parts critical to automotive manufacture, all enjoy a long-standing reputation for product reliability, and all are competitively priced. Yet one of the marketing managers has consistently produced better results than the others—more volume, longer-term contracts, more favorable pricing, earlier involvement in product changes, and the like. For some time, senior management attributed the difference to weaker competition in the one product area. Upon closer examination, however, management realized that this one marketing manager was going about his job in a fundamentally different way. Instead of dealing with the automakers' purchasing departments, he had developed relationships with their key people in engineering, product design, and manufacturing. In fact, he and his staff spent most of their time in plants rather than Detroit offices, they often brought in technical experts to help in the plants, and they enjoyed full membership in product design teams. In other words, this marketing manager's success was not due to random chance. It was due to his systematic application of a different set of management skills, focused on building relationships and solving problems rather than on negotiating prices and delivery dates.

The Complexity Barrier

The final barrier to boundaryless relationships between customers and suppliers is the sheer complexity of the undertaking. No matter how straightforward the business interests, there are a multitude of variables that can influence success—and many of them cannot be fully controlled or predicted in advance. They include shifts in the business climate, changes in government regulations, and developments or frustrations in technology. Collaboration also requires an ongoing match between the business goals and needs of the partners, a fit between company cultures, and the right chemistry among the key players.

The ultimate failure of a strategic partnership between copier makers Savin and Ricoh shows how complexity can break down a successful relationship. Savin was built in the 1960s by American entrepreneur Paul Charlap, who joined forces with Israeli inventor Benny Landa to develop a copier that used liquid toner instead of the powdered toner that Xerox employed. The technological shift allowed the Savin copier to use less energy (no need to heat and liquefy powder) and be much more reliable (no loose powder grains to gum up the works). Savin had no manufacturing capability. To get its invention to market fast, it arranged with the Japanese camera company Ricoh to produce the machines that Savin would distribute and service. The arrangement worked spectacularly well for several years. In the late 1970s, Savin had cut into Xerox's market share and had one of the best distribution networks in the United States. Then, in the 1980s, the complexity factor came into play.

First, Xerox—responding to the threat from Savin and other manufacturers—began focusing on quality and reliability improvement as well as new product development. Then Ricoh, seeing a huge market opportunity, began to sell copiers under its own name, setting up a competing distribution system. And Savin, seeing its success threatened, began to invest heavily in developing technology for color photocopying with liquid toner. Just as Savin was pouring capital into R&D and manufacturing, the dollar-yen exchange rate deteriorated, forcing Savin to pay much more to Ricoh for copiers and spare parts. During the ensuing cash squeeze, Savin allowed its distribution base and service levels to deteriorate, causing further cash problems. Negotiations with Ricoh became increasingly frustrating; there was little common ground between the U.S. managers and the Japanese company. Finally, when the color technology failed, Savin collapsed into bankruptcy. Ricoh entered the U.S. copier market on a major scale. After several years of bankruptcy proceedings and a series of ownership changes, Savin was eventually bought by Ricoh.

Robert Lynch, speaking of the high failure rate of technology-based partnerships and the way their success diminishes with increasing complexity, says, "When explorations into new technologies are coupled with the development of new products for new markets, it is like solving a triple simultaneous equation with three unknowns."[24] Managers moving toward boundaryless relationships must be alert to complexity and realize that the relaxing of external boundaries may allow the dynamics of a relationship to shift rapidly. It is not enough merely to establish a customer-supplier partnership; that is only the beginning. Once initiated, the partnership must be continually recalibrated, adjusted, tested, assessed, and reworked. Otherwise, as with Savin and Ricoh, the complexity may become overwhelming.

From There to Here, from Here to There/ Funny Things Are Everywhere

Given the extent of external boundaries and the barriers to crossing them, getting from here to there for most companies will often seem like the Dr. Seuss tale that provides the title of this section,[25] as companies are beset by things of all sorts in their paths. Although stories of joint ventures, alliances, and partnerships appear daily, many of these new arrangements flounder and fail. For every successful new boundaryless arrangement between companies, there is probably at least one more that collapses. Here are two additional examples.

In the late 1980s, GE Lighting researchers developed a new light source. Called "discharge forward lighting," it provided much more focused, energy-efficient light from a significantly smaller source than before. It presented a possibility that automakers could completely redesign automobile front ends with lighter-weight materials and lower costs. The opportunities for enhanced beauty, safety, fuel efficiency, and cost-effectiveness seemed significant.

GE Lighting searched for and found a joint venture partner among its customers. The partner would get a head start with the new technology in exchange for sharing in some development costs. For the next two years, GE and its partner struggled to create a commercially viable product but found it difficult to resolve the host of technical factors. For example, the auto company insisted that the cost of the discharge forward lamp had to be equal to or less than that of the halogen lamp it would replace. GE, however, argued that the appropriate comparison was between the entire old and new lighting systems, including electronics, wiring, and housing. The complexity barrier was writ large as the partners attempted to deal simultaneously with technical, commercial, aesthetic, and cultural issues. After two years of work, GE Lighting began to look for alternative partners, and the existing partnership was dissolved.

Additional difficulties that might surface in cross-institutional relationships can be seen in the 1993 proposed joint venture between Blockbuster Video and IBM to develop and launch a computer network that would store and download compact discs on demand at Blockbuster stores. A store customer would select entire discs or specific songs from a music catalogue. The selections would be immediately downloaded onto a blank disc, so the customer would never have to leave the store without finding a particular number. For Blockbuster, the system would have allowed diversification from video rental into retail music without the need to build up a big inventory. For IBM, the project would have promoted the development of a system requiring sophisticated high-end computers, an IBM specialty.

For both companies and consumers, then, the idea looked powerful, and it was announced with some fanfare. But Blockbuster and IBM had failed to bring in other key members of the value chain—the music producers. Companies like Sony and Time Warner reacted with concern, worried about losing proprietary rights over their music, losing control of production and packaging, and easy pirating of recordings. Faced with these trust and control barriers, as well as the venture's technical complexity, Blockbuster and IBM let the project drop.[26]

However, while individual companies must still struggle with the complex strategic issues of when to pursue partnerships and with whom, the real question is not *whether* such ventures are worthwhile—they seem to be occurring in almost every industry sector at an increasing rate. The more difficult question in the long run is *how* to make these boundaryless relationships successful—how to get over the barriers of legal and regulatory tradition, competitive confusion, lack of trust, difficulty in letting go of control, slowness in learning new managerial skills, and coping with complexity, and how to forge a new model of collaboration between independent but linked companies.

Getting Started: How Well Linked Is Your Organization's Value Chain?

In this chapter, we have painted a broad picture of promoting success by loosening boundaries between partners in the value chain through joint planning, greater information sharing, development of common measures, a more consultative sales process, and increased sharing of resources. The result will be significantly faster and more focused product development, streamlined manufacturing and distribution, lower-cost support systems, more flexible responses to market shifts, and an overall competitive advantage in relation to competing value chains.

Developing looser external boundaries, however, will not be easy. There are plenty of challenges along the way, including regulatory traditions, competitive confusion, distrust among partners, lingering desire for total control, and the complexity of multi-organizational business efforts. Currently, barriers such as these cause at least as many failures and frustrations as successes.

In our experience, however, it is possible to make progress, no matter the starting point. Before you turn to the next chapter, we suggest that you get a fix on the relationships with customers and suppliers that your company has today. This knowledge will help you select the actions that will be most effective given your current external boundaries.

Each of the five external boundaries that define customer-supplier dynamics—planning, information sharing, measurement, sales processes, and resource utilization—represents a continuum of possibilities, ranging from the impermeable (traditional go-it-alone mode) to the highly permeable (involving considerable sharing and collaboration).

Your company may be at a different point on the continuum of each external boundary. The rigidity or looseness of each boundary will also vary in relation to the particular customer or supplier on the other side. However, since the five boundaries are to some extent interdependent, it is unlikely that your position on one boundary will be vastly different from your position on the others. For example, it is difficult to engage in a great deal of information sharing without also increasing collaboration in other areas. If such a collaboration imbalance were to occur, it would point to the possibility that trust was localized in one relationship between individuals rather than widespread and that the overall relationship was in fact fragile.

Questionnaire #4 allows you to locate your company on this continuum for each of the five external boundaries. To improve the accuracy of your answers, we suggest that you have a specific customer, supplier, or value chain partner in mind as you score yourself.

Questionnaire #4

Stepping Up to the Line: How Well Linked Is Your Organization's Value Chain?

Instructions: Diagnose your company's progress toward a boundaryless relationship with customers or suppliers in your value chain. Select a strategically important customer or supplier (or category of customer/supplier) in your value chain. Circle a number on each scale to reflect where your relationship now stands.

	Traditional								**Boundaryless**	
1. Strategies and operating plans	Developed independently			Shared		Coordinated			Developed jointly	
• Marketing plans	1	2	3	4	5	6	7	8	9	10
• Product development plans	1	2	3	4	5	6	7	8	9	10
• Production and inventory planning (including who owns inventory)	1	2	3	4	5	6	7	8	9	10
• Distribution and transportation planning	1	2	3	4	5	6	7	8	9	10
• Information systems planning	1	2	3	4	5	6	7	8	9	10
2. Information sharing and problem solving	Highly guarded		Selective sharing as needed			Joint sharing and problem solving		Integrated data systems and processes on common issues		
• Cost structure	1	2	3	4	5	6	7	8	9	10

	1	2	3	4	5	6	7	8	9	10
• Profit margins	1	2	3	4	5	6	7	8	9	10
• Quality and production problems	1	2	3	4	5	6	7	8	9	10
• Problem-solving methods	1	2	3	4	5	6	7	8	9	10
• Market information and feedback	1	2	3	4	5	6	7	8	9	10

3. Accounting, measurement, and reward systems

	Related	Understood but unconnected		Consistent but separate			Interconnected		
• Accounting procedures	1	2	3	4	5	6	7	8	9	10
• Quality measures	1	2	3	4	5	6	7	8	9	10
• Costing systems	1	2	3	4	5	6	7	8	9	10
• Rewards and incentives	1	2	3	4	5	6	7	8	9	10
• Communication processes	1	2	3	4	5	6	7	8	9	10

4. Sales processes

	Independent and differing views		Selective collaboration		Two-way understanding			Consultative partnership		
• Establishing sales goals and quotas	1	2	3	4	5	6	7	8	9	10
• Assessing customer needs	1	2	3	4	5	6	7	8	9	10
• Determining optimal product usage	1	2	3	4	5	6	7	8	9	10
• Providing product feedback	1	2	3	4	5	6	7	8	9	10
• Setting terms of the deal	1	2	3	4	5	6	7	8	9	10

(continued)

Questionnaire #4 *(continued)*

5. Resources and Skills	Traditional								Boundaryless	
	Separate	Called upon in emergency			Transfer of knowledge			Shared or co-located resources		
• Technical expertise	1	2	3	4	5	6	7	8	9	10
• Financial expertise	1	2	3	4	5	6	7	8	9	10
• Organizational and management skills	1	2	3	4	5	6	7	8	9	10
• Information systems	1	2	3	4	5	6	7	8	9	10
• Training	1	2	3	4	5	6	7	8	9	10

Questionnaire Scoring

Add up the numbers from each boundary to find your total score. (For example, total boundarylessness—which is probably not possible—would score 250, that is, 10 points on each of the twenty-five scales.) Interpret the numbers as follows:

- *75 or less.* You are probably just getting started on developing a boundaryless relationship with the customer or supplier. Your main challenge is to tune in to the needs of the other organization and find where the opportunities for further collaboration lie.

- *75 to 150.* You have made good progress on the relationship and are probably poised to build momentum toward long-term collaboration. Your challenge is to create action experiments that can generate results and provide further experiences of success.

- *More than 150.* You have experienced a good deal of success in the relationship, and are probably ready to design mechanisms for sustaining progress in the long term. Your challenge is to align and integrate systems and structures and to institutionalize the boundaryless relationship.

Questionnaire Follow-Up

You can also use this instrument with a group of people who are in contact with the particular supplier or customer you have in mind or who are affected by the relationship with that supplier or customer. Asking members of the supplier or customer organization to participate as well will add greater richness and candor to the assessment. One way to facilitate the follow-up discussion is to place an enlarged copy of the blank instrument on the wall and ask people to record their answers on the enlargement using small colored stickers. The resulting visual map of areas of agreement and disagreement can be the starting point for a discussion of how to move the relationship forward most productively.

Both the group discussion and your personal analysis can focus on these follow-up questions:

- On which external dimensions have you made the most progress toward a boundaryless relationship? What have you done to make this progress? What has worked particularly well?
- On which dimensions are you lagging the most? Why are they the most difficult? What have you tried and what barriers have you run into?
- How far do you need to move on each continuum to successfully strengthen this part of the value chain and increase your competitive capability? Which dimensions are most critical to your progress? Where do you want to focus your efforts?
- Is the relationship with the chosen supplier or customer representative of your overall situation in your value chain? Are there ways to leverage learnings from this relationship elsewhere, or vice versa? Are there more broadly based changes that need to occur?

Chapter Seven

Strengthening the Value Chain

In today's business world, strengthening the value chain is critical for increasing overall speed, flexibility, integration, and innovation for every participant. This chapter describes several actions you can take to help loosen external boundaries that have become barriers and forge a new pattern of relationships with customers, suppliers, regulators, and other external entities. It will probably work best to employ a number of these actions together, building on those that work and creating new approaches based on second-order learning. You may also identify some actions that will work best with particular types of customers or suppliers or in certain situations.

This isn't a matter of business strategy—other sources can advise on how to select an alliance partner, how to evaluate the fit between potential partners, how to assess the potential payoffs and risks, and how to structure an alliance and set up the architecture of cooperation.[1] Here we concentrate on ways to overcome the barriers that interfere with efforts to build the relationships, the mindset, and the attitudes necessary for success in boundaryless collaborations between members of the value chain.

The actions we describe for tuning your organization's performance in relation to its external boundaries fit into three categories: getting started, building momentum, and sustaining progress. Questionnaire #4, in Chapter Six, will help you choose the best action category to explore first and the particular actions that suit your organization now.

Getting started actions are for organizations in the early stages of building boundaryless relationships across the value chain. These companies need to break old patterns and introduce employees to the external focus. Therefore the proposed actions identify opportunities for strengthening an entire value chain by helping people see how it is to do business from the various viewpoints of customers and suppliers.

Building momentum actions are for companies in the middle of the boundaryless continuum who want to create tangible successes as a base for further collaborations. The key here is to design short-term, relatively low-risk experiments in strengthening the value chain. Such experiments can give everyone a taste for the results available through collaborative action.

Finally, *sustaining progress* actions are for organizations that are ready to institutionalize the new value chain model. These actions expand the collaborative process, assess the learnings, consolidate the gains, and move companies to the point where quantum leaps in performance are possible through collaboration.

Table 7.1 summarizes these three categories, listing the specific actions discussed in this chapter.

Getting Started Actions

This category includes the tuning switches aimed at enhancing employees' understanding of the company's overall value chain. With this broader perspective, people are likelier to see opportunities for improvement. The box lists five principal actions that can change people's perspectives.

Five Getting Started Actions

- Arrange customer and supplier cameos.
- Take customer and supplier field trips.
- Hold open-agenda dialogues between management teams.
- Map customer and supplier needs.
- Collect customer and supplier data.

Arrange Customer and Supplier Cameos

One of the easiest and most powerful ways to build an external focus is to bring in other members of your value chain to speak to

Table 7.1. Creating Boundaryless Relationships with Customers and Suppliers.

Score on Value Chain Self-Assessment	Appropriate Actions
75 or less	**Getting started**
	Tune in to customers and suppliers and figure out where the opportunities are.
	• Arrange customer and supplier cameo appearances.
	• Take customer and supplier field trips.
	• Hold open-agenda dialogues with management teams.
	• Map customer and supplier needs.
	• Collect customer and supplier data.
75–150	**Building momentum**
	Experiment with collaboration to experience success and learning.
	• Hold customer and supplier town meetings.
	• Organize cross–value chain task forces.
	• Share technical services.
	• Teach sales people to be consultants.
Above 150	**Sustaining progress**
	Align and integrate systems, structures, and processes to sustain gains in the long term.
	• Integrate information systems.
	• Reconfigure roles and responsibilities.

your organization. We have often been shocked by how little contact many people have with external customers or suppliers and how little they understand the pressures, preoccupations, and priorities of key outsiders.

There are as many subjects for these presentations as there are customer and supplier issues, but we have found that these three topics can form the core of any customer or supplier presentation:

- *What is my business:* How does it work? What are the key performance measures and goals? Who are my customers and competitors?
- *What are the keys to further success for my business:* What do we need to do differently? What changes are occurring in the markets that cause me to lose sleep? Where are the risks and problems?
- *How can you help me be more successful:* How can we do business together in more effective ways? If we were one business instead of two, what would we do differently? How can we reduce overall transaction costs or eliminate paperwork or speed cycle times?

GE Lighting once invited several independent lighting distributors to speak at an internal company meeting on the subject "What It's Like to Do Business with Us." In one of the speeches, a customer mentioned that GE shipping schedules were not synchronized with his company's monthly receiving, booking, and inventory accounting schedules. He noted that his orders were pretty consistent each month, but deliveries arrived at different times— presumably due to manufacturing changes, carrier availability, and the like—leading to fluctuations in his inventory levels, periodic stock outages, overordering, late payments, disputed bills, and a host of other administrative hassles. He suggested that GE Lighting might work with customers on a fixed delivery schedule.

Over the next six months, the head of GE Lighting's distribution organization worked with a dedicated trucking company and several customers to create an experimental procedure for fixed delivery schedules from one warehouse. Much to GE Lighting's surprise, the new procedure not only made it easier for the customers but also reduced GE's outstanding receivables and improved shift scheduling and staffing in GE warehouses. The experiment proved so successful that it spread to other warehouses and eventually became standard procedure for over a thousand customers.

While not all cameo appearances lead to such dramatic changes, they do build awareness that the world looks different from different parts of the value chain and that successful cross-organizational interactions take those different perspectives into consideration. This, of course, is a good starting point for loosening external boundaries.

Take Customer and Supplier Field Trips

A second way to increase value chain understanding is to take people to visit customers and suppliers at their locations. The rest of the value chain is often vague and foggy for most employees. Only sales or purchasing people regularly get to visit customers and suppliers, and many of those meetings are restricted to isolated offices and limited numbers of participants. When senior managers visit, they tend to meet in restaurants or executive suites and don't get a broad flavor of the customer's or supplier's organization. But when people are taken off their routine jobs for a day or two for a close look at another organization's business, they can develop a much deeper and more personal understanding of how their work is linked to customers and suppliers. This understanding can lead them to much more targeted efforts at value chain improvement.

As a beginning step in a plantwide quality effort, management at the Allied Chemical Fibers plant in Columbia, South Carolina, now part of Honeywell International, took two busloads of hourly and middle-management people to a nearby carpet mill. There, the mill workers showed the Allied people how certain fiber quality defects (known as drips and fusions) could shut down the knitting machines. Having seen, up close and personally, the impact of these defects on their customers' jobs, the Allied people zeroed in on reducing drips and fusions—without a lot of executive cajoling, convincing, or proselytizing. Everyone at all levels pitched in, and defect levels began to go down within weeks. By repeating this approach and building on it over the next year, the plant not only boosted customer satisfaction but also reduced its own costs through eliminating a number of recurring quality problems.

Employees tend to tune out talk about the impact of quality on customers. It's different when they hear the same message from customers themselves and see with their own eyes how customers are affected by their work. Suddenly, the value chain is no longer an abstract concept but a reality that they can feel and touch.

Hold Open-Agenda Dialogues Between Management Teams

Senior management teams, too, can benefit from understanding the total value chain and their effect on others in it. In our observations, most dialogue between senior managers of companies in the same value chain is transactional, that is, it centers on a particular deal or problem. At times, these senior managers will share common issues or best practices, such as how to deal with a difficult board, how to handle investor relations, how to set up a compensation or stock-option program. But rarely do they step back and take stock of the entire relationship, looking at how each management group can help or strengthen the other. Moreover, most intercompany dialogue between senior managers occurs in one-on-one meetings—senior-level summits that often resemble diplomatic visits, complete with protocol, formality, and ritual behavior. They lack the rich give-and-take dialogue that could lead to joint ways of strengthening the value chain.

To overcome this pattern, companies can organize *open-agenda meetings* between their top teams, that is, meetings with no issues set in advance. The purpose is to share information on each company's methods of working, issues, and challenges and to begin a dialogue about how the companies can help each other be more successful. (Exhibit 7.1 is a sample agenda for such a meeting.)

Exhibit 7.1. Sample Agenda for Senior Management Meeting.

- *Introduction by host executive:* Key issues facing the host company and programs under way to address them; introduction of host team members.

- *Response by visiting executive:* Key issues facing the visiting company and programs under way to address them; introduction of visiting team members.

- *Discussion of the value chain:* Where are we linked? Who are the other members of the value chain? What does the end-use customer expect? What will it take for the entire value chain to prosper and be successful?

- *Work session:* What would each team like the other company to do differently to be a better customer, supplier, or partner? (Each person makes individual notes; people do not respond to each remark but look for patterns and common themes.)

- *Moving forward:* Are there any joint projects or initiatives that should be started, based on the ideas presented about what to do differently? What will each company do on its own? When and how can the dialogue be continued?

GeneralCologne Re has used the open-agenda method to open up dialogue with several key customers. One session, for example, was hosted by company chairman Ronald E. Ferguson and attended by his top team and the chairman and senior officers of a large customer insurance company. Ferguson opened the meeting by emphasizing that the purpose was not to discuss any individual deals or transactions but rather to look at patterns of interaction between the companies, what was working and what could be strengthened. He then talked informally (without notes or slides) about some of the current challenges facing GeneralCologne Re, some of the initiatives it had under way, and some of his concerns for the future. Each member of the GeneralCologne Re team then gave a personal introduction and said a few words about current work. Once this tone was set, the chairman of the customer company, who had come into the meeting not knowing what to expect, began to reciprocate. He informally talked about the challenges facing his company, where it was making progress, and where it was not. The dialogue had begun.

Eventually, Ferguson asked everyone in the room to write down, individually, what they would like the other company to do differently to be a better customer or supplier. At first, the comments were gentle, with neither side wanting to offend the other. After these first suggestions for change, however, Ferguson made it clear that he was not going to be defensive and genuinely wanted to listen. Then things heated up, and the inputs became more pointed. In the next hour, a number of constructive themes emerged. The most significant was the need for more collaborative product development, so the customer could help shape reinsurance products from the beginning rather than have to accept or reject them after months of GeneralCologne Re design work.

On the basis of this meeting, a joint product development team was established, along with further working groups in areas of risk management and subsidiary ventures. Even more significantly, the members of the GeneralCologne Re team realized they needed to strengthen their understanding and appreciation of customer issues. They then refocused their marketing representatives—rather than simply representing GeneralCologne Re product lines to customers, the newly named "client advocates" were charged with discovering client risk management and risk transfer needs and then constructing the most effective response to those needs.

Map Customer and Supplier Needs

Customer and supplier needs mapping is a powerful analytical tool for increasing appreciation and understanding of customer and supplier issues. It can be applied without personal interaction between members of the value chain. Based on quality functional deployment (QFD) tools used in process control, it was simplified and applied to clients by Richard Hilbert of GE's corporate business development staff.

The main premise of needs mapping is that a company's core business processes must be closely aligned with customer and supplier needs or they weaken the value chain. At the same time, however, business processes must meet such internal needs as cost, profitability, and market share. Sometimes trade-offs must be discussed.

Through needs mapping, groups of people can identify the processes with the greatest leverage on various parties' requirements for success. Those processes can then be improved or reengineered, adding strength to the value chain.

Figure 7.1 is an example of a customer needs map for a hypothetical fast-food restaurant. Company processes are arrayed along the top of the matrix. Customer needs are listed down the left-hand side, weighted to indicate their relative importance. A score of high (H), medium (M), or low (L) indicates how important each company process is to each customer need. For example, the first process step, taking the order, has a high impact on how quickly the customer gets the order, so the first cell on the chart ("Quick" and "Take Order") receives an "H" score. As shown in Figure 7.1, scores are tallied by assigning points to each score (as shown in the legend), multiplying the point values by the appropriate importance rating, and totaling the process columns. The processes with highest total scores are those with the greatest change leverage.

In the fast-food example, the process with the greatest impact on both customer and company goals is "plan capacity," that is, the decisions about staff levels, supply inventories, and so on. This suggests that the restaurant manager would want to find cost-effective ways of staffing adequately for peak periods and should be constantly on the lookout for changes in customer traffic patterns. The manager would probably get more benefit from these activities

Figure 7.1. Needs Map: Fast-Food Example.

Process

		Importance Rating	Take Order	Fill Order	Prepare Food	Store Food	Select Food	Purchase Materials	Plan Capacity	Clean	Train Employees	Advertise	Track and Report Costs
Customer Needs	Service — Quick	5	H	H	L				H	M	M		
	Service — Clean	4			M	L			M	H	H		L
	Service — Friendly	1	L	L							H	L	
	Food — Inexpensive	4			L	M	M	H	M		L	M	H
	Food — Good taste	4			H	H	M	L		L	H		
	Food — Healthy	3			H	H	H	L		H			
Business Needs	Market share	4	L	L	L	M	M		M			H	
	Cash flow	5	M		L	M		M	H			H	H
	Total Ranking		65	50	93	94	63	62	126	82	100	94	85

Note: Importance ranking: 5 = most important; 1 = least important. Relationship strength: High = 9; Medium = 3; Low = 1.
Source: Figure developed by Richard Hilbert.

than from working on new and better ways to fill orders, the process with the lowest total score.

In 1992, GE Lighting Europe mapped customer needs to attack a number of intractable quality problems with a major line of fluorescent tubes produced in the United Kingdom. A cross-functional group from engineering, manufacturing, marketing, finance, sourcing, and distribution first mapped the overall process for getting a fluorescent bulb from raw materials to the customer. These process steps were then arrayed against the quality problems—the key customer complaints—and weighted and scored.

This analysis suggested that the greatest quality improvement would come from two activities: improving a certain stage of the manufacturing process and strengthening certain aspects of packaging. After teams deployed against these specific areas and took corrective action, including a redesigned package, customer complaints dropped significantly.

The customer needs map is effective because organizations have finite resources and must be selective in their efforts to change processes. The map is a form of mental discipline that encourages thoughtful selectivity.

Collect Customer and Supplier Data

The final getting started action for changing an organization's value chain perspective is to collect performance feedback from customers and suppliers. Despite being the best-known action step and perhaps the easiest to implement, it is still tremendously underutilized. Many companies are unsure what data to collect, and in what form. Some companies are also hesitant to bother their customers, fearing customers will resent the request.

The truth of the matter is that it almost doesn't matter what you ask or how you collect data. Nor is it necessary for every survey to be statistically valid. The main value of the activity is not the data you get. Rather, it is the data-collection process that is important: it forces people to begin to think externally, and it sends a message to your partners that you are interested in their input.

This can produce surprising results. Several years ago, a maker of large imaging equipment began to wonder why many customers took so long to pay. It had worked very hard to accelerate shipping schedules and get products to customers on the promise date over

90 percent of the time, a significant improvement over previous performance. So why were payments getting even further behind?

To answer that question, the company surveyed a number of customers. Much to the company's dismay, customers were very disappointed. Company-produced equipment was arriving on time, but critical components from other manufacturers were arriving much later. Less than 40 percent of the "90 percent on-time" deliveries provided equipment customers could actually use. And until it asked, the company had been completely oblivious to the problem, which was rectified over the next six months through a concentrated effort to coordinate shipments with the other component producers.

As this case illustrates, other parties in your value chain have much to tell you about how your company does business, and it is important to seek out their views. The challenge will be to convince your people to value input from beyond the external boundary, to welcome it without defensiveness or skepticism. It is all too easy for managers to think that their customers or suppliers "don't really understand our business" or "just want to change things so they can take advantage of us." Getting beyond these attitudes is the underlying benefit of any getting started action. When the readiness to listen begins to flower, a world of possibilities will emerge.

Building Momentum Actions

Once people learn to appreciate the issues facing other members of the value chain, the questions become: How do we translate this newfound understanding into tangible, sustaining action? How do we experience the short-term successes that will reinforce the value of collaboration and make it worthwhile for all value chain partners to keep the lines of communication open?

Four Building Momentum Actions

- Hold customer and supplier town meetings.
- Organize cross–value chain task forces.
- Share technical services.
- Teach salespeople to be consultants.

In our experience, the four powerful actions listed in the box reinforce ongoing momentum, making the process of collaboration so rewarding that it cannot easily be truncated.

Hold Customer and Supplier Town Meetings

By bringing together groups of people from different areas in a safe, structured environment, a town meeting helps them generate innovative recommendations for changing the way their work is done and challenges managers to make immediate yes-or-no decisions on those recommendations. Participants are then empowered to follow up on the approved ideas and make them happen.

Though the town meeting was originally designed at GE to loosen up internal ceilings and walls, GE quickly realized that the process was also a means of crossing external walls and strengthening relationships with customers and suppliers. In the past few years, GE businesses have initiated hundreds of town meetings with customers and suppliers, all aimed at strengthening their value chain.

For many years, for example, Sears Kenmore appliances competed directly against the GE Appliance business. In the late 1980s, however, Sears began selling GE brands, thus becoming a customer as well as a rival. With the advent of the Sears Brand Central concept in 1989, Sears positioned itself as a distributor more than a proponent of one brand, and the time seemed right for GE Appliances and Sears to overcome the old competition and forge a new relationship. GE Chairman and CEO Jack Welch described the town meeting process to Dick Lieberman, the Sears national merchandising manager, and found a receptive audience. As Lieberman later reflected, "The lightbulbs went on. The timing was right because Sears had undergone recent changes: a more integrated, vertical organization; a new philosophy of everyday low pricing; and the introduction of power formats, like the Brand Central concept in Sears Home Appliances. With the potential to reduce unnecessary work, increase productivity and derive more synergy out of the Sears–GE relationship, the [town meeting] seemed a perfect fit for the new corporate direction Sears was taking."[2]

A joint Sears–GE Appliances design team identified five major areas of opportunity to address: appliance delivery, billing procedures, inventory management, in-store merchandising, and customer and market information. The team also developed an agenda for the first session, selected five teams of participants (one for each area), and considered how the process could unfold.

The first session was fraught with difficulty. Participants were used to thinking of each other as competitors and, despite preparatory remarks by Lieberman and Welch, came to the session with a basic sense of distrust. Over three days, however, a shared sense of understanding began to emerge, and the five teams generated productive ideas. When the ideas were immediately accepted by the Sears and GE senior managers, the group's skepticism was replaced by a sense of accomplishment. One Sears participant later recalled: "The actual . . . sessions were some of the most encouraging ones we've ever spent with a supplier. We questioned procedures that had outlived their usefulness, examined ways to remove redundancy, and tried to reduce the business equation to its bare essentials. Although we haven't seen all the implications of the [town meeting], it has created a mindset for progress."[3]

Following the initial town meeting, progress on the joint projects and recommendations was reviewed at each organization's senior staff meeting. Sears then held two internal town meetings and GE Appliances held one, all aimed at addressing issues raised by the partner organization at the joint session. In July 1990, a second joint town meeting reviewed the first round of projects and began a second set of more ambitious efforts, such as coordinating the production-sales-inventory systems and integrating systems across the companies. A sustaining process had been created.

Encouraged by GE's early experience, many companies since have taken to town meetings to strengthen relationships with a supplier, a customer, or with multiple members of the value chain all at once.

In many instances, companies have used a *customer-supplier expectations questionnaire* (Exhibit 7.2) as part of the preliminary session to set the stage for an open discussion. To use this tool, participants first rank the twelve characteristics of the buyer or supplier relationship (as appropriate), in order of importance according to their own expectations. They then form company teams to develop a consensus ranking of the characteristics. (This step often proves to be a team-building activity for participants.) Next, each company team speculates about how the other company team has ranked the items. Then the teams share their guesses. A rich discussion usually ensues around the perceptions and misperceptions each side has about the other, about what each company is really looking for in the other, and what each company has in mind when it speaks about partnership.

A group of General Motors purchasing people and their suppliers derived some surprising insights from the questionnaire, over and above the issues it addressed. The GM team resorted to a strict mathematical calculation that produced a "product" very quickly—but very little satisfaction or buy-in among team members. Meanwhile, the suppliers argued about each item and agreed to disagree when they could not reach consensus. They took a long time to complete the assignment but were much more personally engaged. Witnessing the different approaches gave everyone a better understanding of the style differences that might be shaping the overall relationship between the companies.

Organize Cross–Value Chain Task Forces

Another way to orchestrate immediate successes in collaboration is to form a task force that draws members from different parts of the value chain. It should operate like any other organizational task force, but the emphasis is subtly different:

The task force should have an urgent and compelling business goal. Moreover, the goal should promise a significant payoff for *all* parties. This mutually beneficial goal is a key element for overcoming the inevitable parochial views, interests, and perspectives of task force participants.

The task force requires a clear leader. This leader must be able to pull things together, and must be accountable for the results. Some companies prefer to have co-leaders from the different organizations, but this arrangement often reflects a trust barrier at work, with neither side trusting that someone from the other can be an impartial leader. The leader (or leaders) must be able to go beyond the organizational view, take a value chain perspective, and convey that perspective clearly to all team members.

The task force must engage in up-front team building. While task force team building is always helpful, it is vital for a cross-company effort. Not only do members often not know each other, they also come

Exhibit 7.2. What Aspects of the Buyer-Supplier Relationship Are Most Important?

There are hundreds of ways to describe an effective relationship between buyers and suppliers. The following list of characteristics or qualities has been compiled from a number of studies of salesmanship and vendor relations. All seem to be important. Your task—first individually, then as a team—is to rank the characteristics from 1 to 12, in the order you feel should be the most important to the buyer-supplier relationship.

	Your Ranking	Team Ranking

Part 1: Characteristics important to suppliers

1. Reliability. Always keeps commitments and delivers on promises. ___ ___

2. Candor. Provides us with all the information we need; willingly shares information. ___ ___

3. Authority. Has the authority to make final decisions. ___ ___

4. Loyalty. Values a long-term relationship; sticks with us over the long haul. ___ ___

5. Trust. Believes that we have the customer's best interests in mind; does not take advantage of the relationship. ___ ___

6. Openness. Is open to new ideas and alternative ways of doing things. ___ ___

7. Fairness. Negotiates fair contracts; prices product fairly. ___ ___

8. Clarity. Knows what he or she wants; clearly communicates performance requirements. ___ ___

9. Organizational savvy. Gets things done effectively within the customer organization; works "the system" well. ___ ___

10. Honesty. Gives us a straight answer; never misrepresents things. ___ ___

11. Competence. Understands the product development process; knows what is required for us to produce a quality product. _____ _____

12. Flexibility. Is always willing to compromise to create a win-win situation. _____ _____

Part 2: Characteristics important to buyers

1. Reliability. Always keeps commitments and delivers on promises. _____ _____

2. Candor. Provides us with all the information we need; willingly shares information. _____ _____

3. Quality. Meets our expectations in terms of product quality. _____ _____

4. Consistency. Provides us with a consistent level of overall service over time. _____ _____

5. Trust. Has our best interests in mind; does not take advantage of the relationship. _____ _____

6. Creativity. Offers us new ideas and product improvement; develops new products to meet our needs. _____ _____

7. Fairness. Negotiates fair contracts; prices the product fairly. _____ _____

8. Responsiveness. Goes the extra mile for us. _____ _____

9. Organizational savvy. Gets things done effectively within the supplier organization; works "the system" well. _____ _____

10. Honesty. Gives us a straight answer; never misrepresents things. _____ _____

11. Competence. Thoroughly understands the product features and how the product can meet our needs. _____ _____

12. Flexibility. Is always willing to compromise to create a win-win situation. _____ _____

into the project with different views of the problem, different assumptions about how to tackle it, and different ways of working.

The task force needs a great deal of project management discipline.
Whether team members are assigned full or part time, they need
to be used well because each organization is making a significant
commitment of resources. In addition, members will carry the
story of their collaboration back to their home organizations. If
they have clear task responsibilities, feel a constant sense of progress, and receive periodic short-term feedback and reinforcement,
they are likely to feel enthusiastic about the collaboration and take
a positive report back to their companies. Nothing will make them
feel more positive than the achievement of short-term results.

For example, as part of an effort to accelerate new product development and reverse a business growth slowdown, the PPG Industries fiberglass products group set up several teams to tailor
fiberglass applications for specific customers. One team decided to
take a collaborative approach with its customer, an automotive parts
manufacturer that was developing a fiberglass-reinforced plastic sus-
pension spring for one particular model produced by a major automobile company. The spring had the potential to be lighter and
stronger than a conventional metal spring, and the PPG team recognized that if the spring were successful a much broader market
could be developed.

Given the potential, both companies were willing to innovate.
But the goodwill did not translate initially into a successful product.
No matter how PPG formulated the fiberglass, the customer couldn't
get a strong enough bond to the plastic materials and the product
kept failing. To resolve this problem, the PPG team worked out an
unusual agreement—the customer would help PPG recreate the customer's highly confidential proprietary bonding process. That
agreement allowed PPG and the customer to work together to test
different types of fiberglass and different conditions for the bonding process. The result was a successful new application for fiberglass, which later expanded beyond the one automobile model
originally targeted.[4]

This success would not have been possible without a loosening
of the traditional external boundaries of the sponsoring organization. Moreover, people worked together in real time on an ongoing
urgent effort, rather than separately on isolated tasks in a remote

and little-understood project. The more enduring value of the effort, however, was the way it built bridges between members of the value chain that could grow and evolve over time, making it easier for future collaborations across boundaries to occur.

Share Technical Services

A third way to produce tangible, short-term improvements across the value chain is to extend your company's expertise to suppliers and customers. You might offer your value chain partners help in using your products, financial management, inventory control, distribution, sales, and many other areas. Such help, of course, must be provided in the spirit of strengthening the entire value chain; it should not be offered simply as an incentive for doing further business or as a way to gather proprietary information. Also, partners must feel ready to accept such help—not forced to accept only to maintain good relationships. For example, as we mentioned before, many GM suppliers felt coerced into accepting help when José Ignacio Lopez headed GM procurement. Although many of them welcomed the expertise provided by GM engineers, they did not appreciate what accompanied that help: unilateral price reductions and the threat that if the recommendations weren't implemented, GM would take its business elsewhere.

There are many examples of extremely positive technical support between collaborators. As mentioned earlier, shared technical assistance has benefited fiber manufacturers and carpet mills. Production and engineering experts in Honeywell's customer service department take the time to learn consulting skills so they can effectively translate their expertise into customer results. In many carpet mills, they work in such close collaboration with regular employees that they are indistinguishable from them.

Other firms use similar technical exchange tactics. Many financial institutions lend not only money but also financial expertise to their customers.[5] The Swedish furniture company IKEA has one of the most extensive and successful programs of supplier assistance. Consultants Richard Normann and Rafael Ramirez report that "long-term suppliers . . . receive technical assistance, leased equipment, and advice on bringing production up to world quality standards. . . . For example, the company employs about a dozen technicians . . . to provide suppliers with technical assistance. The company's Vienna-based Business Services Department runs a computer database that helps suppliers find raw materials and introduces them to new business partners."[6]

Teach Salespeople to Be Consultants

As mentioned in Chapter Six, when companies lower their external boundaries, they also stop pushing product on customers. Instead, they practice consultative selling. The salesforce tunes in to customer needs, shapes product offerings and configurations to meet those needs, and then works with customers to help them take full advantage of the product. In this context, the job of the sales rep is less about transferring specific products or services from one organization to another and more about building a mutually beneficial collaborative relationship.

Consultative selling requires several abilities:

- Understand the customer (both the individual and the organization) in terms of business pressures, internal politics, information access, readiness to change, and so on.
- Map the customer organization to know who is who, what are the points of entry, who needs to be involved in decisions, and so on.
- Interact with the customer in ways that build the relationship, empower the customer, and develop trust.
- Provide products, services, and solutions in a variety of ways so as to match the unique needs of the customer.
- Help the customer use products or services in creative ways.

Traditionally, salespeople are trained first in technical product knowledge and second in selling, that is, in making contact, presenting the product, negotiating price, and closing the deal. They are rarely trained in the skills listed here. Therefore, a major action for building momentum across the value chain is to build such skills through both training and on-the-job experience. If combined with appropriate changes in sales compensation, performance measurement, and management follow-up, such training can have a significant impact.

For example, in 1991, the IBM Business Professional Institute, in collaboration with consultant Robert Schaffer, developed the "Consulting Skills Workshop," a three-day course for IBM sales reps. (The course agenda is outlined in Figure 7.2.) Its purpose was to give members of IBM's 8,000-person salesforce the skills, work methods, and strategies that would enable them to be perceived by customers as allies in the pursuit of the customer's business objectives.

The course was offered first as a pilot program over a six-month period. The ticket of admission for the fifteen to twenty attendees in each of the ten sessions was a specific customer situation in which the rep wanted some assistance. During each course, the attendees applied their learnings from each module to these situations, and "consulted" to each other about them. By the end of the three days, each sales representative had a detailed work plan to take back to the field.

Many reps who took the pilot courses developed new business in ways they had not previously thought possible, and there were other benefits. One senior account rep, for example, related how he found a way to avoid losing a multimillion-dollar account at one company:

> I stopped by to make a courtesy call on the president, [and] he started complaining how he was still not getting the information he wanted and that huge systems expenditures had been a waste of money. In the past, I probably would have gotten on my high horse and argued with him that he had the best possible equipment and plenty of reports. But instead, I asked him what was missing. Before I knew it, we were engaged in a long conversation which made me realize that his own systems people didn't have a clue about the kind of information he wanted. I promised to work with his systems people to reconfigure some of the reporting, and help them tune in more to what he was looking for. It didn't take long at all to make some changes . . . and we went from being cast as the villain to having a much more solid relationship.

After such successes, the IBM sales organization developed a cadre of internal trainers to teach the course, rolling it out to hundreds of sales reps each year ever since.

It's relatively easy to introduce consultative selling to a salesforce that sells to end users and can apply the new methods directly. But how do you introduce consultative selling when salespeople sell to a

Figure 7.2. Agenda for IBM's "Consulting Skills Workshop."

Day 1	Day 2	Day 3
A. Marketing in the 1990s • The Competitive Challenge B. Diagnosing Consulting Opportunities • Hidden Factors • Readiness: Identifying the Client's Issues • Demands: Making Sure the Client Makes Measurable Demands • Agendas: Mapping the Client Organization	C. Consulting Face-to-Face • Mastering Anxiety • Versatility: Preparing for Client Visits • Consultative Interviews and Meetings D. Consultative Tactics and Strategies • In a Specific Sale • Building Key Relationships	E. Moving Into Action • The Breakthrough Strategy F. Action Plan: Creating and Presenting a Work Plan for a Client • Building a Support System in the Branch

network of distributors? That was the question facing Kevin Sullivan, PPG's director of fiberglass sales in the late 1980s. To boost distributors' sales of fiberglass products, he realized that the PPG salesforce would have to strengthen the sales and managerial skills of the distributors. This would require a profound shift in approach, from pushing product to teaching and consulting. To start, PPG salespeople ran some goal-setting and work-planning sessions for a few distributors, designed to demonstrate how to get a greater return on time invested in selling PPG products. They also scheduled formal follow-up reviews to evaluate progress and see what further support the distributors might need.

Very shortly, the new approach paid off. For example, one low-performing PPG distributor had been concerned that sales of other product lines would suffer if he focused on PPG products. The PPG sessions helped this distributor see how to increase all his current sales while expanding his focus on PPG products. In one year, he tripled his sales of PPG fiberglass and became one of the top ten PPG fiberglass distributors.[7]

As with a number of our change actions, consultative selling is not an event—not something time-bound that happens at one given moment. Rather it is an evolving shift in perspective that causes people to gradually acquire an additional set of skills. Moreover, while the skills can be taught and practiced, the mindset must emerge out of a conviction that the best way to succeed is to help customers succeed. Once your company evolves to the point where this premise is a given, consultative selling can be a powerful action for change, deepening ties across the entire value chain. In addition, your organization is probably ready to move to the next level of boundaryless external relationships and to institutionalize partnership arrangements.

Sustaining Progress Actions

Even with tangible successes in your partnerships and collaborations, you still face the challenge of sustaining progress. You need to lock in the gains made. To prevent backsliding, you have to institutionalize the new approach to the value chain.

This phase of becoming boundaryless involves restructuring the structure. That is, to institutionalize seamless collaboration between value chain partners, it is not enough to make the boundaries more permeable, you have to move them. The points where the supplier ends and the customer begins must be changed in an ongoing process, a continuing dialogue about shifting boundaries over time.

Companies currently achieving a sustained reformulation of the customer-supplier relationship use the two methods listed in the box.

Two Sustaining Progress Actions

- Integrate information systems.
- Reconfigure roles and responsibilities.

Integrate Information Systems

At its core, the customer-supplier relationship is held together by information—accurate information. When information is inaccurate, incomplete, or untimely, members of the value chain expend enormous resources compensating for these deficiencies. Many if not most value chain problems can be traced to faulty information flows: for example, billing errors, order filling and shipping problems, stock-outs, and customer inquiry issues. Untold costs pile up in the resolution of these difficulties. Smooth, quick, and accurate information transfer and the subsequent elimination of these costs will therefore represent a quantum leap in competitive advantage for value chain members. Equally important, as customers and suppliers integrate their information flows, they institutionalize their working relationships.

Though information can certainly be shared verbally and through the exchange of reports, the most significant benefits accrue when members of the value chain link electronically through integration of computer systems. Electronic linkages eliminate transcription errors, misunderstandings, and reams of paperwork. They also speed up cycle time considerably.

A powerful example concerns GE Lighting and its relationship with a large North American retailer. For many years, this chain sold GE lightbulbs. However, it also carried competitors' bulbs and often pushed for lower prices by pitting suppliers against each other. Such price reductions meant a continually deteriorating profit picture for GE Lighting.

In 1990, in an attempt to change the downward spiral, GE Lighting approached the retailer about establishing a partnership. The idea was to tighten up the order-ship-bill cycle between the two companies so as to speed delivery, cut costs, and also provide customer-service benefits. Called the "21st Century Partnership Plan," the idea worked like this: GE Lighting and the retailer would exchange information on the retailer's warehouse stock, shipments from warehouses to stores, stock outages, and so on through an electronic data interchange (EDI) network. GE Lighting would then use the information to determine product needs, create orders, and trigger the shipping process to replenish stock in the customer warehouses. In other words, GE Lighting would not have to wait for someone at the retailer to call in an order, and the retailer would not have to worry about inventory levels. GE Lighting would also use EDI to transmit shipping notices and delivery dates and to send invoices. Both would hook up with a bank so that payments also would be electronic (see Figure 7.3 for a diagram of the process).

By early 1991, the partnership was active, and both companies were reaping benefits. The retailer reduced inventory levels and avoided stock outages. Both companies reduced paperwork and all the associated costs of purchase order processing, invoice preparation, and disputes. Cost savings were passed along to the consumers. It all worked so well that the retailer made GE Lighting its sole supplier of lightbulbs.

Building on this success, GE Lighting and the retailer expanded the partnership even further, arranging for point-of-sale data to be sent electronically to GE Lighting's computers. In this way, GE always knows which types of bulbs are being sold in which of the customer's hundreds of stores, and it can further refine ordering and shipping patterns, even shipping directly to the stores instead of a warehouse.

The GE Lighting case illustrates how productive value chain partnerships can continue to evolve over time. As the two companies experienced success and built trust in each other, their view of new possibilities for collaboration and mutual benefit widened and deepened.

The ultimate systems integration is with the end-use customer—and it's come faster than anyone realized it would. Tens of thousands of people use the Internet to pay bills, manage their investments, and

Figure 7.3. GE Lighting Stock Replenishment Process.

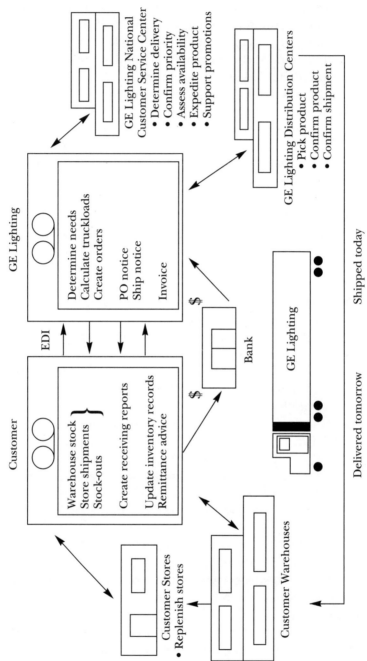

order consumer goods directly from manufacturers. Consumers now use personal computers to shop, order movies and other forms of entertainment, get financial advice, and more. The potential benefits of such integration are virtually unlimited and will continue to evolve.

These examples illustrate the power of systems integration in strengthening relationships between customers and suppliers. Such integration, however, is not easy. It must be built on a foundation of understanding and then on concrete experiences of success. And it takes a great deal of trust and faith on both sides. Installing and operating integrated systems requires a real commitment to supplier and customer partners and substantial investments of time and money. It should not be entered into lightly. But it offers almost unlimited potential for gain, so it's clearly a change worth exploring.

Reconfigure Roles and Responsibilities

The ultimate strategy for strengthening a value chain calls for a shift in the roles and responsibilities of the members. The goal is to add value all along the chain at the right times, with the best resources, and at the lowest overall cost. Meeting this goal often means that tasks or activities traditionally done by one member of the value chain must be eliminated altogether or shifted to another place in the chain. The organizations involved must map out their various tasks and processes, assess their value, and determine how best to get them done (if they are needed at all), regardless of who has done them in the past.

This reconfiguration can be a by-product of many actions described earlier in this chapter, but here it is an explicit goal. For example, several years ago a group of Pittsburgh Yellow Cab drivers, all of whom owned their own cars, banded together to form a more customer-focused taxi service. Over several dinners at a local restaurant, they thought through the traditional Yellow Cab setup and decided to try some modifications. First, they agreed to keep the Yellow Cab name, since it was recognized and respected by consumers. This decision also allowed them to continue to obtain reduced automobile insurance rates and group health and life insurance and to use the Yellow Cab garage for maintenance and repairs. But they would not be employed by Yellow Cab. Basically, they negotiated with

Yellow Cab to transform their previous employer into a supplier of maintenance and insurance services.

Second, they changed the way they handled information, replacing the office dispatcher with a rotating driver/dispatcher. Customers called in to a cell phone in the current driver/dispatcher's cab, and the driver/dispatcher then used the existing radio system to find out who was in the best position to pick up the customer. So a task once done by a central organization was now done by the drivers themselves.

Next, the group decided to create partnerships with local hotels, restaurants, hospitals, universities, and corporations. In exchange for their business, the drivers promised them such benefits as higher levels of service, charge accounts, and clean and smoke-free cabs. The drivers struck the deals themselves, again taking on a former function of the central organization.

Finally, to further streamline the organization, the taxi drivers agreed to eliminate central accounting and profit sharing. They would proceed on the assumption that if they all worked together for the betterment of the group, everyone would do better than under the previous arrangement. Therefore, all fares were kept by the driver who made the run, and each driver operated as an independent business. To cover expenses such as the cell phones, each driver contributed a small monthly fee, which was more than made up by additional revenues.

Although clearly different from the transformation of a large corporation, the Yellow Cab case illustrates two kinds of task reconfiguration. The first was the shift of centralized functions from the supplier organization to the next party in the value chain, the taxi drivers themselves. Moreover, after the drivers shifted the functions, they distributed them, sharing tasks among themselves. The second reconfiguration was the elimination of central accounting, which the drivers felt did not add enough value to be done at all.

In the Yellow Cab example, task reconfiguration led to a new kind of organization, creating more value for everyone in the chain. Such reconfigurations can move whole units or functions to a new part of the value chain. For example, in December 1991, Continental Bank (now BankAmerica) outsourced management of its entire information technology (IT) services function to an IBM subsidiary, turning over people, equipment, and responsibilities. This shift resulted from a conscious, ongoing reassessment of core competencies and a decision to focus limited resources on basic bank strengths in banking and customer relations.

Although the bank had already outsourced in-house service departments ranging from food to legal services, Richard L. Huber, the executive then in charge of the IT outsourcing, recalls initial concern that the bank would lose control of its "crown jewels" if it gave up control of systems development. However, by reconfiguring the relationship between the bank's business units, the IBM subsidiary that would run systems, and Ernst & Young (now Cap Gemini Ernst & Young) for systems development support, necessary control was maintained, previously never-ending projects put to bed, and costs substantially reduced.[8]

In this case, the reconfiguration was based on the notion that different value chain members have different strengths and that the greatest overall value comes from concentrating on those strengths, not on ancillary functions. Continental decided it was in the banking business, not the systems business. In contrast, the IBM subsidiary was in the systems business. So the determining factor was not cost alone but rather where in the value chain the most value could be added without sacrificing cost, control, or customer service.

Sometimes, however, cost will be the main factor—especially when the value added is virtually the same in different locations. For example, as part of its ongoing effort to reduce costs, Federated Department Stores asked apparel suppliers to ship clothes on better hangers, so Federated would not have the expense of changing hangers to display the clothes. For Federated's suppliers, of course, this change made sense only when they considered the overall value chain picture and not just their added costs.[9]

Similarly, reconfigurations in the value chain can change or diminish roles for distributors. Many manufacturers have traditionally used distributors as sales outlets. This requires merchandise to be shipped twice, first to the distributor and then to the consumer. Some manufacturers are exploring the possibility of delivering direct to consumers' homes, using distributors only as sales showrooms and follow-up services. In the newly defined value chain, distributors no longer carry inventory or provide shipping and installation services. In other cases, former retailers have become delivery and cross-selling sites. For instance, Cannondale customers order high-end bicycles directly from the manufacturer, but the finished product is shipped to an authorized retailer. This arrangement helps the manufacturer control costs associated with returned merchandise, and positions the retailer to cross-sell bicycle accessories at the time of customer pickup.[10]

The last type of reconfiguration involves the shifting of functions from the selling organization to the end user, asking the customer to do things previously done by the retailer. Discount or generic brand supermarkets ask customers to bag their own groceries; salad-bar restaurants ask diners to put together their own dinners. One of the best examples of this trend is the strategy of IKEA, a Swedish furniture retailer. As described by Normann and Ramirez:

> The company offers customers something more than just low prices. It offers a brand new division of labor that looks something like this: if customers agree to take on certain key tasks traditionally done by manufacturers and retailers—the assembly of products and their delivery to customers' homes—then IKEA promises to deliver well-designed products at substantially lower prices. . . .
> At the front door, customers are supplied with catalogues, tape measures, pens and notepaper to help customers make choices without the aid of salespeople. . . . IKEA's goal is not to relieve customers of doing certain tasks but to mobilize them to do easily certain things they have never done before.[11]

Today's shifting boundaries between suppliers and customers are a reality not just for organizations but for individual consumers as well.

In summary, reconfiguring a value chain is a major undertaking that needs the insight, collaboration, and full cooperation of value chain members. It cannot be done unilaterally, nor can it be done without the interests of the entire value chain in mind. Thus manufacturers such as GE Appliances work closely with dealers and third-party delivery services in formulating home-delivery pilot tests, and they monitor customer reactions. Continental Bank has worked closely with internal constituents as well as outside IT suppliers to reconstruct its systems value chain. IKEA has constructed a business system that tries to make it easy for consumers to play their new roles.

Once started, however, the reconfiguration of a value chain and the resulting permeable boundaries between participants can fuel an evergreen process of learning, change, and improvement. To return to an earlier example, GE Lighting began its close customer relationship with a straightforward attempt to protect its profit margin by becoming a more strategic supplier. From there, the relationship developed into a model of information systems integration, first through EDI and then through direct systems access. That integration eventually led to reconfiguration of roles and responsibilities, with GE Lighting taking on inventory management, store replenishment, and other tasks. Through this collaboration, the retailer's innovative management processes became visible to GE management, which expressed an interest in learning about them. Consequently, the retailer's CEO and several senior executives spent a day visiting with the GE Corporate Executive Council (the heads of the GE businesses), and the council members also visited the retailer's headquarters to watch the management process firsthand. This sharing has had a profound influence on GE's management style. In turn, GE has sponsored an introduction to town meeting and process-mapping technologies for the retailer, which now uses these tools in its continuous improvement efforts.

The boundaryless world will be full of opportunities for such fruitful learning, change, and growth. The challenge will be to use them to best advantage.

Making It Happen: Permeating External Boundaries

In the final analysis, the actions described here are merely tools. And, like any set of tools, they require proper use. To use these tools effectively, organizational leaders, CEOs, and other senior executives must first assess the current *reality* of relationships with customers and suppliers and then, based on that honest assessment, select suitable actions. If this diagnostic step is skipped or skimmed over, it is all too easy to create unrealistic expectations for customers or suppliers or to waste money on things that do not pay off. For example, integrated information systems are usually little more than fantasy if a foundation of trust, experience, and success is not already in place among institutional partners. To build such actions on sheer expectation is probably a time-consuming diversion at best.

At the same time, it's essential to resist the temptation to dwell on a point-by-point diagnosis of every relationship with every customer and supplier. You can spend years in such assessments without ever starting the next step of doing something together. In fact, in some organizations, people use extended diagnosis as a means of avoiding change—hoping that if they study the situation long enough, the pressure to do anything will go away.

A more effective approach is to select a few strategic relationships where more permeable boundaries could have a significant impact and concentrate your efforts on moving these relationships forward quickly. The learnings from these experiences can then be used to help loosen boundaries with other institutional partners, as it makes sense to do so.

One caution: it is not necessary to have a boundaryless relationship with every customer and supplier in your organizational universe. As is true for all relationships, one size does not fit all. It is likely that you will always have various arrangements, all evolving at different speeds, with your many customers and suppliers. The key to success will not be the number of boundaryless partnerships formed. Rather it will be the development of your organization's capability and competence to advance customer and supplier relationships toward boundarylessness *when it is appropriate to do so*. As conditions change, as they certainly will, value chain configurations will also shift. When that occurs, your organization will need the ability to respond quickly, creating appropriate levels of boundaryless relationships with new or transformed members of the various value chains of which you may be a part.

Part Four

Free Global Movement

Crossing Geographic Boundaries

First Person: **Mieko Nishimizu, Vice President,
World Bank South Asia Region**

The South Asia Region of the World Bank is a six-hundred-person organization that functions as a multibillion-dollar investment banking concern for poverty reduction in countries such as India, Pakistan, and Sri Lanka. A Japanese national trained in economics, Mieko began her career as an academic before joining the World Bank in 1980. After a series of technical assessment and financial advisory assignments, Mieko was appointed country director for several countries in South Asia in 1995, and regional vice president in 1997.

Since becoming vice president, Mieko has been leading her organization on a journey to transform the way that institutions such as the World Bank address issues of economic development and poverty reduction. This journey has led her to see economic development not as a process of expert technical analysis, policy adjustment, and lending but as a process of change wherein people in a society take control over their own destiny, and institutions such as the World Bank function as partners, catalysts, and providers of resources. To make this happen, Mieko has worked to create an organization with "porous boundaries"—where economists and villagers can work as a team, where experts from different disciplines can construct holistic solutions, and where distinctions between headquarters and the field are meaningless. This shift has helped the World Bank to regain its relevance in many of the countries of South Asia, and to play an increasingly powerful role in the fight against poverty. Following are Mieko's thoughts on leading this shift:

Leading the South Asia Region has been an emotional journey with many colors and layers. One of the first lessons from the journey is that in facilitating organizational change, I needed to start by being true to my own convictions. There is great value in a leader's being open, speaking from the heart, and being willing to change. Organizational transformation builds into everyone's life a degree of chaos. And no matter how smart people are, most human beings crave stability. So the challenge was how to encourage the group to own change while still going through instability. As it turned out, my consistency was critical for this process. At a time when everything else was changing, people knew that they could count on me to be open, to say what I meant, to walk the talk.

Being true to my core, however, meant that I needed to learn how to change my relationship to people from an intellectual relationship to an emotional one. And this was not easy for me, given my training as an academic economist. The start of that shift was what you would call in the business world "getting close to your clients."

When I first became a country manager, I told people my vision and values, as any good manager would do. And I said that "reducing poverty" was our mission. But then I realized that I didn't really know what this meant. So I arranged to spend six weeks in a remote area of Pakistan, living with poor people in rural villages. It was a mind-boggling experience. I went in with the mindset of an economist and came out as something else. I learned about the wisdom of poor people, what they do to control their lives and expand their horizons. And I saw the World Bank through their eyes.

From that experience, it hit me that our clients, the poor people in South Asia, don't give a damn about the boundaries that are so important to us. They don't care if support comes to them from the "education department" or from the "infrastructure department," or from people who live in Washington or in Delhi, or from the World Bank or a local NGO. They just want a holistic solution that helps them to lead their lives more fully and realize their dreams.

This emotional shock has driven everything else that I have done. For example, I have always had an intellectual understanding of the pitfalls of organizational hierarchy. But looking at it from poor people's eyes—particularly poor women's eyes—made me truly appreciate the importance of equality. People in power need to learn how to relate to marginalized people as human beings. The traditional Western colonial mentality is that "we" know better about how to provide assistance. But the experience of living with poor people wiped away that notion. We don't know better. Our clients need us to be humble, to listen to them deeply, to understand their needs, and to holistically help them to solve their own problems without regard for our boundaries. Otherwise we end up building a girls' school without bathrooms, or setting up agricultural extension services without roads.

These insights from our clients have deeply influenced my thoughts about how to make the South Asia region more "boundaryless." From the start, I talked to my staff about these ideas and this vision. And I got an immediately positive reaction because our dreams were the same. But the intellectual understanding was not the same as an emotional understanding and it did not necessarily translate into a shift in how we behaved. So I encouraged my staff to have the same experience that I had, and we began what came to be called the "village immersion program." We used local NGOs to arrange invitations for our staff members to live the lives of the poor in their villages for two weeks, and to help them with the stress, and with a debriefing process. Eventually we made participation in this process mandatory for categories of our staff—so that over two hundred people have participated in the past few years. It is now a well-known program in our countries, and it has sent an enormous signal about the attitude of the World Bank to listen and learn, rather than dictate and impose.

But to create holistic solutions for our clients, we also needed to change the way we worked inside the World Bank. To serve our clients well, we need open dialogue across disciplines, one without deference to authority. To communicate this symbolically, I never draw a traditional organization chart for our region. And if I have to draw anything, I put myself at the bottom. I say all the time that "my colleagues are my bosses," and that I am the least important person in the region. At the same time, I've also had to learn over the years how to be more open and easy to talk to. Having somebody call me "dumb" is what I consider to be a pinnacle achievement! But it's still not natural.

Horizontally, we still have not done enough. It is probably impossible to have no boundaries when there are different disciplines like finance, energy, health, economics, and education. People want a "home base" of colleagues that do the same work that they do and that they respect and can learn from. So that is why my initial suggestion to not have sector groups was rejected. People wanted professional homes. So I honored that. But I wanted a commitment that people would work across boundaries and not get stuck in their "homes." And though we have all agreed on this, we still have not succeeded relative to our own standards. Yes, there are pockets of success, but we still have a long way to go.

A boundary that we have had more success in breaking down is the geographic one. When I became vice president, 75 percent of our staff was based in Washington. Now we have four hundred people in the field and only two hundred at headquarters. More important, we have changed the roles of people in the field. Most of these people are hired locally, and they are first-rate people. They are judged by exactly the same criteria as those in Washington; they are engaged on teams in the same way and they bring a local perspective to our assistance that just didn't exist before. This approach was unimaginable when we started. The overseas staff was just an expensive post office that took our work and delivered it to clients. It was a classic colonial relationship where all the power was at headquarters. Now that mentality is a thing of the past. We don't worry about where someone is located—only about whether they are the best to be part of the team.

For other leaders who are beginning this journey, I can offer three pieces of advice. First, know yourself deeply. Shed the traditional cultural and managerial biases that hold us all prisoner. Second, be driven by your clients' needs. Listen to them deeply to understand what they want and how you can help. And third, whatever change you make needs to come from your team. They need to own it, and you can't drive it top-down. So you also need to listen deeply to your people. And realize that all of this is hard—but there is no other way.

Chapter Eight

Toward the Global Corporation

Like Marco Polo discovering new realms of trade, organizations today are exploring vast new markets. The process is nothing less than a revolution, breaking down once-sacrosanct boundaries of space, time, and nationality. Suddenly, we find ourselves in a global village, exchanging trade, business, and information so rapidly that the dichotomy between domestic and foreign has vanished. Global boundaries between companies, markets, and people have become irrevocably blurred.

It used to be different—simple, one might say. Companies could be characterized by national origin. Ford was an American company, headquartered in Detroit, producing American cars with American employees. Some of its business involved other parts of the world, but both literally and symbolically, Ford was clearly an American enterprise.

By the 1990s, Ford's business was far more complex, with a relatively small percentage of the typical car consisting of American–made parts. And the process of organizing to produce these cars was equally changed. Thus, for its Ford 2000 project, the company engaged a team of 170 executives to develop a new global organization. North American and European operations were merged, and Ford centers of excellence and activity could be found in different places around the globe. Ford 2000 took advantage of global economies of scale and streamlined global business processes. A subsequent reorganization along brand and regional lines (four geographic units focusing on the Ford brand, global units for premier brands, global units for automotive service brands, and global organizations for product development, quality, purchasing, and so on) was designed to preserve the strengths of global scale and collective knowledge while creating smaller, more customer-responsive business units.

In short, managers must now think in terms of a world soon to be populated with stateless, borderless, virtual corporations. Take Unilever, for example. Although originally an Anglo-Dutch operation, Unilever now comprises more than five hundred companies in seventy-five countries. In size, it is among the top ten companies in the world. How has it achieved such a global presence? Among the many reasons are its small home markets, its headquarters location in the Netherlands—the crossroads of Europe—and its comfort with multiple languages and cultures. Seven nationalities appear on Unilever's board.

For companies such as Unilever, ABB, and GlaxoSmithKline, globalization has become a natural aspect of business, an integral part of their mission and culture. For most companies, however, truly globalizing mindset, staff, and market seems a stretch. Although the opportunities are tempting, the effort, knowledge, and skill required are much greater than for running a domestic operation, and the risks are equally enormous.

Why Go Global?

The rationale for going global is perhaps not as evident as that for breaking down vertical, horizontal, and external boundaries. While loosening the latter clearly helps the organization apply the new success factors of speed, flexibility, integration, and innovation, attacking global boundaries seems, on the surface, to be of minor consequence to companies successful in domestic markets.

However, global reach is becoming a new business standard, and loosening global boundaries will be a necessity for the successful organization of the twenty-first century. According to the U.N. Conference on Trade and Development, more than twenty-four thousand transnational firms already originate from the world's fourteen richest countries.[1] Some of these firms are seeking new markets, some are taking advantage of new cross-border trade agreements, some are exploiting new technology, some are looking for less expensive labor or new sources of capital.

The box lists ten of the most significant causes of the urge to globalize.

> *Top Ten Reasons to Globalize*
>
> - Competitive survival
> - Cost spreading
> - Trailblazing
> - Rule of Three
> - Domino effect
> - Evolutionary forces
> - Technological revolution
> - Search for innovation
> - Ripple effect
> - Benchmarking against other companies

Competitive Survival

Survival in a competitive world is perhaps the single most potent reason to globalize. Survival often requires reducing costs and increasing margins—which can mean finding cheaper labor by setting up shop in whatever country offers the least expensive labor pool. This issue is less clear-cut than it once was, however. For decades, globalization largely involved North American, European, and Japanese companies seeking cheap labor in South Korea, Taiwan, Malaysia, and Thailand. Then wages in those countries began to rise, triggering an unexpected turnaround. In the mid-1990s, scores of South Korean and Taiwanese firms set up plants in Britain, where the growth of wages was expected to be slower than in Korea.[2]

Another aspect of competitive survival is the quest for larger economies of scale. For example, a manufacturer whose breakeven twenty years ago was a million units may well face a breakeven double or triple that to compensate for years of research, design, and new tooling and setup costs. At the same time, manufacturing standardization can create savings of 20–30 percent, as a company operates fewer plants, buys from fewer suppliers, and reduces duplication. Globalization thus gives companies the leverage to reduce costs, achieve breakeven earlier, and increase profits.

Globalization can even help some companies address local preferences that cannot be satisfied by standardized or universal products. Such companies must work in many locations and create or adapt new products to match specific customer tastes in each cultural region. They lose some economies of scale, but they gain the ability to compete in a market in which a standardized product is not acceptable. For example, the Japanese giant Matsushita set up a microwave division in Europe to be closer to its European customer base. The move allowed Matsushita to discover the distinctions among various European tastes, that British people like crispy fat on top of meat, so you need a stronger heating element in their ovens. Germans like their potatoes overcooked, but the British like them almost crunchy, so you have to design the cooking controls differently. As a Matsushita marketing specialist observed, It's hard for product engineers sitting in Japan to understand all that.[3]

Cost Spreading

Practically no industry today escapes the trend toward mergers, alliances, and joint ventures among the largest North American, European, and Japanese firms. One cause of these alliances is the desire to spread or share costs for various capital-intensive investments. For example, the cost of R&D in high technology, communication, transportation, pharmaceuticals, and medical equipment drives many companies to join up with other firms around the world. Neither the smallest nor the largest firms can afford to go it alone in funding the level of research necessary to many new products, much less pay for the large-scale product launches now required.

As GE's Jack Welch wryly pointed out, GE's medical equipment business has spread its cost and operation everywhere: "Boundaryless behavior in our company leads a medical business based in Milwaukee . . . to empower a Swedish manager in Asia . . . to use a Japanese associate . . . to make diagnostic equipment with components sourced from India and China . . . for sale in Europe.[4]

Trailblazing

For many companies, expanding into new territory is a trailblazing strategy—exciting, aggressive, and demonstrating the capacity to win. But it can also be a necessity. Like the great explorers of history who opened up new trade routes, many companies cannot help but seek new adventure because there is nowhere else to go.

Although trailblazing is often founded on the drive of a single executive or management team, it can benefit the entire organization. Leading the industry pack increases a company's value and enhances its image. Coke, Sony, Toyota, and Citibank are recognized throughout the world precisely because they have led their fields. Today, many small firms are recognizing the merit of crossing boundaries to set themselves up as industry leaders. For example, Lycos, the Boston-based start-up Internet site, merged with Terra, a Spanish Internet and telecommunications firm, to form terraLycos—with the assumption that a globally based company would have a better chance of succeeding in the emerging Internet industry. And when Murray Robinson took over as CEO of Delta & Pine Land, which led the U.S. cottonseed market but had no international presence, he realized that it would have to participate globally to have any hope of long-term growth. Today, the seventy-plus-year-old company sells its conventional and herbicide-tolerant, insect-resistant genetically modified cottonseeds in China, Australia, Turkey, and thirteen other countries. Overseas sales represent 10 percent of revenues and are growing by 35 percent annually.[5]

The perspective an organization needs for an aggressive stretch is summed up in the classic tale of two shoe sales reps far from home. The first cables back to headquarters, NOBODY WEARS SHOES HERE; COMING HOME. The second cables, NOBODY WEARS SHOES HERE; SEND 100,000 PAIR ASAP. Trailblazing is a matter of vision. The risks may paralyze some companies. But those with sights set on being first in their industry will recognize the value of crossing borders—and the opportunities on the other side.

Rule of Three

Related to trailblazing, the Rule of Three pertains to the truism that three companies will snag the lion's share of any market while latecomers receive only crumbs. Over and over, it seems to work out that an industry has three major players, followed by lots of small, usually niche players. In long-distance telephones, the major players were AT&T, BT/MCI, and Sprint. In the automotive industry, the stars were the U.S. big three until Toyota virtually knocked out Chrysler, which slid to fourth place, typically a difficult position and usually closer to the laggards than the leaders. As a result, when untapped markets open, the need for market share makes companies compete to maintain or capture a place on the winners' dais. Today, many companies realize they must gain a major presence if they are to recover the high start-up costs of simply entering a new market in the first place. Coca-Cola and Pepsi, for example, are fighting local soft drink producers in many developing countries to gain a position in the top three. Similarly, Nike, Adidas, and Reebok are fighting for position in Southeast Asia. The goal is to become major players in targeted local or regional marketplaces while preserving worldwide top-tier positions.

Domino Effect

The new century's domino effect is the sequential benefit that companies gain when they cross one global boundary and realize that success makes it easier to cross another—just as toppling the first domino in a chain is the hardest, but the others are ready to tumble once that first move has been successfully made.

The domino effect is especially valid when cultures and customs are similar from country to country, and the challenges overcome in the first new market correlate with the challenges in the second. For example, a company that learns how to do business in one Latin American country often has fewer problems setting up business in another. But even with dissimilar markets, some degree of learning will still transfer and will still be an important enabling factor. To put it another way, the domino effect begins simply by getting one's feet wet.

Evolutionary Forces

Globalization is also a natural growth process for certain types of organizations, particularly those that originate in small countries and cannot afford to make a distinction between domestic and foreign. They are forced to see their natural market as lying beyond their national boundaries. For example, Lila Pause, a German chocolate manufacturer, established its products as a Eurobrand right from its start, placing them in ten European countries. Some companies evolve more slowly but reach the same conclusion. Italian pasta maker Barilla SA was well established in its home country as a maker of premium and mass-market products before it decided to expand into other European countries, and later into the U.S. market.[6]

The increasing world homogenization contributes to such growth. Whereas it was once a truism that people are more separated by their differences than joined by their similarities, today's world is quickly getting smaller and its cultures more similar. Furthermore, companies are also learning to modify some local preferences with the right mix of marketing and product design. For instance, a *Wall Street Journal Europe* survey showed that more than half of Europe's twenty best-selling brands, ranging from detergents to pet foods, are available in all ten European countries. Global homogenization gives companies a substantial motive to take advantage of expansion to lower production, advertising, and packaging costs.[7]

The same force also affects companies in maturing markets with waning growth potential. For these companies, globalization is a natural response to stagnating sales and declining profits. Some of the largest U.S. companies, for example, draw more than half their revenues from outside the United States. In 1999, Exxon Mobil generated 71 percent of its revenues from foreign sales; Motorola, 57 percent; Coca-Cola, 62 percent.[8]

Technological Revolution

Technology is an enabling factor in globalization and levels the playing field for smaller companies. Whereas the cost of travel once meant only the richest companies could compete on a worldwide scale, today just about any company can conduct overseas business relatively inexpensively through Internet, e-mail, phone, fax, and videoconferencing. Time differences are minimized when voice mail, e-mail, and Internet allow fast, extended, and precise communication without the need for both parties to come together in real time.

In short, technology has made borders and time zones essentially meaningless in separating people from other people or from information. Organizations that can maximize communication technology and take advantage of the wealth of information available electronically, regardless of company size or location, are poised to succeed on a global scale.

Search for Innovation

Another reason why companies aggressively seek to cross global borders is to pursue innovation, perhaps one of the most critical survival factors in the modern world. Going global enriches the innovative spirit by tapping into worldwide trends that may lead to new products or services. Moreover, as the time and cost of R&D increases, innovation often requires new sources of ideas and financing that can only come from an increasingly large base of operations.

America Online (AOL), now AOL Time Warner, demonstrates how a firm can use alliances, both domestic and international, to supplement its creative efforts and obtain new technology. AOL's alliances reach beyond the United States into Asia, Europe, and Latin America. They span Internet companies and traditional media, computer manufacturing, and satellite technology, positioning AOL to take advantage of innovations in all these sectors, and to create new products and markets. For example, its investment in Hughes Electronics Corporation, a unit of General Motors, should provide access to high-speed Internet delivery via satellite. Computer maker Gateway, another alliance partner, is designing AOL-friendly Internet appliances. And media giant Time Warner opens the door to the development of new types of Web sites and services based on the convergence of entertainment, information, communications, and online services.[9]

Ripple Effect

Suppliers to companies that go global tend to feel the ripple effect. That is, they often face the decision to follow the customer abroad or risk losing its domestic contract. Typically, what happens is that the globalizing company prefers to start foreign ventures with the same suppliers it uses domestically, reducing its costs and getting it up and running quickly and with predictable quality. The supplier must follow the customer or lose the local business to someone who will serve both markets. You can see the ripple effect in the automotive industry, as suppliers to U.S. carmakers establish plants in Eastern Europe and Asia while suppliers to Japanese carmakers open up shop in the United States.

Benchmarking Against Other Companies

Benchmarking, the process by which organizations compare their business practices with those of other companies to ascertain their own soft spots, is more than simple intelligence gathering. Done properly, it pushes a company to examine its own operations, compare them with others' performance, and set up programs to improve its methods to meet world-class standards.

Widespread benchmarking pushes companies toward globalization in two ways. First, companies often see how other companies break through global boundaries, thus gaining confidence about their own global potential. Second, benchmarking is easier and yields richer data for a company that already has global operations. In other words, going global makes benchmarking a more effective tool. As an article in *International Business* puts it, "Learning about the best practice from foreign companies bedevils large and mid-size [U.S.] companies alike because American culture, in particular, is much more open than most European and Asian cultures, experts say. . . . Of course, any company with foreign operations, or in a joint venture with a foreign partner, has an advantage."[10]

From Intention to Implementation:
Challenges for the Globally Minded

Many organizations will recognize at least one of the ten reasons as a sufficient rationale for crossing global boundaries, and most will recognize far more than one. The challenge, however, does not usually lie in finding a rationale for globalization but in finding the right path and implementing it in a fashion that suits the organization. As with other boundaries, theory and practice are often miles—or kilometers—apart, giving rise to the familiar horror stories of failed alliances, conflicting cultural values, rampant parochialism, and shaky structures.

Consider, for example, a common ploy: the acquisition, merger, or joint venture with a foreign or overseas firm. The hot M&A market of recent years has been characterized by a stream of highly publicized multibillion-dollar cross-border deals. But their early promises have not always materialized. Consider German Daimler-Benz's merger with the number three U.S. automaker, Chrysler Corporation. The deal promised to deliver $3 billion a year through purchasing efficiencies and technology-sharing synergies. But cultural differences and the lack of a clear integration plan eventually led CEO Jurgen Schrempp to announce that that he would continue to operate the two as separate business units. Business performance has been mixed, savings have fallen far short of the goal, and the stock price has declined steadily. Other companies have also struggled against a range of obstacles to make their cross-border acquisitions successful, as with Deutschebank's takeover of Bankers Trust and Marks & Spencer's difficulties integrating its Brooks Brothers acquisition. Such highly visible failures among cross-border marriages are reminders that the path to globalization is strewn with problems.

The other side of the story is that a multitude of companies and joint ventures have benefited richly from globalization. Some of these companies—Shell, Matsushita, and Unilever, for example—are among the world's largest firms and have financial and technological resources that certainly helped their international success. But it's not necessary to be huge. When ASEA Brown Boveri (ABB) formed from the merger of a Swedish engineering group named ASEA with Swiss competitor Brown Boveri, it created a strong pan-European firm that eventually had the clout to take on another hundred acquisitions and joint ventures, encompassing over a hundred thousand employees. Successful globalization changed ABB from a localized engineering organization to a worldwide leader in electric power generation, high-speed trains, automation and robotics, and environmental control systems.[11]

We have investigated the winners and losers of past decades to identify not only the challenges but the factors that sustain success. And it is clear that a wide variety of integrated and consistent shifts are required of the organization that becomes truly global. In our experience, companies seeking to globalize must first struggle with the seven critical challenges listed in the box.

Challenges for Breaking Through Global Boundaries

- Challenge 1: Establishing a workable global structure
- Challenge 2: Hiring global supermanagers
- Challenge 3: Managing people for a global environment
- Challenge 4: Learning to love cultural differences
- Challenge 5: Avoiding parochialism and market arrogance
- Challenge 6: Designing unifying mechanisms and a global mindset
- Challenge 7: Overcoming complexity

Challenge 1: Establishing a Workable Global Structure

Establishing a workable organizational structure has always been one of the first issues faced by companies seeking to cross geographic boundaries, along with the same centralization, decentralization, and matrix choices that we discussed as horizontal boundary issues. A landmark study by J. M. Stopford and L. T. Wells showed that many worldwide corporations typically adhered to the following structural progression as they expanded globally:[12]

Early stages: centralized approach. In the early stages of foreign expansion, when both sales and product diversity are limited, companies typically manage international operations through export departments or international divisions. They maintain control using the managerial skills and technical expertise at the center.

Growth stages: decentralized approach. Next, as sales abroad expand into new regions, many companies adopt a regional structure. If there's a substantial increase in product diversity, companies may adopt a worldwide product division structure. In either case, the decentralization allows initiatives based on local or market needs and often on a manager's own managerial and technical resources.

Peak stages: matrix approach. In the third growth phase, when both sales and product diversity are high, companies often turn to a global matrix structure—organized by region/product, region/function, or product/function—with dual reporting lines connecting product and geographic management structures.

For a period of time, globalization reinforced centralized structures for a variety of reasons:

Global clients began to demand worldwide coordination of their needs. Economies of scale in sourcing and purchasing necessitated greater global coordination, as did technology and manufacturing. Duplication of local initiatives in MIS, QM [quality management], and the like had to be avoided, and the transfer of learning from one business or country to another became more important. Greater control was needed to enter and leave the growing number of joint ventures, alliances, sales and acquisitions of operations. Closer relations between local detection of opportunities, central research, regional manufacturing, and local marketing became important to speed up time to market, which in some industries was becoming a major source of competitive advantage.[13]

However, as business globalization increased, three formal structural approaches began to be prevalent among major international companies:[14]

- *Multinational.* Multinational companies have a decentralized structure and a diversity of strategy that allows them to be sensitive and responsive to local conditions. Essentially, this structure creates a federation of national entities stemming from a single parent. External organizations have some degree of independence and operating autonomy, as with Philips, Unilever, and ITT.
- *Global.* Global companies such as Matsushita, NEC, and Kao are significantly more centralized than multinationals in structure and strategy. Organized around a strong headquarters, they focus on scale efficiencies. They treat the world market as an integrated whole, with universal consumer demand more dominant than local market demand.
- *International.* International companies such as GE, Procter & Gamble, and Ericsson are structured to adapt and transfer the parent company's knowledge and competencies to foreign markets. The parent maintains substantial influence and power but less than global companies do. National units may adapt products and ideas from the parent to suit their localized needs.

The companies that were first to globalize employed classic structural solutions based on either hierarchical or functional approaches. As more companies entered the global arena, however, many analysts began to recognize that the global centralization/decentralization debate was as pointless as the domestic one. Bartlett and Ghoshal, for instance, proposed a new model that would be more responsive to the forces of global integration, local differentiation, and worldwide innovation. To compete successfully in this environment, a company has to develop global competitiveness, multinational flexibility, and worldwide learning capability simultaneously. Building these strategic competencies is primarily an organizational challenge, which requires companies to break away from their traditional management modes and adopt a new organizational model.[15]

Bartlett and Ghoshal named their new model the *transnational organization* and described it as neither centralized nor decentralized but containing pieces of each strategy. In a transnational structure, the parent organization may centralize core processes such as R&D—keeping them either at headquarters or at another site—to benefit from shared expertise. However, functions such as marketing, pricing, sales, and distribution are handled locally so as to respond to market demands for speed, innovation, and responsiveness.

The difference between a multinational and transnational was aptly described by Henry Wendt, then CEO of SmithKline Beecham:

> The difference in outlook between transnationals and multinationals is the difference between a globe and a map. The surface of a globe has neither a beginning nor an end, neither a center nor a periphery; it is a continued integrated whole. A map has a definite center, peripheral places, and remote corners; it is a discontinuous, hierarchical fragment. And for the traditional multinational, the home market and the headquarters stand at the center of the map and send out expeditions to progressively less important provinces. In sum, transnational corporations view the world as one vast, essentially seamless market in which all major decisions are grounded solely in the desire to gain a global competitive advantage.[16]

The structural debate continues today, but in our view, the evolving boundaryless solution, founded on Bartlett and Ghoshal's transnational format, might best be described as *glocal* because it aims to merge a global strategy with a respect for local presence. The glocal structure is like the improvisational jazz ensemble that provided a metaphor for the domestic organization, except that this ensemble consists of players from around the world. The glocal company does use solo players at times (local control), but it also calls for ensemble work (central integration and economies of scale). Above all, the glocal ensemble keeps a constant ear open, listening for whatever song the customer requests, and making changes to accommodate that request.

Ford Motor Company is a prime example of this new type of glocal structure, and its periodic restructurings reflect the interplay between economies of scale and responsiveness to local customers. The Ford 2000 project merged North American and European operations, replacing the old multinational structure with five global product divisions. The divisions were split according to basic design (small front-wheel drive, large front-wheel drive, rear-wheel drive, pickup trucks, and large trucks). Each group was quasi-autonomous, designing and developing new models and handling their manufacture, marketing, and profitability. However, decision making in each group was coordinated and checked by worldwide vice presidents for product development, marketing, and manufacturing at Ford headquarters in Dearborn, Michigan. Many vehicle designs aimed to satisfy global demands, and so drew upon R&D efforts and market research across both the United States and Europe. At the same time, other designs reacted to significant local market differences (for example, Americans' love of big cars versus Europeans' preference for smaller ones). Furthermore, the global divisions were not isolated from each other. Engineers and executives talked to each other via videoconferencing and computer networks to transfer best practices and learnings.

Under this structure, Ford leveraged global economies of scale and streamlined its global business processes, increasing its product offerings, improving quality and productivity, reducing total costs by $5 billion, and achieving consistently improved profits. However, management felt the need to become more responsive to local customers, so the company reorganized again in January 2000 into strategic business units that aligned more closely with target consumers' needs. This new structure features four geographically defined business units focused on the Ford brand (Ford North America, Ford Europe, Ford Asia Pacific, and Ford South America), the Premier Automotive Group (with global strategic business units for Jaguar, Aston Martin, Volvo, and Lincoln and Mercury), and four business units focused on Ford automotive service brands (Ford Credit, Hertz, Customer Service, and a new global enterprise focused on e-business initiatives). Ford thus began the new century by calibrating again the balance between global mechanisms and local units.

PriceWaterhouseCoopers is another example of a large multi-national firm engaged in the glocal balancing act. It is organized along a three-dimensional matrix: by geography (local); by products and services (global); and by clients and industries (either local or global). While this seems to meet the extreme demands of global coordination and local responsiveness, it is a challenging structure for the organization and its individual professionals to work in. Difficulties include complexity, cost, and achieving the necessary alignment and consistency of approach, and there are constituencies who argue for simplifying the structure by removing one of the three dimensions.

As these descriptions make evident, structure affects decision making, flexibility, competitiveness, and many other critical areas of a global concern, and the question of the right structure is highly complex. Many organizations struggle continually to gain the global synergies and coordination they desire. In our own experience, we have noted a structural paradox worth highlighting. On one hand, every boundary-crossing company we deal with is constantly examining, reexamining, and redesigning its organizational charts to enhance global coordination. On the other hand, many executives we talk to stress that the real key to working across borders is less a matter of structure than of people and processes. The remaining challenges we have identified for globalizing organizations deal precisely with these issues.

Challenge 2: Hiring Global Supermanagers

Following structure, the second key challenge is finding the right global managers to lead the organization into new territory. But to some, a good global manager is just an effective manager operating globally. After all, they argue, good management is good management wherever it is practiced. To others, however, the qualities and characteristics of a global manager are different from and go beyond those of a domestic manager because managing a global operation differs from managing a domestic operation.

We agree with the latter view. In the broadest sense, a true global manager is someone with deep knowledge of and appreciation for international issues—both geopolitical and cultural—and their impact on business. Some have said that worldwide companies need supermanagers who have all the attributes of basic management skills plus advanced linguistic, cultural, and people skills. That is, managers who not only know how to order in foreign restaurants but are also trilingual and can handle a variety of jobs anywhere in Europe (or elsewhere).[17]

The challenge, then, is learning how to identify or grow global managers. To date, two factors appear significant: origins and global management competencies.

Country and Culture of Origin

Nationals of small European countries (for example, Sweden, Holland, and Belgium) seem to have a natural bent for global management. As products of minority cultures, they often realize innately that the world neither starts nor stops at their doorstep. In addition, many have lived and studied outside their home countries and speak one or more foreign languages, often fluently. And they are used to thinking in terms of worldwide markets. Third-country nationals are also good candidates to become global managers. They took the first step toward leaving their home culture when they went to work for a multinational based in another country and thus are more open to work in yet a third country.

Another positive demographic factor is cultural heritage. Individuals whose parents are of different nationalities, or who spent their youth in several countries, are likely to be strong candidates. In short, experiences of diverse nationalities through parents, schooling, jobs, and street addresses equate to the breadth of experience and exposure that builds a global supermanager, and a promising interview might include an exchange not too different from this imaginary one:

Interviewer: Where are you from?

Candidate: Well, it's a long story. I was born in Italy, my father is French, and my mother is Argentinean. My father worked for a Swiss company, and he was assigned during my high school years to Japan, so I learned

Japanese. I went to school in the United States and had my first assignment in Germany. But now I'd like to come back to my birthplace, Italy, for a few years.

When you hear such backgrounds, you may be left wondering where the person is really from. Nonetheless, you can be sure you have more than likely found a global manager.

Global Management Competencies

The search for the global supermanager can also be based on developing key competencies, because global managers are not just born. They need experience and management training. What competencies does it take to routinely operate across geographic borders? One profile, developed by Stephen Rhinesmith, argues that the global mindset contains six dimensions.[18] Each has a corresponding personal characteristic and competency, as shown in the following list:

Global Mindset	Personal Characteristic	Competency
Bigger, broader picture	Knowledge	Managing competition
Balance of contradictions	Conceptualization	Managing complexity
Process	Flexibility	Managing adaptability
Diverse teamwork and play	Sensitivity	Managing teams
Change as opportunity	Judgment	Managing uncertainty
Openness to surprises	Reflection	Managing learning

Another study translated the training in the Jesuit order into an ideal model for the international manager. The model suggests the development of six qualities: an aptitude for searching and combining things in new ways, the ability to communicate ideas and turn them into action, the command of several languages and knowledge and sympathy for several cultures, honesty and integrity, the willingness to take risks and experiment, and faith in the organization and its activities.[19]

The precise characteristics of the global supermanager are still emerging. Nonetheless, it does appear that the successful global leader sees the larger worldview, is focused on process, and is willing and able to manage global complexities.

The Search for a Global Manager

Global organizations require leaders with equally global perspectives. For example, consider Ford's CEO, Jacques Nasser. Nasser is an Australian citizen, speaks English, Arabic, Spanish, and Portuguese, and has worked in Australia, Europe, North America, Asia, South Africa, and Latin America. Or Antony Burgmans, chairman of Unilever N.V. and vice chairman of Unilever PLC. Burgmans speaks Dutch, English, and German, as well as some French and Bahasa Indonesian. He has worked in various countries in Europe, and in Indonesia. Such strong global managers are becoming more common, but demand for them still far outpaces the supply. Furthermore, it is particularly rare to find Americans with this linguistic range and international experience.

Disney ran into the challenge of finding a global manager a few years back, when it needed someone to head up its Paris-based consumer products group. At the time, Disney had a loose federation of eight wholly owned subsidiaries in Europe, each in a different country, and it wanted an integrated cross-border business. With the new Euro-Disney theme park and several new lines of business, Disney believed the time was right to establish a headquarters in Paris and to hire someone to oversee and coordinate its entire European operation. All eight country heads were loyal, long-serving, and effective managers, but none were considered appropriate candidates for the job.

Disney's new European head would have to build a team out of individuals with varied and often conflicting cultural backgrounds, and the job came with an ambitious growth plan requiring cross-business synergies and a high degree of uncertainty. In the end, Disney chose Dennis Hightower, one of the first global supermanagers, and one of the rare Americans with the experience and abilities required by the role. Aged forty-five at the time, his background in-

cluded eight years as an Army intelligence officer in the Far East, a
Harvard MBA, four years at McKinsey, and a stint as a country manager for GE in Mexico. He'd been Mattel's vice president of corporate planning during its European expansion, and had worked
with international clients for a recruiting firm. Overall, he had lived
in over fifteen countries, spoke six languages, and had worked in
many different industries in staff and line roles. He operated with
values and style similar to the Jesuit characteristics described earlier. In addition, he was an African American, which, he said, was
good preparation for being sensitive to different cultures.

Disney's choice was astute. Hightower achieved significant growth
for Disney in Europe year after year, despite the initial difficulties of
the Disney park in France. Later, he reflected on the challenges
of being a Euro-global manager:

> You must have a large propensity for risk to take a job like this.
> It requires an out-of-national experience. The most important thing
> is the attitude and mindset; managing in a multinational is a frame
> of mind. While there are certainly many universals in management
> practice, you must come to understand that how you execute varies
> from culture to culture. I understood that I had to listen to people
> and not have everyone adjust to me. For example, I found that issues
> took three times as long to discuss and debate in the Italian office.
> In Germany, [similar issues] took often just a matter of minutes.[20]

Hightower's observations reflect the many special qualities
needed in global managers. Organizations must be highly sensitive
to this management challenge and strive to find or grow a new
breed of leader for the future. Indeed, Hightower himself was ultimately succeeded by a Frenchman who had a wide range of geographic, functional, and global company experience.[21]

Challenge 3: Managing People for a Global Environment

A natural corollary to the second challenge is the challenge of ensuring the preservation and development of human resources once
found and hired. However, developing global talent often runs into
three obstacles.

The perception of a career block. The adage "out of sight, out of mind"
often looms large in the heads of bright, sophisticated, qualified

personnel who are assigned to foreign sites. In the old organizational paradigm, foreign assignments usually meant a form of exile from the real action at domestic headquarters, so the new global company must work hard to redefine such assignments and highlight their value both to the organization's bottom line and to the manager as a stepping-stone to career advancement.

The fear of undesirable locations. As more and more territories throughout the world open up to global business, some people inevitably wind up in locations that are inconvenient, distant, lonely, or extremely foreign. For example, when PriceWaterhouseCoopers won a contract to audit a factory in China, the team wound up more than ten hours by train from Shanghai, the nearest city, and staying in a hotel two hours away from the plant. Job assignments such as this have minimal appeal, so organizations must develop programs to maintain fairness when hardship is an issue.

The disruption to families. An equally important obstacle is employees' concern over assignments that split up families or move them to uncongenial locations. While managers may accept these assignments, cultural differences and language barriers can be hard on a spouse and children, who may not be willing to tolerate the move. Such stressful situations require new incentives and supports to counteract the inevitable feelings of loss and abandonment that many people experience in a globalized company. People willing to accept overseas or foreign assignments are essential to a global company, but the management of such assignments is a critical challenge.

Challenge 4: Learning to Love Cultural Differences

It is a rare company that doesn't find itself managing cultural conflict when it does business in global settings. People living in foreign cultures invariably find themselves disturbed by personal habits, dress, customs, holidays, language, beliefs, and eating and drinking patterns that differ from their own.

Unfortunately, cultural clashes are often vastly misunderstood, leading to a number of disastrous problems. One major problem is what might be termed *cultural paralysis.* Many global relationships fail because people come to believe they cannot work with foreigners—usually as a result of misunderstanding and miscommunication based on cultural stereotypes. For example, a joint venture between a U.S. company we know and a French company was plagued in its fifth year by numerous cultural and operational differences between the groups. When the firm brought in a consultant to help people overcome the clashes, he initially asked each group to describe what they thought of the other group. Both groups produced documents typifying the difficulty of breaking down stereotypes and appreciating authentic cultural differences. Exhibit 8.1 shows the American description of working with the French.

Exhibit 8.1. A U.S. Company's Perceptions of Its French Partner.

- French experts can't be objective and [they] hinder objective evaluations. In France, it often seems that anyone can be an expert, and that philosophy spills over into other scientific evaluations. Reports are biased.
- The French don't tell the whole story and tend to take the easiest route (give the easiest explanation). They don't delve into other explanations or don't share that information.
- Reports are done initially in French, then translated to English when they have people on staff who could have written the reports in English from the beginning.
- The French abide by gentleman's agreements—they abide by the spirit and intent of the agreement at the time it is reached, whereas we abide by "if it isn't written then it's subject to interpretation or changes."
- In France, working up to the event is as important as the event itself: pre-meeting dinners, toasts after dinner. They recognize and affirm relationships. Americans have a bottom-line mentality—get to the bottom line—cut the B.S.
- Protocol is important in France; in the U.S. our attitude is, what does it take to get the job done? The French use a lot of body language/facial expressions and these expressions are sometimes interpreted by the U.S. as the French reacting negatively to an issue, and so on.
- Communication: the French are more talkative than Americans. French people are more emotional but Americans are not sensitive to the emotions of the French.
- Each company should have a mutual understanding and sensitivity to the other's needs, such as financial requirements and how research is conducted. But why can't the French do more to meet our needs?

To overcome cultural paralysis, companies must learn that many cultural differences are real, reflecting deep-seated values and attitudes that cannot simply be subsumed into the home company's mindset. One study, for example, distinguishes six basic viewpoints or attitudes that can vary greatly from culture to culture:[22]

- Universalism versus particularism (behavior based on general versus specific relationships)
- Collectivism versus individualism (group-based versus individual behavior)
- Neutral versus expressive emotional attitude (open versus closed manner of emoting)
- Achievement versus affiliation view of status (personal versus positional power)
- Attitude about time, especially the future
- Attitude of molding the environment versus going along with it

Given these cultural variations, the study concludes that company cultures may be viewed as various combinations of these attitudes. For instance, the study identifies the *family* culture, centering leadership in an authoritarian father figure said to know more than subordinates, which makes delegation difficult and matrix-reporting structures impossible (a culture typical in Japan, India, Belgium, Italy, and Spain). It also lists the *Eiffel Tower* culture, which is highly hierarchical, rule driven, and impersonal (typical in France, Germany, and Holland), and the *guided missile* culture, which tends to be more egalitarian and individualistic but also impersonal (typical of U.S. and U.K. companies).

The point is that cultural attitudes affect nearly all aspects of working and living abroad, including conceptions of management's role, of performance appraisal and reward systems, and of priorities. Moreover, these differences are often subtle and may not be detected until it is too late. Learning how to be a multicultural multinational where many cultures and ideas coexist is therefore a major challenge.

Companies must also remember that cultural variations occur even at regional and urban levels. For example, employees of a large pharmaceutical R&D lab in north London resisted its plan to move to south London because they resented the difference in lifestyle, accent, and environment that the new location would have imposed on them. The same can be said about nearly every country with major regional differences, like those found in the United States from north to south and east to west.

Challenge 5: Avoiding Parochialism and Market Arrogance

Parochialism and arrogance are corollaries of cultural stereotyping. Parochialism is any narrow-minded view that does not accept outside ideas; it frequently stems from ethnocentrism or egocentrism, and it is counterproductive. As the *Economist* once phrased it, an organization that relies on one culture for ideas and treats foreign subsidiaries as dumb production-colonies might as well hire a subcontractor.[23]

Parochialism often keeps global organizations from hiring native managers to run foreign operations or moving company headquarters to new countries. It also appears to be a factor in explaining why many organizations refuse to hire foreign nationals as senior managers or to include them on boards of directors. For example, a survey of more than seven hundred international managers from over a dozen countries indicated that an overwhelming number believed their companies did not have enough foreign nationals at any level in corporate headquarters, nor did they have policies to recruit and promote foreign nationals to top management positions.[24]

North American corporations appear to be particularly xenophobic. According to a study by the Accord Group, a global network of executive search firms, fewer than 40 percent of the fifty largest U.S. stock companies have even one foreign board member.[25] A study by Korn/Ferry International showed equally disappointing results: of 348 U.S. companies, less than 14 percent had a non–U.S. director. In contrast, nearly every one of the top fifty stock corporations in France, Germany, Hong Kong, Spain, the United Kingdom, and Sweden had from 3 to 15 percent foreigners on its board.[26]

Arrogance is related to parochialism in that it reflects resistance to outside opinion. The most crippling arrogance, of course, is failure to understand one's market—as when McDonald's offered the "McPloughman" lunch in its British outlets to compete with the traditional pub repast of bread, cheese, and pickle. After a brief, disastrous test period, McDonald's backed off and admitted it hadn't researched interest in its fast-food version of the lunch. Not only did consumers hate the concept, feeling that it trivialized a proud English tradition, McDonald's own employees were embarrassed to offer the meal.

Market arrogance happens frequently, reflecting serious flaws in design and marketing processes. While homogenization of tastes is occurring in some areas, most products must still be customized to local preferences and cultural demands. (Apparently, McDonald's learned a lesson from its British experience; it now serves teriyaki burgers in Tokyo and wine in Lyons, France.)

The value of avoiding parochialism and arrogance is clear. Organizations must recognize the importance of other cultures and take action to understand, appreciate, and respect them. Narrow vision and misplaced pride cause companies to lose out on the development of a truly open environment, a better awareness of overseas trends and markets, and improved communications between headquarters and foreign sites. Combating these forms of myopia requires a commitment to worldwide recruitment and promotions and a strong orientation toward learning.

Challenge 6: Designing Unifying Mechanisms and a Global Mindset

Going from a domestic to a global organization is like moving from a one-room schoolhouse to the bullpen of an international stock exchange. That is, you go from a small space in which everyone speaks the same language, knows everyone else's business, and is accustomed to certain set of rules to a vast tangle of different languages, staffed by people with many different values and attitudes who have to function without a solid foundation of trust and respect. Furthermore, the new organization must operate over time and distance and handle substantially greater amounts of information and data. The result, of course, is most often a feeling of chaos—the organization lacks the internal mechanisms and mindset to hold itself together.

Global organizations, therefore, require unifying mechanisms, what Paul Evans calls "glue technology."[27] *Glue technology* allows the global company to integrate its functions over time, distance, and culture without resorting to the stifling power of centralization. It consists of a hierarchy of tools that range from simple to complex, inexpensive to sophisticated:

- *Regular face-to-face meetings* help eliminate stereotypes, break down interpersonal barriers, and develop networks of people who trust each other based on personal relationships.
- *Horizontal project groups* learn teamwork and problem solving without an imposed management structure delivered from headquarters.
- *Communication tools* such as e-mail, the Internet, and telecommunication technology bring people together quickly and easily.
- *Project-oriented training* develops competencies.
- *A career and mobility management program* helps people develop long-term skills and cross-cultural competency to meet the demands of global management.
- *Shared vision and values,* built through the definition of business goals and organization-wide values, mobilizes energy and action.
- *Human resource development programs* use all the rest of the tools to make the integrated organization self-perpetuating.

These tools create an organic network. Some ties are stronger and some weaker, but everyone is nevertheless linked and interconnected at many points. The network acts as the nervous system of the organization, keeping it responsive to the outside world. As Evans writes, an organizational nervous system that functions effectively requires "loose ties"—knowing someone who knows someone who knows someone. Network theory and research show that a relatively small number of strong ties among appropriate gatekeepers can provide a vast set of potential linkages. Moreover, the nervous system facilitates responsiveness. Signals and information on competitive moves, technological shifts, and the like flash through the network rather like gossip along the proverbial grapevine.[28]

A related means of unifying the global company is to develop communication and information systems that enable the free exchange of data and ideas and help bridge operations from office to office. Especially as global companies grow larger and more diversified, they must have compatible computer systems, e-mail, videoconferencing, and other high-tech solutions to help them routinely and naturally communicate over time and space. Without such communications, organization members cannot maintain the glue that binds them.

Challenge 7: Overcoming Complexity

Although much of this chapter is predicated on the assumption that the world is growing smaller and simpler, globalizing organizations cannot forget that their business is still often subject to the vicissitudes of bureaucracy, politics, and ethical dilemmas. Throughout vast regions of Eastern Europe, Asia, Latin America, and Africa, operational complexity is the rule. What could occur without a hitch in one's home country requires endless hours and money in another culture due to differences in negotiating styles, time perceptions, and financial dealings. When automotive supplier Loranger Manufacturing Corporation, as just one example, established a plant in Hungary, it spent eight months and $8 million to overcome political blocks and fix ancient facilities before it could even start operations.[29]

Complexity can also be an internal dilemma. Many organizations stumble in developing and implementing the right structure for their global effort and must then backtrack and reconfigure at great expense. Many fail in their attempt to globalize through joint ventures or acquisitions. Still others overcommit themselves, going into too many regions at once, draining their resources and management capabilities. Cultural clashes can also stop a globalizing effort in midtrack.

In short, the complexity challenge can affect all globalizing firms, ranging from those that are just starting to those that have been global leaders for decades. In fact, global leaders often risk running into more complexity barriers than newcomers find, simply by virtue of being involved in more areas of the world or in more ventures.

Crossing Global Boundaries: How Much Progress Have You Made?

We suggest that you pause here to use Questionnaire #5 to identify how far your organization has progressed toward going global. This will enable you to customize the action ideas that follow. The three levels—global learner, launcher, and leader—are discussed further in Chapter Nine.

Questionnaire Scoring

Add all the circled numbers to figure your total score. You can also view your scores in four key areas: human resource practices, organizational structure, organizational processes and systems, and overall global mindset.

Total score: Add scores for all items.   _____

Human resource practices:
Add scores for items 2, 9, 10, 11, and 17.   _____

Organizational structure:
Add scores for items 3, 7, 14, 16, and 18.   _____

Organizational processes and systems:
Add scores for items 4, 8, 12, 13, and 19.   _____

Overall global mindset:
Add scores for items 1, 5, 6, 15, and 20.   _____

Total score: 20–55. Your organization is probably a global learner, at the beginning stages of globalization. At this time, many organizational supports are not developed, and resistance must be overcome.

Total score: 56–75. Your organization is probably a global launcher. It has made considerable progress on the path toward removing global boundaries, but certain areas must be improved.

Total score: 76–100. Your organization is likely to be a global leader. It has demonstrated a serious commitment to removing global boundaries and is probably in the midst of solidifying and institutionalizing this way of operating.

A comparison of your total scores in the categories of human resource practices, organizational structure, organizational processes and systems, and global mindset will show you which boundary-crossing characteristics are strongest and which are weakest in your company. This can help you determine if barriers to globalization are equally in evidence across all the categories or if your company has conspicuous gaps in one or two categories.

Questionnaire #5

Stepping Up to the Line: How Far Along the Path to Globalization Is Your Organization?

Instructions: Assess your organization's efforts to remove global boundaries and operate across space, time, and nationality. Use the scale to indicate the extent to which each of the following statements characterizes your organization, circling a number from 1 (not true at all) to 5 (very true).

	Not true at all			Very true	
1. Managers in our company have a global outlook.	1	2	3	4	5
2. Managers in our company speak more than one language.	1	2	3	4	5
3. We have managers responsible for global products, services, or customers.	1	2	3	4	5
4. We communicate well across borders.	1	2	3	4	5
5. We respect cultural differences in management styles.	1	2	3	4	5
6. Top management constantly stresses its desire to become a global competitor.	1	2	3	4	5
7. We routinely engage in cross-border task forces on projects.	1	2	3	4	5
8. Top management's calendars (daily schedules) reflect their commitment to globalization.	1	2	3	4	5
9. Training programs include significant exposure to global issues.	1	2	3	4	5
10. Leadership positions in our company include people from culturally diverse backgrounds.	1	2	3	4	5

11.	Accepting international assignments is a stepping stone to future success.	1	2	3	4	5
12.	Information about global competitors and customers is well known throughout the company.	1	2	3	4	5
13.	Travel budgets enable us to take necessary international trips.	1	2	3	4	5
14.	Our structure allows us to operate seamlessly across borders.	1	2	3	4	5
15.	Our customers recognize our ability to operate across borders.	1	2	3	4	5
16.	We operate across borders significantly better than our competitors.	1	2	3	4	5
17.	We recruit in places where "globally minded" candidates can be easily found.	1	2	3	4	5
18.	We have many examples of culturally diverse teams.	1	2	3	4	5
19.	Our culturally diverse teams generally work together in a way that the whole is greater than the sum of the parts.	1	2	3	4	5
20.	Other companies have, or could, benchmark our efforts to remove geographic boundaries.	1	2	3	4	5

Questionnaire Follow-Up

Ask several colleagues to complete the questions and then compare responses. For this questionnaire, involving associates from operations outside your domestic base (if you have them) would be especially useful.

Chapter Nine

Actions for Global Learners, Launchers, and Leaders

It isn't enough to make a goal of loosening geographic boundaries—to adapt to a global world, you have to take action. This chapter presents a set of digital switches—specific geographic boundary–breaking techniques and practices—for tuning your organization's outermost boundaries, along with some thoughts on pitfalls to avoid in the process.

If well managed, the actions described here can help global learners become global launchers and global launchers become global leaders. (Refer to Questionnaire #5 in Chapter Eight to identify your organization as a learner, launcher, or leader.)

From Global Learner to Global Launcher

Most companies today would probably class themselves as global learners. That is, they are interested in developing some level of cross-border contacts or sites to expand their markets and resources, and may feel competitive pressure to do so. Yet they are inexperienced in international business. How can such learners transform themselves into launchers?

There's no one-size-fits-all solution, of course. Cross-border relationships and a truly global approach to business depend on many factors, including the industry, the level of competition, the trade-off between opportunities and costs, and the legal, social, and cultural hurdles of the specific locale. However, we can describe a wide range of actions (summarized in the box) that an organization may initiate to take its first steps into the global arena.

Human Resource Practices

- Supply language and cultural sensitivity training.
- Standardize forms and procedures.
- Set up an overseas presence via joint venture, modest acquisition, or establishment of a headquarters.
- Engage in extensive cross-border relationship building.

Organizational Structures

- Arrange short-term visits and international assignments.
- Staff for more diversity in management and board of directors.
- Use e-mail and videoconferencing to maintain day-to-day contact.

Organizational Processes and Systems

- Establish worldwide shared values, language, and operating principles.
- Conduct fact-finding missions.
- Design ad hoc transnational teams.
- Hold global town meetings and best-practice exchanges of information.

HR Practices: Focus on Cultural Awareness and Diversity

The most basic task in any globalization effort must be to sensitize people to the vast landscape beyond their own doors. The place to start is with some degree of foreign language learning. Although English remains the international business language, most non-English speakers feel that Anglophones should not be immune to language training. At the least, people need the ability to speak basic phrases in the language of the locale where they do business and to follow light social conversation. Almost everyone appreciates any efforts businesspeople from other countries make along these lines.

Even more important, however, is cultural awareness training. People doing global business must become familiar with critical cultural differences, business practices, cultural attitudes and values, and socialization customs. The best global companies have extensive orientation programs, often including computer simulations of special cultural circumstances, especially ones likely to be perceived as problems. They also present factual information and discussions about cultural differences.

For many managers in U.S. companies, cultural awareness training is not a trivial issue—they often have, to put it mildly, a parochial outlook, little international exposure and experience, and a false sense that the world revolves around American habits. This is often due to the distance between the United States and other countries. To see the world in its true diversity—and to learn to understand, respect, and appreciate its cultural and traditional differences—is a challenge that requires commitment and an open frame of mind.

Home-country programs in foreign languages and cultural awareness training are the first step in preparing people for foreign travel and work with international counterparts. Next, short-term visits are the necessary spark for the beginnings of any globalization process: fact-finding missions, exploratory discussions, and setting up legal and financial arrangements. A bigger step, when the time is right, is to assign selected staff to live abroad for a year or two, establishing a permanent office or representative site. This longer time frame produces a much better acquaintance with the business methods and cultural values in the host country than do short-term visits. It also helps build personal relationships with local customers and suppliers. As an example of how far a company can go with this, Samsung once sent about four hundred of its brightest junior employees overseas for a year with a specific mission to goof off. Some went to the United States to hang out at the malls, watching American consumers. Others went to Russia to live, eat, and drink with the Russians for a year, study the language, and travel to every republic.

Beyond cultural training, the next most significant HR building block is the establishment of a set of global values and principles that will form the basis of a shared mindset for all members of the organization. This action can range from creating mission statements on corporate globalization goals to writing policy manuals that document standard operating procedures everywhere the company has business. Of course, mission statements tend to be dismissed as nothing more than pretty words unless they are truly backed up by action and frequent review.[1] Therefore, as ASEA Brown Boveri former CEO Percy Barnevik pointed out, these statements must relate directly to people's behavior:

> Our policy bible, which was produced at the inception of ABB and presented at our Cannes meeting for 250 managers, . . . describes our mission and values, where we want to be several years from now, and gives guidelines for overall behavior. It also describes how we should behave internally. To illustrate, one value is that it is better to be roughly right than exactly right with respect to speed. Then there are rules about minimizing overhead, about integrating newly acquired companies, about rewarding and promoting people. But the most important glue holding our group together is the customer-focus philosophy—how we want to be customer driven in all respects. The values describe how we want to create a global culture, what can be done to understand each other, the benefits of mixed nationality teams, and how to avoid being turf defenders. Our policy bible is not a glossy brochure with trivial and general statements, but practical advice on how we should treat each other and the outside world.[2]

A second aspect of developing a shared mindset involves making sure that key administrative and corporate procedures are implemented in the same manner throughout the organization. Such standardization helps ensure a one-firm concept and has four additional beneficial results.

- *Efficiency.* People at each location should not be developing their own forms or procedures; this is both time-consuming and costly. All forms should be usable worldwide.
- *Common metrics.* The global firm will function better when people use measures that have meaning regardless of geography (for example, cash flow).
- *Common strategy and vision.* Standardized procedures reinforce the organization's shared goals and vision.
- *Consistent image to the marketplace.* A global company benefits from promoting a consistent image regardless of location.

All the actions just discussed point to many fundamental HR steps that can be taken to prepare an organization for doing business in different countries. Each clearly reflects the need to expose employees to other cultures and business practices—a prerequisite for avoiding debilitating stereotyping and misunderstandings.

Organizational Structures: The Dilemma for Learners

Most learner companies hesitate to overhaul their structure when planning their first expansion across borders. A fact-finding task force is therefore a useful way to open the organization to new information and to identify opportunities. The task force can carry out data collection and market research that familiarizes the company with the targeted territory. For example, the French public utility company Électricité de France (EDF) was once primarily a domestic provider of electrical energy and services. However, given the saturation of its domestic market, opportunities to export its technology to other countries, and increasing competition and privatization in utilities, EDF set out in the early 1990s to expand its exports. To identify opportunities and better understand the challenges of cross-border business, EDF took a very simple and modest first step: it set up an eight-person task force to study the international arena and to prepare a report for top management. The group served as a change catalyst by making recommendations as well. EDF began to expand modestly into the international arena as a result of the recommendations of the fact-finding exercise. Since that time, EDF has continued to grow its international operations, and today would be considered more of a global launcher than a learner.

Beyond this simple kind of exploration, the global learner must opt for some kind of first structural step. At minimum, doing business globally requires the organization to initiate an overseas presence, if not an autonomous headquarters, moving part of itself away from its traditional base and closer to the new customers. On-site location is a powerful indicator of a firm's intent to participate in a foreign market, and management based on site rather than in the home country has a constant reminder that it must adapt to a new business climate and culture.

Alternatively, global learners can penetrate a geographic boundary using what we call a *soft structure,* meaning a structural change that is reversible and can be limited in length, commitment, and financial investment: a joint venture, for example, or a small acquisition. At this early point in a globalization effort, soft structures make sense because they keep options open while the firm explores markets and develops expertise. Soft-structure arrangements limit risk because they leave the main organizational structure intact. If the firm needs to rethink its plans or if a soft structure fails, the firm's core is not damaged.

A joint venture is perhaps one of the safest ways to get your feet wet. Its value is to combine expertise and capability from two firms, forming a more powerful and efficient operation than either could mount on its own. In the global context, a joint venture using the knowledge and on-site presence of a foreign firm may be one of the best strategies for a monocultural organization that wants to break out of its boundaries.

However, joint ventures do commonly disintegrate over time, as corporate differences emerge after the sparkle of the first meetings. One McKinsey study showed that fully 70 percent of all joint ventures (not just international ones) break up within three and a half years.[3] Other studies have indicated that even the survivors do not achieve their participants' expectations. Of course, joint ventures with overseas companies are even more complex than domestic ones, given the language and cultural barriers to be crossed as well as the potential for substantive differences in operating style and strategy.

As a result, we suggest approaching international joint ventures without counting on big direct paybacks. You'll get most value from them as learning experiences: discovering the success factors in the new culture, making connections and contacts with industry leaders, obtaining benchmarking information and new technology to use in your own processes, and exploring new markets. And the significance of this learning process is not to be underestimated. Many studies have shown that the joint venture partner who learns the fastest can dominate the relationship and dictate the terms. Yet some show that Japanese organizations excel at learning from others while North American and European companies have more trouble with it.[4] That observation suggests that this is an area deserving an organization's close attention.

Two additional elements will enhance the success of an overseas joint venture. First, choose a compatible partner—one where you can develop a personal relationship based on trust and mutual respect. That's a critical part of the glue that holds partners together. Personal incompatibility is thought to cause more failures among joint ventures and alliances than any other factor. Second, take time to fully evaluate the venture and its goals. Do not rush headlong into a deal without clearly identifying the market opportunities, potential drawbacks, and long-term gains.

In some cases, acquiring a small company abroad can move an organization into the international arena more quickly than a joint venture. In theory, an acquisition also carries less risk. The company comes under your control and the chances of disagreement with its management are reduced. Nevertheless, the word *modest* should be emphasized when it comes to a foreign acquisition. Without experience in a culture or market, the global learner may wind up throwing resources away on improvements, restaffing, training, or accommodating constraints imposed by the foreign government. The keys to a successful acquisition, like the keys to a joint venture, are to ensure that the planning phase has covered every decision point in depth and to keep expectations and investment low. As is also true in joint ventures, an ability to learn from the experience is vital, as is the ability to adapt quickly if it becomes clear that the original plans are failing.

As the company gets deeper into foreign operations, its domestic structure should include increasingly diverse senior people. The global learner should begin to seek the involvement of top managers representing a range of nationalities, experience, and professional backgrounds in the geographic area of its globalization. We have seen the dynamics of companies change significantly with the arrival of a few foreign members. Managers with diverse experiences often yield different insights into the cultural impact of decisions. Diversity can be difficult to manage initially, but companies need to recognize that a long-term perspective is required when establishing a new global mindset.

In particular, adding foreign directors to the board yields many benefits. Knowledgeable foreign leaders can expand company perspective and open doors to new contacts. They can often improve negotiations in their home countries. Smaller companies, especially, can gain from the advice and intelligence a foreign director brings—advice that would cost far more if bought from an international consulting firm.

Organizational Processes and Systems: Global Colleagues and Meetings

More and more, the starting point for crossing borders effectively is getting to know your global colleagues. In many companies in the early stages of globalization, people literally do not know their counterparts from different countries. And even when they've met, they may still have distancing stereotypes that interfere with normal business processes. An important tuning action here is to give people intense, even if not frequent, opportunities to be together in both social and task situations. Both will socialize them, and a socialization process, says Paul Evans, builds a network of personal contacts that "becomes the nervous system of the organization. [Moreover] a network does not require everyone to know everyone else." This is the essence of what Evans calls "loose ties"—connections to one or another of a small set of gatekeepers who maintain connections to each other that are strong enough to keep the whole network functioning.[5]

Consider the example of a multibusiness conglomerate with its central headquarters in London but much of its business in Asia. Every year, the company sent a group of managers—consisting of equal numbers of British managers and Chinese managers—to a month-long business school program specially designed to upgrade management capability for the company. Program faculty met with senior management to discuss each year's training. But training was not the program's sole or perhaps even its primary purpose, as the company chairman made clear when he reputedly instructed the faculty, "I don't really care what you do in the classroom as long as they are getting drunk every night together. That's the best way to break down cultural barriers and create a lasting bond!" Of course, a drinkfest isn't the only technique to accomplish this end, but intense socializing experiences do go a long way toward removing barriers between people and breaking down stereotypes.

Another global learner was the former Chemical Bank Europe, now JP Morgan-Chase. When Chemical originally merged with Manufacturer's Hanover Trust, its people had to get to know the other company, reaching across not only geographic but also corporate cultures. Despite the cost-cutting climate, the merged bank's European head decided to convene a three-day off-site workshop in which his top hundred marketing managers gathered to clarify common goals, work on serving the needs of common clients, and build mutual trust. The workshop combined intense work and intense play. Every meal table, every breakout discussion, and every sports and recreational activity was carefully designed to socialize a different group of people. Over the three days, each individual had the opportunity to meet virtually all the others. This workshop became an annual event and a valuable source of bonding, supplementing many of the bank's other global processes.

It is important to note, however, that the emerging trust that people build across national and organizational cultures may be fragile. Years later, after another merger, the bank tried the same off-site relationship-building approach that had worked so well before. The first two days were successful. Then at the final banquet, one of the speakers began making off-color jokes with sexual and culturally insensitive overtones. As a result, two days of building trust were undone in fifteen minutes. The bank learned that trust can take many years to build, and only an instant to lose.

A novel approach to building relationships between managers from different cultures is practiced by AXA, which set out to create a global insurance services company. It operates in a "multidomestic" fashion in multiple countries, but integrates these units through pursuing global synergies, best practice sharing, and personnel exchanges. AXA has grown through acquisitions over many years, and faces challenges of both cultural and organizational integration. The company's CEO is committed to creating an international, multicultural ethos that permeates the organization. One way he does this is through offsite conferences held every two or three years for the top management team, which represents all the acquired companies. Three things make these conferences unique:

- Each one is held in a different, exotic location where few if any participants have ever been before (on a boat in the Bosphorus, in the Sahara desert, in a remote village in the Amazon jungle). The location ensures that no culture or individual feels comfortable or conversant enough to dominate, and the group truly engages in the experience together.
- For each conference, participants are given uniform clothing to wear that is appropriate to the location and climate, but also creates a common look and feel.

- Content sessions are designed to raise awareness of multicultural issues while also emphasizing the organization's shared values, overall strategy, and emerging global brand platform. Participants represent sixteen languages, and the meeting is conducted in English and French with simultaneous translation available as required.

These conferences are immortalized in stories that symbolize AXA's multicultural value system, and are told again and again throughout the company. They also provide AXA's managers with firsthand experience of how to operate within and benefit from cultural diversity, while creating something larger than any one unit or culture.

The global learner must carefully balance universal and local needs in designing and developing new products or services. This makes ad hoc transnational teams useful as another action for global learners to develop projects that can benefit from a global perspective. Such teams used to be much harder to manage, but modern communications have essentially eliminated many of the barriers of time and distance that once interfered with their use. Both e-mail and videoconferencing have many advantages besides speed and cost-effectiveness. E-mail provides a real-time record and allows people from different cultures and with different language capabilities to communicate without having to cope with pronunciation or cultural conventions. Videoconferencing allows participants to see facial reactions and body language and perhaps gives a better picture of attitudes and behaviors.

Moreover, technology is essential to making managers' offices geographically boundaryless. As Philippe Chevaux, head of an AT&T business located near the French-Italian border, says (speaking of his ability to communicate with clients or his home office), "We are a global business, open twenty-four hours a day. My office is anywhere I am." That mentality must be part of the mindset for any global company.

Two final processes recommended for learners are global town meetings and best-practice exchanges. The global town meeting works very much like the domestic variety we described earlier. People from related functions among multiple worldwide locations come together for the purpose of identifying common problems or challenges that cross borders. For example, an international bank might conduct a town meeting to resolve conflicts over originating new products, addressing questions like these: Should the products be uniform for all markets or tailored to individual locales? Who owns the market intelligence that determines the decision—headquarters or the field? If one country develops products on its own, what mechanism does it use to share those ideas with other countries? As in any town meeting, people must feel able to exchange information honestly and openly and to resolve differences of opinion on the spot or in a timely fashion. They must go back to their home countries knowing that issues raised have been resolved.

The objective of the best-practice exchange, again, is to see whether what works in one territory might work in another. Too often, international borders reinforce a not-invented-here mindset. People want to reinvent the wheel each time a problem comes up, because that makes it their wheel. Best-practice exchanges counter this wasteful mindset. They are ultimately a form of sanctioned plagiarism of good ideas from any and all geographies and locations within the organization, and they should be explicitly encouraged through newsletters, e-mail, and conferences.

The Clifford Chance Experience

Clifford Chance, a law firm with roots in the United Kingdom, illustrates how one global learner became a global launcher.[6] It is a prototype for companies with long-standing reputations for domestic or regional success that then realize their marketplaces can be, or must be, far more expansive.

Traditionally, legal service firms were strictly local. However, the growth of the Euromarket in the 1970s, followed by the emergence of the global financial marketplace in the 1980s, prompted a few law firms from the advanced economies to consider global opportunities. In subsequent years, more and more law firms began restructuring and globalizing.

By no stretch of the imagination would the British-based law firms of Clifford Turner and Coward Chance have seemed likely candidates to become global players. But after the two merged in 1987 to become Clifford Chance, they worked hard at internationalization. By the beginning of the twenty-first century, Clifford

Chance was the world's largest globally integrated law firm, with thousands of lawyers representing dozens of nationalities in offices throughout the world. Its strength—both strategic and organizational—catapulted it to a position of international renown. It now serves business clients worldwide in areas of corporate finance, banking, tax, property, and international law.

How did Clifford Chance make its transformation? What actions for change did it use? How did it move from being a global learner to a global launcher? And what lies ahead as it deepens its attempts to serve other multinational clients?

Some premerger history is relevant. The firm of Coward Chance, founded in 1881, had sixty-one partners in 1987. Its reputation was built on a combination of technical knowledge and understanding of the needs of fast-developing financial markets. In 1976, it had been one of the first law firms to enter the Middle East, and it had served the Southeast Asia financial markets from Hong Kong and Singapore offices from the early 1980s. Clifford Turner, founded in 1900, was slightly larger, with eighty-seven partners, and its strength was corporate finance. It served many large British retailers, but it had also established a practice in Japan in the late 1970s. It had several offices in continental Europe and, from 1986, an office in New York to specialize in transatlantic legal matters.

Thus both firms had been global learners, with a presence in several foreign locales, although both still largely operated as U.K.-minded law practices. One critical goal of their merger was to become more international. But the leadership of the new firm quickly discovered that achieving this goal would not happen by itself.

The newly merged company faced many real barriers to further globalization. Nearly 80 percent of the lawyers were in London, giving the firm a strictly English feel. Its potential clients and even its young recruits around the world thought of it as an English firm. Moreover, the older lawyers at the home office cherished their English traditions, personal independence, and lack of bureaucracy in operations. To themselves, they wondered why partners from high-earning offices should invest in less profitable operations in developing countries. As a result, international expansion required changes not only in structure, systems, and processes but also in mindset.

As a first step, Clifford Chance set out to establish a broader presence in several European cities. It could have done this by buying up established law firms. Instead, management opted for a more flexible structure. The firm set up its own offices in each location and slowly hired people according to the client needs that presented themselves. It then opened six additional offices—in Barcelona, Frankfurt, Rome, Warsaw, Budapest, and Shanghai—starting very small in each locale.

As the offices developed, management sent lawyers from London to temporary postings in these offices. "One of the ways you integrate cultures," said Geoffrey Howe, the senior managing partner, "is by moving around. Increasingly the people who make partner in Paris or Madrid will have spent a year or two in London and vice versa. There is a direct cost, but it is the best way you integrate the people: it is not done by statements or strategies on paper."

But new locations and international assignments were not enough, because people were still thinking in the old domestic ways. Many of the lawyers still thought of Clifford Chance as an English law firm with offices in foreign places. As a result, service to clients was not seamless across borders. One indication of the problem was the use of words and phrases that reinforced the old mindset. Management thus introduced another tuning switch: the "Unwords Campaign," for which the firm newsletter printed a set of linguistic rules—words that had to be removed from everyday parlance and the new words that would replace them:

Unword	*Global Word*
City firm (British equivalent of "Wall Street firm")	Business and financial firm
English firm	International firm
U.K. firm	European-based international firm
Assistant solicitor	Lawyer
Overseas offices	International offices
The [Paris, Madrid, and so on] office	My colleagues in [Paris, Madrid, and so on]
Cross-selling	Integrated service

The technique of teaching employees a new vocabulary to encourage them to think in new ways is not unusual at all. Clifford Chance simply made it more explicit and more mandatory than in many companies.

Finally, to reinforce the global mindset, the firm redesigned its procedures and systems to instill more consistency across all offices and geographies. It asked secretaries worldwide to use the same typeface for all documents, right down to the cover sheets for faxes. It increased the use of standard templates to draft frequently used commercial documents such as leases, loan agreements, joint venture agreements, or board minutes. The clear signal sent to all employees at every level was, "We are one firm worldwide—with the same image to the marketplace and internally no matter where we are in the world."

The actions just described exemplify some of the steps that have moved Clifford Chance from a global learner to a global launcher. Given the firm's starting point, its progress was substantial. Nevertheless, senior partners still felt they had a long way to go, since their ultimate aspiration was to become, in our term, truly glocal, the hallmark of the global leaders. As one partner in Amsterdam said: "Each office should be a link in the international chain as well as having a focus in its national marketplace. Our strategy is to be recognized not only as part of a major international firm but also as a Dutch law firm in [our] own right."

In January 2000, Clifford Chance took another major step along the path to globalization, propelling itself from global launcher to global leader. It merged with two other law firms, Frankfurt-based Punder, Volhard, Weber & Axter, and U.S.-based Rogers and Wells, both of which had also been pioneers in international expansion. The result was the world's largest globally integrated law firm, with twenty-nine offices throughout Europe, Asia, the Americas, and the Middle East, and three thousand legal advisers representing more than fifty nationalities.

Beware of Learner Landmines

All globalization efforts carry risks. Experience tells us, however, that the following are the typical landmines lying in wait for global learners:

Indecision. Jumping into the global waters demands a greater understanding of management, financial, geopolitical, and cultural issues than that required for a domestic operation. Many companies naturally become indecisive when attempting to determine how to dedicate time and resources when many options are available.

Lack of planning. Planning is an essential element of business when cultural and physical distances are involved. You must decide certain questions in advance, such as: How far do you want your company to go? How aggressive and ambitious is your global strategy? Do you intend to develop a business that will become 20 percent nondomestic, or 50 percent, or 80 percent? The answers to such questions have a direct impact on a firm's willingness to make investments of time and financial resources.

Cultural hypersensitivity. In developing greater cultural awareness, global learners often go overboard and become hypersensitive to differences in work styles and management philosophies, causing them to excuse problems rather than face them. Recently, a senior manager, about to leave his post in France after two years, told us an anecdote that typifies the phenomenon. While reflecting on what he learned about doing business abroad, he recalled receiving extensive cross-cultural sensitivity training at the beginning of his assignment. Although he originally felt this made him more understanding about performance problems, he now believed he had bent over too far to accommodate cultural differences when he should have followed universal principles of good management—holding all employees accountable for target dates they set for themselves, for example. In short, cultural awareness shouldn't supersede basic management principles, hard-core analysis, and market experience.

One of the best detection systems for many of the landmines learners face turns out to be an early mistake. We often find that organizations learn from mistakes that surface at the beginning of a venture and make adjustments rather painlessly compared to those that discover a mistake only after a significant investment of time and resources. The more effective way to avoid stepping on landmines, however, is to benchmark other companies that have recently traversed the same territory. For example, an Israeli company contemplating the acquisition of a privatized Hungarian firm closely studied GE Lighting's experience with Tungsram before making a decision.

Finally, the global learning organization requires a leader with exceptional personal courage and humility—as well as ambition—to support whatever stumbles happen among first steps. As in any infancy, the leader must encourage celebration of any early accomplishments with pride. Clifford Chance has had such leadership. Along with other decision makers in the firm, managing partner Geoffrey Howe has helped ensure the consistency, courage, and continuity to enable the firm's success. The importance of this leadership task to breaking down global barriers cannot be overestimated.

Global Launchers to Global Leaders

For organizations that have become global launchers, moving to the next stage of global leadership entails a new set of challenges.

Human Resource Practices

- Seek complete fluidity of human resources: recruit outside the domestic base; place foreign recruits within the domestic base; promote the best people to global assignments; rotate people internationally; use twinning.
- Aim for a glocal structure.
- Map global processes.

Organizational Structures

- Provide continuing global leadership training and regular transnational training to reinforce the global mindset.
- Remove or minimize country management and replace with global managers and focus on global customers.
- Routinize real-time global communications.

Organizational Processes and Systems

- Use global reward systems.
- Multiply ongoing transnational project teams.
- Work for global integration (for example, total global sourcing, global design, global engineering, and global purchasing).

For the most part, a global launcher has developed a global strategy and vision. It has some experience under its belt at trying to remove geographic boundaries, and it appreciates how difficult the challenges will be. It has also seen the progress born of some of the steps described in the global learner section. What launchers must do next is to deepen commitment to removing geographic boundaries. They must also (as summed up in the box) recalibrate their human resource practices, their organizational structures, and their systems and processes accordingly.

HR Practices: Make Human Resources More Fluid

Global launchers need to develop a more fluid workforce, so that they can pour it into whatever vessel they must fill. The rationale for resource fluidity is that, in a completely globalized market, companies need to move people with flexible sets of skills from location to location or task to task to respond to customer needs. For example, ABB routinely moves its managers laterally to positions in other countries so they develop a wider understanding of local markets. Many professional service firms, such as McKinsey and Accenture, have also developed systems for rotating professionals to projects around the world for periods of three to six months, as their clients require.

To develop fluid human resources, the global launcher organization needs high-quality HR programs that attract the best people and assign them to top global positions, regardless of their country of origin. Such programs send out a clear message that international assignments are valued and critical positions, not career dead ends. As openings arise, HR must fill them with individuals who are recognized as among the most talented and successful in the company at working globally. Launchers benefit particularly by making good use of the different educational backgrounds and viewpoints of their personnel, demonstrating that the firm is able to do business from a multicultural perspective, without prejudice or ethnocentrism. In short, launchers moving to leaders must promote the free flow of individuals from country to country, without regard to national origin.

Launchers also progress globally by bringing recruits from operations abroad to work in the domestic base, as Gillette's international trainee program does. Several hundred trainees have

passed through the program since the early 1980s. Begun originally as an internship operation, the program turned into a formal
training tool when Gillette realized that many interns wanted to
return to work in Gillette plants in their home countries. University graduates from business schools around the world begin by
working for Gillette plants in their home countries for six months.
The best and brightest of these people are then transferred to one
of the three Gillette headquarters (in Boston, London, and Singapore) for more intensive work. Successful trainees are assigned to
management positions back in their home countries or in other
Gillette facilities. Many eventually become general managers or senior operating managers in their home countries.

Another critical element in making human resources more
fluid is the same kind of regular rotation of people around the
world that ABB and McKinsey engage in. Rotations give managers
the experience and enlarged perspective to tackle a wide range of
problems. International experience allows people to

- See local conditions firsthand and obtain direct exposure to
  markets and ways of doing business abroad.
- Live in others' shoes for a while to learn others' ways of thinking.
- Develop loyalties to multiple regions or segments of a business.

Another value of regular rotations is the development of alternative worldviews that boost the quality of decisions. We hear
many U.S. managers with global experience take a healthy contrary
stance in discussions, saying, in effect, "We don't see it the same
way as you do in the United States." Living and breathing a different culture has shown them new points of view. This is so desirable
that many firms hesitate to have a local person run an important
center unless that person has proved effective in another country
as well as in a headquarters or central staff role. Ultimately, rotations help all members of the organization learn and grow.

Launchers moving to leaders also benefit from consistent transnational training that continues to develop a global mindset and
shared values among all organizational members. PriceWaterhouse-
Coopers periodically brings newly appointed partners from around
the world together (at a new location each year) for education on
the firm's basic values and principles. This serves both purposes of
training and international socialization.

Another technique to foster continual training and learning is *twinning*, the process of assigning one local and one foreign person to the same job for a time. GE Lighting employed twinning at Tungsram so that GE managers would learn about global issues while Tungsram people learned about Western business practices.

Although perhaps more subtle than the actions just described, restructuring reward systems is another important adjustment that helps global launchers become leaders. Their new systems reward a broader view of performance than formerly and encourage managers to use their expertise more flexibly in such areas as improving market penetration worldwide or helping sister companies in other countries. For example, Goldman Sachs implemented a new compensation and organizational structure that promotes cooperation. In this system, "because compensation is based more on subjective criteria than on transaction count, officers in different departments don't constantly bicker over how much credit they should get for a particular deal. And unlike other firms that are organized by geographical region, Goldman brings in the firm's heaviest hitters . . . to pitch in on a transaction in any region."[7]

Organizational Structure: Resolving Complexity

The global launcher is likely to have numerous sites or headquarters in countries around the world. To become a leader, the launcher must resolve the complexities this multidomestic approach entails. It must develop a structure that will balance the centralizing needed for pooling of resources and economies of scale at the global level with the decentralizing that allows catering to local preferences with speed and precision.

For many firms, the choice boils down to converting to a loose matrix that interlaces management by product, customer, and function with a continuing country or regional structure. This solution offers the advantages found in centralizing certain kinds of decision making and expertise with those of maintaining a strong product or local orientation. As the *Economist* summed it up, "In theory, this means that management can make decisions without regard for national borders—but only if they want to."[8]

However, no one solution is guaranteed to fit the advanced stages of globalization for every company. The best answer for any given company most likely depends on a number of variables: type of product, number of markets, methods of distribution, and long-term strategy. Nevertheless, the active and ongoing search for a solution to complexity in the best global companies suggests a definite move away from a multidomestic structure and toward more product, customer, or brand-driven arrangements. For a number of years, Sony used a four-zone global operation—Japan, America, Europe, and the rest of the world—while maintaining product managers as well. It recently reorganized to focus on key strategic thrusts. This involved trimming its sprawling global network of seventy manufacturing companies down to fifty-five, placing all of its electronics businesses under a separate upper-management group, and establishing a new division to focus exclusively on mobile phones and strategy. IBM reorganized into fourteen worldwide industry groups—such as banking, retailing, and insurance—but also kept its geographic chieftains. It then refined its structure further, focusing on five overarching business segments. Having traditionally used a regional structure, Unilever now operates with two global divisions. Reporting to their divisional executive directors are the regional presidents, responsible for driving profitability in their regions. A third division is managed on a global basis.

Each of these is a solution that is somewhat unique to the industry, size of company, and individual leader preferences. However, they share the intention to achieve clout and focus, to find a balance between global synergy and local responsiveness, and to deal effectively with the tensions inherent in maintaining this balance.

Organizational Processes and Systems: Technological Solutions to Complexity

Successfully managing complexity in processes and systems is a major challenge for launchers who want to become global leaders. Launchers typically have extensive R&D, manufacturing, sourcing, purchasing, and distribution networks that cover wide territories and consumer needs. A key action for strengthening and globalizing these systems is process mapping (see Chapter Five). Examples of processes to be mapped include development of a new product from design through warehousing and fulfillment of an order from customer request to delivery. Global process mapping reveals the links and kinks in operations and where companies may be able to save time, money, or space.

For example, the global company at the launcher level may have orders from around the world going to a central order bank, which then transmits them to manufacturing or distribution centers at other locations. However, if a process map shows that most orders for certain products arrive from one region, the organization might decide to adjust warehousing and distribution to accommodate that regional pattern.

Launchers who want to become leaders make more use of technology than learners do, and at higher levels, to achieve real-time global communications. Dedicated trunk lines, intranets, e-mail, groupware, paging devices, and portable computers with fax and modem cards allow people to communicate at length and instantaneously across time zones, at any hour of the day or night, and with a common language.

Two organizations that emphasize the use of technology are PriceWaterhouseCoopers and GlaxoSmithKline. PriceWaterhouseCoopers, the largest professional service firm in the world, has increasingly focused its attention on serving multinational clients. This adjustment entailed abandoning the long-standing tradition of treating the local office as supreme in favor of a worldwide operating structure and decision-making process that could mobilize human resources, investment advice, and technical information from any office as needed. To accomplish this, it turned to groupware technology that connects everyone through an elaborate electronic system.

Groupware is particularly useful in the development of client proposals. Formerly, the originating office had to communicate with other parts of the firm by phone or fax across time zones, a process that was time-consuming and had a high rate of incomplete contacts. Today, the groupware system allows an office developing a proposal to collect data and information easily from any of the resources throughout the twenty-six offices worldwide. Within days rather than weeks, the lead partner can draft a proposal, send it electronically to others for review, receive feedback, and even recruit colleagues to help rewrite the proposal.

GlaxoSmithKline's "R&D Team Connect" groupware allows researchers throughout the company to hook their personal computers or terminals to a common set of databases for information sharing. Team members can also carry on electronic conversations to get comments and feedback about their experiments or clinical results.

In short, launchers becoming leaders recognize that technology supports their ability to be global. They track new technological developments and install the latest equipment if it can save time and contribute to gathering information and making decisions that otherwise would require unwieldy meetings, exorbitant travel costs, or excessive investments of time.

Finally, launchers becoming leaders must identify opportunities for global sourcing and purchasing, global design, and global engineering to reduce costs and maximize economies of scale. An additional common benefit from centralization of these processes is the transfer of learning across the organization.

The Alcatel Bell Experience

A leading supplier of telecommunications equipment, Alcatel Bell is moving from global launcher to leader in an industry that has seen intense competition to take advantage of both emerging markets and the increasingly sophisticated needs of advanced economies. As a result, the challenge for Alcatel Bell has been to globalize as effectively and quickly as possible.

Alcatel Bell is a Belgium-based subsidiary of Alcatel Alsthom, an international producer of technologically advanced infrastructure equipment for the communication, energy, and transport sectors. Alcatel Alsthom ranks among the world's leaders in all its areas of activity. Highly aggressive and ambitious, it has dedicated itself to internationalization through growth and almost two hundred acquisitions.

At one time, Alcatel Bell was a very local business, with long-term secure contracts for serving the Belgian telephone company and a reliable revenue stream from its Belgian world of business. In the 1960s, 70 percent of its business was local. In the 1970s and 1980s, its business widened, becoming 50 percent global but largely through export and licensing agreements. However, in the 1980s and 1990s, it began globalizing substantially, attempting to become a global leader. Through joint ventures, start-ups, mergers, and acquisitions, Alcatel Bell sales today are only 30 percent Belgian; most of its attention is focused on the international world. (Alcatel Bell's global development is summarized in Table 9.1.)

What switches has Alcatel Bell used to enable the radical retuning of both its business mix and its business mindset? What did it take to transform this rather localized business into a leading world player?

One major step was to fill critical senior positions with people (insiders and outsiders) who had extensive international experience and orientation. The new players understood the structures, people, and systems required to build and sustain a global business. They shaped a new strategy and direction of deepening globalization in such places as Russia, China, and Turkey.

The new leaders also filled key slots in Belgium with people who were comfortable in an international context and who had lived as expatriates elsewhere. As joint ventures and acquisitions were made, the leaders relied on this select group to serve as managers in resident positions abroad. They also called on a cadre of functional specialists from engineering, finance, and technical operations—no functional specialty was excluded from international assignments. Specialists had to be prepared to go to any country in which Alcatel Bell operated.

In addition, Alcatel Bell invested heavily in ongoing people development. Employees from newly acquired subsidiaries spend three months to two years in Antwerp for technical training. New customers also are trained on equipment in Antwerp, while managers

Table 9.1. Alcatel Bell's Globalization.

Period	Local Sales (Percent)	Global Sales (Percent)	Strategic Steps
1960s	70	30	Local manufacturing; exporting to international locations; first licensing agreement (Romania)
1970s	50	50	Multiple licensing agreements and turnkey contracts (for example, India, Taiwan, Yugoslavia)
1980s	50	50	Joint ventures in China, Mexico, Russia, Turkey; centralized engineering; exporting to seventy-two countries
1990s	30	70	Starting new companies (for example, in Russia and Colombia); making mergers and acquisitions; managing businesses worldwide

are familiarized with Alcatel Bell management techniques there. On any given day, the number of languages spoken at the training center mirrors the United Nations, even though the training is conducted in English. In addition, in China and Russia, people trained by Alcatel Bell train other people locally, in their local languages.

In these ways, Alcatel Bell has instituted many of the practices summarized at the beginning of this section, namely, HR practices that enable top talent from different parts of the world to work together regularly, processes and systems that integrate key functional areas and expertise, and many ongoing transnational project teams.

To understand the progress of Alcatel Bell, we interviewed one of its key regional managers, Stan Abbeloos, at the time the Alcatel Bell general director in Russia. A Belgian by birth, Abbeloos has an engineering degree and speaks English, French, German, and some Russian in addition to his native Flemish. (Every one of the Alcatel Bell general directors speaks two or three additional languages.) In 1994, at forty-two years of age, he was completing his third year in Russia. Prior to that, he had worked for Alcatel Bell in China for four years. A glimpse into a month of his life is telling of the kind of energy and work needed by global leaders:

> I started the month traveling to Anadyr, Russia, near Alaska. It took five days to get there because of the weather. But we signed a contract for $4 million by the end of the day. Then we waited two additional days to get the plane back. And you must fly Aeroflot—you have no choice! If you want, you could take the train, but it would take a lot longer to travel, often up to thirty-six hours between cities.
>
> Then I next went to Novosibirsk, in the middle of Siberia, where we have one of our offices. It's actually a joint venture in which we have 75 percent control. I had to negotiate next year's delivery of product.
>
> Then I went to Surgut, also in Siberia, where the temperature was minus twenty-six degrees centigrade, but I got final acceptance to sell a System 12 toll exchange, and they signed a maintenance agreement.
>
> I then went back to St. Petersburg, where for one week I was managing the creation of a space for refurbishing our products. Then I went to Anadyr to finalize a contract, then on to Moscow for a steering committee meeting to coordinate international activities across Alcatel Alsthom, and finally I was sent to France for one week to attend a "High Potential Leaders" training program!

What does this hectic month of activity show? First, it is an excellent example of a glocal executive's focus. Although the better part of the month represented intense attention to local matters, the end of the month provided two global links—the corporate task force on global coordination and the leadership training with worldwide representation. Such agenda balancing is crucial if a company is to become a global leader.

Second, the example reveals the stress tolerance required of global leaders. Operating in this mobile, fluid fashion was not unusual for Abbeloos and the other general directors, especially in emerging marketplaces. It is the grueling, stressful life of a pioneer, albeit challenging and gratifying. Abbeloos found that "one of the major limiting factors [of operating this way] is family. You have to have a fluid family or give it up, especially in places like Russia and China." While that principle by no means applies for all aspiring to be global leaders, there is no denying that people operating across the world stage must accept a heavy wear-and-tear factor.

Finally, the example reveals how Alcatel Bell created a multiplier effect as it expanded and integrated. It opted to create a roving team of global leaders such as Abbeloos, all willing to accept the sacrifices and stresses inherent in such assignments. The members of this transnational team could then learn from each other as they came to truly understand the cultural differences required to operate across the world. For example, owing to cultural differences, marketing in China is done by local Chinese. Alcatel Bell people are rarely involved. But in Russia, Alcatel Bell people do the marketing because Russians are not interested in selling. In Russia, then, knowing the language becomes more critical for foreigners doing business there.

Alcatel Bell's process of becoming a global leader is not over. It still needs better ways to integrate people with international experience back into their home countries and ways to hand new assignments to local talent. But Abbeloos is confident that Alcatel Bell has built global leadership: "In terms of operating in Europe, we have all [the] languages and capabilities required. Our real opportunity now is across the world. Here we have the flexibility required. . . . And we have marketing and sales people who can be deployed from throughout Alcatel Bell to be 'door-openers' and a full organization behind them able to serve customers wherever they are."

Beware of Launcher Landmines

Beyond the sheer complexity of running an international firm with a slew of variables including diversity of workforce cultures, varying raw material suppliers, currency fluctuations, political swings, and a multitude of other unpredictable factors, several specific landmines lurk in the ground global launchers must cross to become leaders.

First, firms pursuing leadership often find themselves triggering unexpected—and unpleasant—domino effects. They solve one problem only to see the solution engender another. Sometimes they end up in seemingly no-win situations, such as growing so large they compete with themselves. For example, Matsushita now finds that its cost-effective and productive subsidiaries in southeast Asia produce so much and export so much to Japan so cheaply that Matsushita employees back home cannot keep up. The one-time slogan of Matsushita's Malaysian plants, "Let's catch up with Japan," is outmoded—these plants outperform the Japanese plants in both quality and efficiency. Similarly, Fuji Xerox, the Japanese affiliate of Fuji Film and Xerox, found itself embroiled with its parent company Xerox over sales territory and R&D independence.

A second landmine is sociopolitical and cultural embroilment. As launchers become players in more and more places, they automatically face a greater probability of encountering political, social, cultural, and ethical values that differ significantly from their own and lead to turbulence and moral dilemmas. For example, several global launchers have been fined for obtaining contracts in certain countries by using a form of bribery that in their view was acceptable if not required in those cultures. Meanwhile, companies such as Levi Strauss withdrew their initiatives to open up plants and operations in China because of continuing human rights violations that they viewed as contrary to their corporate values and principles.

Overall, global launchers require a perspective that guides them toward grand but realistic ambitions. Many companies look at China, for example, and imagine that if one billion persons each bought a $1 product, they would produce $1 billion in revenues. Unfortunately, doing business in China today is far more difficult than the scenario suggests. A realistic ambition in this situation would recognize the market potential but at the same time plan to explore all the cultural and political differences in the Chinese market and to understand the complex arrangement of structures, processes, and systems that would support success in that market.

Similarly, at the individual level, the familiar adage "Think global, act local!" captures the required perspective. Managers in global launcher and leader companies must maintain a vision of the world that is complex and sophisticated but also simple from where they sit. It is analogous to playing chess. The players must be able to think strategically and continually about the overall course of the game, but must also be able to focus on one move at a time.

The Global Village of Tomorrow

As companies like AXA, PriceWaterhouseCoopers and many others will testify, becoming a global leader is a tough transition. Many tools are available, and we have described a good number of them here. But senior management must have the skill and foresight to use the right tools in the right way, at the right time, and in the right sequence. There are no magic bullets, no matter where you are in the global learning curve. Each stage requires structures that enable the crossing of boundaries, systems and processes that drive global behavior, and people who can extend their thinking beyond their present outlook. If these goals are consciously set and strongly pursued and achieved, the ultimate reward is an international organization rich in multicultural diversity, a complex and sophisticated management outlook, and successful global products and services.

Chapter Ten

Conclusion

Leading Toward
the Boundaryless Organization

Through much of the twentieth century, management theory and practice fostered the creation of well-structured, unbending organizational boundaries. These boundaries allowed a relative handful of managers to control vast organizations, harness a variety of specialized skills, and extend the reach of mass-production and mass-service organizations around the world. In recent years, however, new success factors emerged that make rigid boundaries increasingly dysfunctional.

Organizations now need to become *boundaryless*—that is, to make their internal and external boundaries more permeable. In our experience, however, such boundaryless organizations don't just happen. They require deliberate changes in structure and process, actively driven by leaders who ignite the sparks of transformation, fan them to keep them alive, and then control the flames to make the transformation productive.

Leadership Change Challenges

Leading the way to the boundaryless organization is among the biggest but most exhilarating tasks facing senior executives today—largely because it requires executives to overcome the five challenges listed in the box during the course of the transformation.

Most executives already have the skills to cope with one or two of these challenges but can benefit from experienced support for the others, either from colleagues or outsiders.

Leadership Change Challenges

- Transform for tomorrow while doing business today.
- Manage an uncontrollable change process.
- Lead to an unclear destination.
- Deal with disruption.
- Confront the need for personal change.

Transform for Tomorrow While Doing Business Today

No one can simply ignore today and focus exclusively on the future. Companies need to secure their present if they mean to have any future at all. Former GE CEO Jack Welch once made this point when one of us asked whether he worried that his focus on short-term results would compromise his long-term agenda. Welch said: "It's been ten years so far, and my businesses keep delivering the numbers *and* doing the right things for the future. They have to do both. People keep telling me that at some point things will fall apart, that [doing both is] not possible. But I haven't seen it yet."

It's challenging enough to create and maintain this dual focus— to be an ambidextrous manager, with one hand steering the course of today's business while the other hand manages for tomorrow. Meanwhile, you constantly have to face down subordinates who say, "Boss, if you want us to make these long-term changes, we'll have to sacrifice some of our profits this year"; or "Boss, if you want us to make these profits, we'll have to delay our long-term changes."

A dual focus on the present and the future requires managers to put in place and believe in a balanced-scorecard approach to assessing performance; they must look beyond the numbers.[1] After all, in most companies, financials are lagging indicators that draw a static picture of past performance. They rarely offer insights about future threats and opportunities or about what to do in either situation. Managers with a balanced scorecard look not only at financial performance but also at hard and soft "leading indicators" that probe into the future—employee satisfaction, customer service levels, speed of new product introductions, key process cycle times, competitor and industry innovations, and more.

When leaders follow these indicators with the same passion they give to operating numbers, they signal that the future and the present must both be preserved. But this change requires breaking long-standing habits of focusing only on numbers that require reports to the board and analysts and that make stock prices rise and fall. The temptation to stick with the numbers is great, but it is making the numbers while also creating the future that is the real challenge.

Manage an Uncontrollable Change Process

Books like this one can be written in sections and chapters. Real organizational life defies such neat frameworks, so executives pushing organizational change cannot limit themselves to one variable at a time. Inevitably, for example, shifts in hierarchical patterns will influence the ways functions work together. Moves to give more autonomy to manufacturing operator teams will almost always result in the teams' seeking more cross-functional participation. Often, this leads to greater vendor participation and a greater focus on both internal and external customers. In a global company, teams often seek out peers in other plants around the world to share best practices, coordinate material supplies, and so on. In other words, once the boundaryless transformation begins (and no matter which boundary you attack first), it's likely to snowball. This is particularly true when people get turned on, excited by the chance to control their own destiny. At this point, effective leaders follow Peter Drucker's often-repeated dictum and "get out of the way."

The challenge, then, is to live with the ambiguity and uncertainty of an uncontrollable process. Transforming organizational boundaries is more akin to genetic engineering than industrial engineering; it unleashes tremendous energy and chain reactions with the potential to evolve in ways difficult to predict. For many managers, this kind of uncertainty is unnerving and may lead to a conscious or unconscious avoidance of boundaryless change strategies. For others, it is exhilarating—the essence of creative management.

Lead to an Unclear Destination

Another kind of uncertainty is the lack of definable outcomes, or end states. Probably the most productive view of the transformation to a boundaryless organization is similar to the view summed up in the total quality mantra, describing quality as "not a destination but a journey." Many managers struggle with such concepts, but trying to define the ultimate boundaryless organization is like trying to define infinity. There is no time when the process is complete and thus no ultimate static state to talk about. There is no "after." While writing this book, we interviewed a number of senior executives who were actively engaged in creating boundaryless organizations. Every one of them asked the same question: "Can you tell me about an organization that has already done it, that has succeeded in becoming boundaryless?" Even the executives many managers consider models of boundaryless leadership are still searching for their own models; they are unclear about where the process is taking them.

But the indefiniteness of the end state is entirely appropriate. After all, the boundaryless corporation is a living and growing entity. As with the human race, it is impossible to predict how much more potential exists in the life-form.

Although it is possible to look backward and define what the boundaryless organization is not, each new development leads to new insights about what else is possible. Companies begin dialogues with their customers, and from these, new possibilities such as shared information and recalibration of roles and responsibilities emerge. Such identification of new possibilities, we suspect, is never ending, limited only by the imagination and creativity of the participants.

The challenge for executives is to get comfortable with the anxiety that an undefined end state can generate. This can be especially difficult for managers who are used to setting attainable goals, strategic plans, and definable objectives, all of which depend on specific measurements and indicators of progress. Conversely, when Jack Welch began the GE Work-Out, he described it as a "decade-long quest" and insisted he would not create any new measures to assess Work-Out success. When pressed about how he would assess progress, he said, "If we start to measure it, we'll kill the process. We have to just let it evolve. We have enough measures already to tell us how we're doing. Let's just use those." Later, when many GE managers continued to ask for clarification about the ultimate goal of Work-Out, Welch designed a presentation slide that showed success as the point at which GE was "the most productive company on earth."

Of course, when the quest for the boundaryless organization makes GE or any other company the most productive company on earth, that will only be a starting point for seeking galactic excellence. The process will continue as long as participants master their anxiety and transform it into excitement.

Deal With Disruption

Another cause of anxiety is the real or imagined organizational disruption involved in loosening boundaries. The drive toward a boundaryless organization may or may not make companies smaller, but it will definitely make them different, and the shifts spurred by these differences will be hard on some people, perhaps even personally painful. A common example is the way reducing hierarchical boundaries changes the role of middle managers and supervisors. This shift is an exciting opportunity for managers who can learn new skills and change their roles from controlling and directing to coaching and deploying resources. But for those who cannot change or change fast enough, there may be no opportunity. Similarly, managers who grew up equating career advancement with climbing a hierarchy may be repelled rather than intrigued by the idea of careers as series of lateral moves, each one requiring new skills.

All the boundary changes described here require such shifts in roles and career definitions and have enormous implications for the opportunities people can expect in organizations. A major challenge for executives who want to embark on the boundaryless journey is to deal with their own anxiety about such shifts. It is one thing to plan organizational strategies and drive the organization toward greater speed, flexibility, integration, and innovation. It is another thing entirely to be responsible for career disruptions, layoffs, and family crises. Most executives, like most everyone else, want to be liked and loved rather than feared and hated. Unfortunately, there is no easy way out of the dark side of the boundaryless transformation. Avoiding or even delaying it can cause even greater disruptions due to flagging competitiveness and knee-jerk layoffs, as seen all too often in the past decade. Perhaps the only solace is to trust in human resilience and creativity. If people are given the straight story and challenged to change for good reasons that they can understand, then they're apt to make the best of the situation. The challenge for leadership is not to be hard-hearted but to help everyone be realistic about how to succeed in the boundaryless world.

Confront the Need for Personal Change

While helping others grapple with the new realities, senior executives must also confront their own needs for transformation. This is probably the biggest challenge of all. Most of today's corporate executives grew up with leadership models that were extremely effective in the 1970s and 1980s. ITT's Harold Geneen, GM's Roger Smith, Chase Manhattan's David Rockefeller, and many others were tough decision makers who ran their companies with an iron hand, fought hard with unions and governments, and tolerated little dissent. Moreover, they were deal-doers who bought and sold companies, and they were financially astute control people who squeezed money out of every operation.

Having learned at the knee of such leaders, many of today's senior executives are steeped in leadership patterns that lost much of their effectiveness in the 1990s and may prove disastrous in the twenty-first century. Today, instead of driving decisions, leaders need to drive discussion and create buy-in. Rather than confronting unions, governments, suppliers, and customers, leaders need to build partnerships based on mutual respect and trust. Instead of controlling, leaders need to be empowering, coaching, counseling, encouraging, and supporting their people—freeing them to use their talents to the greater good of the corporation.

This does not mean the old skills are unusable. On the contrary, senior executives today and tomorrow will still need to make tough decisions, understand financial issues, and be prepared to reconfigure their organizations both through buying and selling and through constant restructuring and unstructuring. But there is no doubt that the boundaryless world will be a new world for leadership as well as for the troops. It is unrealistic to think that the loosening of hierarchies, functions, and other boundaries will not require new kinds of personal leadership—both to make it happen and to provide ongoing direction. The challenge of making a personal transition is one that executives, too, will face. It is always easy to tell others to change. It is much tougher to say the same thing to that familiar face in the mirror.

Learning from Experience: Leadership Leverage Points

As the four "first person" accounts in this book demonstrate, there is no simple, straightforward formula or magic strategy for meeting the five change challenges. Leaders will deal with them in their own way—probably with lots of hard work, an almost Zen-like tolerance for ambiguity and uncertainty, and a large degree of courage. The shift toward a boundaryless organization requires you not only to fight through your organization's immune response but also to overcome your own natural inclinations for control, clarity, and certainty. Success at dealing with these challenges will depend on your openness to learning and your willingness to change.

Throughout this book, we have cited examples of leaders who have demonstrated openness to learning and change, grappled with the five challenges, and moved their organizations toward a boundaryless paradigm. Their experiences suggest three major guidelines (listed in the next box) for executives determined to transform their own organizations.

Guidelines for Boundaryless Transformation

- Start by focusing on measurable short-term business results.
- Create an iterative vision, not a grand plan.
- Bust the boundaries to bust the boundaries.

Start by Focusing on Measurable Short-Term Business Results

Perhaps the most important lesson to be learned here is that measurable business results must be the initial focus of change. The ultimate purpose of loosening boundaries is a more effective, competitive organization, capable of achieving whatever results are necessary to ensure its survival.

In our experience, one of the most dangerous mistakes executives can make is to reverse figure and ground, that is, to emphasize the new organizational forms and relationships as primary and assume results will automatically follow transformational change. Nothing could be further from the truth.

Widespread experience with Total Quality Management (TQM) illustrates this point all too painfully. Thousands of organizations rushed into TQM with the honest belief that if they changed enough organizational variables, bottom-line results would emerge like Venus from the sea. They crafted quality-oriented mission statements; trained managers and employees; set up contests, assessments, and awards; and organized cross-functional steering committees and conferences. The only thing missing in many of these ambitious efforts was a focus on results. In fact, in the orthodoxy of many quality projects, short-term results were anathema, a product of limited thinking. Managers were told not to pressure people to achieve results quickly because it would prevent them from changing their fundamental values and relationships. A number of well-known corporations even proudly published charts showing a TQM time line: year one was the Year of Understanding; year two was the Year of Training; year three was the Year of Fundamental Change; and year four was to be the Year of Results.

Unfortunately, all too many of these corporations never made it to year four. Many closed up their total quality programs. Others shifted to reengineering or reinventing—and fared no better. It rarely helps to move from one program to another if you still fail to focus on results as the fundamental driver of change.[2]

Professor Michael Beer and his associates at Harvard have studied dozens of corporations engaged in major change programs, and they, too, have concluded that successful companies had an unrelenting focus on results. Less successful companies focused on activities that kept people busy but were aimed at changing intermediate variables (such as organizational structure, communication patterns, and job skills) rather than bottom-line results.

Beer and his colleagues pointed out that "while in some companies, wave after wave of programs rolled across the landscape with little positive impact, in others, more successful transformations did take place. They usually started at the periphery of the corporation . . . and they were led by the general managers of [the] units, not by . . . corporate staff people. The general managers did not focus on formal structures and systems; they created ad hoc organizational arrangements to solve concrete business problems. . . . They focused energy for change on the work itself, not on abstractions such as 'participation' or 'culture.'"[3]

The importance of focusing directly on results as a driver of boundaryless change is also supported by another Harvard researcher, Nitin Nohria. Looking at U.S. industrial trends over the past several decades, Nohria found an inverse correlation between competitive market position and expenditures on organizational change programs. He suggests that companies have actually lost competitive advantage by focusing on "organizational fads" instead of on getting results by using the various change programs. To reverse this trend, he calls for managers to become more "pragmatic," that is, to aim directly at results, using whatever works from the panoply of powerful tools at their disposal.[4]

Whenever we have seen leaders succeed at reducing boundaries—leaders such as Jacques Nasser at Ford or Jack Welch at GE—never has the change been made for purely ideological or intellectual reasons. The focus was always on business results. If reconfiguring boundaries looked like a good way to get there, then that is what was tried. There is little doubt that if these managers had not achieved bottom-line business gains, they'd have scrapped those specific boundaryless configurations and tried something else. The goal was never to be boundaryless. The goal was to be a successful, effective, competitive organization.

Create an Iterative Vision, Not a Grand Plan

The second lesson that emerges from the cases described here is that a boundaryless transformation does not need a grand master plan—and, in fact, should not have one. The move to looser boundaries is (like tuning with digital switches) iterative and empirical, based on constant experimentation in the context of a flexible vision. Anything more structured would be useless or even counterproductive. The world is changing so rapidly that any fixed master plan is outdated before the ink dries.

For example, who would have imagined how extensively facsimile technology would permeate organizational life, only to be eclipsed by the Internet within a decade of its rise to popularity? In the late 1980s, executives who received faxes were unusual, and Federal Express lost millions trying to promote Zap Mail, a type of fax. By 1994, however, fax transmissions accounted for up to 36 percent of some Fortune 500 phone bills,[5] fax modems were becoming standard in personal computers, and the home fax market was booming. For several years, most organizations could not imagine life without the fax machine. Today, faxes are quickly being replaced by links to documents "published" on the Internet. The possibilities of facilitating boundaryless behavior through these technologies are enormous. Real-time document sharing has sped up the pace of business and effectively opened up entirely new channels of communication. And this is only the effect of one technology! Add to it wireless communications tools, videoconferencing, mobile phones, miniaturized personal computing devices, face- and voice-recognition, global satellite networks, and more—and the possibilities for further organizational transformation become mind-boggling. In addition, the world is speeding through vast social, economic, and political changes that are redrawing the maps of commerce and creating whole new markets. In this kind of world, planning is virtually impossible. The executive of a large financial services company told us: "If people ask me where we'll be in a couple of years, I tell them that I don't know. I can make a few guesses, but my guesses probably aren't any better than theirs." Most of the executives we talk to who are engaged in boundaryless transformations make similar statements.

Their attitude—their *reveling* in uncertainty—is contrary to the popular wisdom of strategic planning with its extensive data collection and analyses. It is more akin to what McGill University professor Henry Mintzberg calls "strategic thinking." In Mintzberg's view, strategic thinking is what successful companies use to track changing social and economic trends, to assess their implications, to experiment with new ways of doing business, and to build on empirical experience. It is a continuous process, inculcated into the fabric of the organization, rather than a one-time planning exercise that aims to complete a series of forms and concludes with a fancy presentation. It is "about synthesis. It involves intuition and creativity. The outcome of strategic thinking is an integrated perspective of the enterprise, a not-too-precisely articulated vision of direction. . . . Such strategies often cannot be developed on schedule and immaculately conceived. They must be free to appear at any time and at any place in the organization, typically through messy processes of informal learning that must necessarily be carried out by people at various levels who are deeply involved with the specific issues at hand."[6]

The boundaryless companies we have seen are strikingly kaleidoscopic; they keep changing form and feel. Like the transformer toys popular in the late 1980s, they are always changing shape. In fact, while we were writing this book, several of the companies we work with completely reorganized several times. Yet none of the reorganizations were laid out well in advance in some sort of strategic plan. Rather, they were the result of constant dialogue between members of the management team, between managers and employees, and between everyone and customers. In the course of this dialogue, managers kept revising their vision of the business, its opportunities, its threats, and its challenges. Then the boundaries, the structure, and the strategies were adjusted to the changing vision, and adjusted again and again.

As organizations navigate through this white-water world, they must keep a finger on the pulse of the future as well as the present. This means they must develop the ability to identify emerging trends in politics, society, consumer behavior, technology, and other diverse areas, almost like having sensors that can probe the future. In recent years, a whole consulting industry has sprung up around futuristic projection, and many of the boundaryless companies we have seen incorporate such consultant inputs. They also keep probing into new fields of knowledge, looking for applicable lessons or ideas outside their own industry or technology, and they visit other companies, even when they are not in the same business, just to learn and grow.

No matter the tools used, iterative strategic thinking and visioning must be an ongoing process for any organization engaged in the transformation of its boundaries. Given the pace of environmental change, static strategic planning can't keep up.

Bust the Boundaries to Bust the Boundaries

Although it sounds like a tautology, the third leadership lesson is that boundaryless mechanisms themselves are pathways to the boundaryless organization. The best way to design a corporation with more permeable boundaries is not for senior executives to sit at the head office and redraw organization charts but for those same executives to pull together people from different constituencies and let them loose to reshape their own destiny. Their experience of working together on a meaningful assignment is what breaks down the boundaries.

Several years ago, two of us invented the concept of "organizational dialogue" as a way of explaining why GE's town meetings were such successful vehicles for organizational change.[7] The essence of this theory is that effective organizations intentionally engage their people in ongoing dialogue across boundaries to get things done. In large traditional organizations with solidified boundaries, dialogue is often stilted and difficult, constrained by suspicion, fear, and lack of skill. People lack common language and social conventions or the basic ability to listen to each other. The first thing they need is to learn how to talk. Town meetings are a relatively safe forum in which to begin this learning process, to develop a common language in a sheltered environment with the help of a neutral facilitator.

As people learn how to talk, they also need a second stage of development, which we call "learning how to walk." They learn how to translate the results of dialogue into action. Dialogue by itself is not enough for an organization to be effective. People must be able to work effectively across boundaries, carry out cross-boundary tasks, implement agreed-upon changes, and perform numerous other essential actions. Town meetings produce only recommendations for action. The follow-up process of carrying out the recommendations is just as critical.

Finally, the continuing health of organizations requires that they learn how to "walk the talk," to institutionalize the cycle of dialogue and action. Thus, town meetings shift from "unnatural acts in unnatural places" to "natural acts in natural places," that is, accepted, ongoing processes for getting work done across permeable boundaries.[8] Ongoing dialogue and action require organizations to change their basic supporting infrastructures to reinforce and encourage cross-boundary collaboration. Organizations make these changes with the various actions we have talked about here, rewards and incentives, communication of information, and so on.

Most of the transformations we have described demonstrate that when leaders put people from different places together and encourage them to begin the process of dialogue, boundaries become more permeable. The GE Capital credit card business described in Chapter One is a good example. Throughout almost two decades of change, Card Services' leaders constantly created opportunities for dialogue across boundaries and gave people the freedom to act on the insights they generated. The earliest dialogue (which continues to this day) was with customers. Subsequently, forums were created for systems and business people to grapple with the nature of their collaboration. Similarly, the development of self-managing work teams in the business centers resulted from dialogue between managers and associates about ways to improve customer service while reducing costs. Even today, the primary vehicle for fostering innovation in Card Services is a cross-boundary team.

Of course, GE Capital's cross-boundary teams, as in most boundaryless organizations, always serve a specific goal; they're not just an excuse to get people talking. Katzenbach and Smith, in their study of effective teams, note that one of the defining characteristics of high-performing teams is their mobilization around a shared goal.[9] In boundaryless organizations, the power of teams comes from their drive to achieve goals. And in the process of achieving those goals, they foster the continuing permeability of the organizational boundaries.

Making It Happen: An Evolutionary Process and an Evolutionary Attitude

By following, either consciously or unconsciously, these three guidelines, the leaders we have cited created ongoing engines of change that continue to evolve every day. Managers who want to emulate these leaders must also make the shift from the traditional mindset of controlling and directing to focus on unleashing the powers of the organization, from reducing uncertainty to actually creating ambiguity, and from long-term planning to minute-by-minute experimentation. It is this shift in attitude that is perhaps the most challenging part of the boundaryless journey. It will be especially daunting if you grew up in a centralized structure, learning the managerial style based on personal control, micromanaging numbers, running major client relationships, making all major decisions from the top, and essentially keeping the entire business close to your vest. In this style, you need to know all the details, and your managers need to know them, too, if only to answer your questions.

In the boundaryless organization, you still need to ask questions of your colleagues—but different questions. Now you need to be concerned with processes, growth, and trends. You will want to know whether a potential acquisition is a good fit or how best to use your customers to attract additional customers. In particular, you will want to stimulate your people at all levels, to keep them thinking, questioning, probing, and looking for new ways to do business. You will encourage experimentation, set up teams to explore new ideas, and regularly pull people off their regular jobs for intensive participation in projects. Under your leadership, the organization will be in constant ferment, ready to reorganize quickly to meet emerging market needs, always talking about new ideas with clients, and always looking for new opportunities.

Most important, you will never be satisfied. No matter how much your organization achieves, you will always realize that it can all turn around in a moment, that there is no rest for the winners, only the exhilaration of faster laps around the track. But if you can inspire your colleagues, your customers, your suppliers, and all your constituents to run this never-ending race together, then you will have created the boundaryless capability that can propel you into the future.

In a world where seemingly invincible companies like IBM, United Airlines, and Xerox suddenly become vincible, an on-the-brink attitude makes sense. And perhaps that is the final key. No structure in the world, no matter how boundaryless, can ever substitute for the innovative leader, the individual inspired by vision (or even by fear) who can instill a sense of urgency and a demand for change throughout an organization. That is the ultimate boundary to be crossed—the boundary in your mind and soul. Effective, competitive, and boundaryless organizations are possible only when leaders cross their own invisible, self-limiting walls and believe that nothing is impossible, that motivated people can achieve the highest heights, and that organizations in the twenty-first century will have no constraints other than those they impose on themselves. Technology alone will not make it happen; strategy will not be enough; luck will come and go. But leaders who push, inspire, motivate, and demand—who bring out the creativity in their people—such leaders can move mountains. And when mountains move, there are no boundaries.

Questionnaire #6 gives you the opportunity to assess your progress toward boundaryless leadership on five dimensions. Because different organizations and situations require different degrees of boundarylessness, the questionnaire is constructed as a gap analysis. That is, it defines the distance between where you are currently on each dimension and where you want to be. You measure yourself against your own needs, not against some abstract standard.

Questionnaire Scoring and Follow-Up

Add your eighteen individual gap scores to find your overall score. Interpret the results as follows:

Gap of 25 or less. Either your expectations are very low, or you have already achieved an exceptional level of boundaryless leadership. How far to the right-hand side of the scales are your *O* scores, your vision of the leadership needed in your organization for the twenty-first century? If most of your *O* scores are 7 or lower, you might ask colleagues, customers, board members, or subordinates where they would place the *O*'s on the eighteen scales. Do they share your views about the kind of leadership needed for the future? Be sure you are not simply extrapolating your current situation into the future rather than imagining possible new markets, technologies, competitive threats, and customer demands.

If your *O* scores are already over on the right-hand side, congratulations! You may be a model of the leadership needed in the next century. You may want to ask some of your leadership colleagues to assess themselves or even to assess you. Consider the value of having a dialogue with colleagues to confirm your sense of the leadership needed and where you and they are on the continuum from traditional to boundaryless leadership. If you are already a boundaryless leader, this dialogue is probably ongoing in your organization, and perhaps the questionnaire can add talking points to that dialogue.

Gap of 26 to 75. You've begun the journey and made progress, but there is still a long way to go. A middle-range score probably means key boundary areas need your attention. Look through the questionnaire to see if any categories stand out as having larger gaps than others. For example, companies often make progress on breaking down internal barriers before they see progress on external barriers. If some gaps are indeed bigger than others, you might consider targeting them, selecting from the preceding chapters strategies that apply specifically to closing the largest gaps.

Also, consider whether the larger gaps are reflections of your own leadership challenges. Most executives, at all levels, have a range of skill sets and comfort levels. For example, you may be very effective in producing cross-functional team collaboration but still uncomfortable allowing your teams to go ahead without checking in with you. Or perhaps you are successful at the hard work of developing successful partnerships with customers but much less clear about how to provide global leadership. If one of these situations or a similar diagnosis rings true for you, you might ask some colleagues or close friends, people who can give you candid feedback, to discuss your findings with you. Remember that your own ability to break through self-imposed boundaries is one of the critical determinants of your company's ultimate success.

Gap of 76 or more. You are just getting started, and there are lots of opportunities to pursue. If your gap score is above 75, then the fun is just beginning. It is probably time for you to pull together your management team, review the strategies we have discussed (particularly those keyed to getting started), and have some concentrated work sessions. Remember, of course, that you cannot change everything at once. Pick your targets, create some successes, and get the process going. Return to this questionnaire and its predecessors periodically and take stock of your progress. As long as you keep learning along the way and building your learning back into your organization, you will keep making progress toward the boundaryless organization of the twenty-first century.

Questionnaire #6

Stepping Up to the Line: Are You a Boundaryless Leader?

Instructions: On each 1-to-10 scale, place an O where you think you need to be, or want to be, to move your organization forward into the twenty-first century. Then place an X where you think you currently are on the scale. The difference between the two scores (O–X) is your gap score.

Gap Score
(O–X)

1. Leadership to break down vertical boundaries

You and your senior management team make most decisions. 1 2 3 4 5 6 7 8 9 10 Most decisions are made close to the action. ——

You hold information close to the vest—and promote a need-to-know approach to information sharing. 1 2 3 4 5 6 7 8 9 10 You share information about overall performance and business strategy with as broad base of constituents as possible. ——

Your recognition and reward system is based solely on individual contributions. 1 2 3 4 5 6 7 8 9 10 Your recognition and reward system is primarily team based. ——

2. Leadership to break down horizontal boundaries

Your people have narrowly defined roles, responsibilities, and skills. 1 2 3 4 5 6 7 8 9 10 You encourage people to develop multiple skills—so everyone feels ready to do what it takes to get the job done. ——

You have clear functional agendas that determine the way things get done and the pace of implementation.   1 2 3 4 5 6 7 8 9 10   You ensure everyone is focused on shared goals, across functions.   ———

You have put in place strong controls—with multiple hand-offs and sign-offs—to get work done effectively.   1 2 3 4 5 6 7 8 9 10   You push for integrated end-to-end processes with a single point of accountability to get work done— streamlined, efficient, and value-added every step of the way.   ———

3. Leadership to break down internal boundaries

You and your senior management team focus most of your attention on your own company's current performance.   1 2 3 4 5 6 7 8 9 10   You are focused primarily on maximizing value to the end user.   ———

You encourage a tough negotiating approach to interacting with customers and suppliers.   1 2 3 4 5 6 7 8 9 10   You actively seek partnerships and relationships of trust with customers and suppliers.   ———

You spend a significant portion of your time in internal meetings and in running in-house committees.   1 2 3 4 5 6 7 8 9 10   You spend most of your time with customers, suppliers, and other outside constituents.   ———

(continued)

Questionnaire #6 *(continued)*

	Gap Score (O–X)

You look for new business opportunities solely on the basis of your company's capabilities.

1 2 3 4 5 6 7 8 9 10

You formulate new business in partnership with your customers—based on their needs and changes in their markets

___

4. Leadership to break down geographic boundaries

You promote a look-alike culture—hiring and promoting people who look like you.

1 2 3 4 5 6 7 8 9 10

You seek diversity in the people you hire and promote.

___

To get a shot at the top positions, executives need to "punch their ticket" in a series of domestic positions.

1 2 3 4 5 6 7 8 9 10

Significant international experience is a prerequisite for top positions.

___

You try to apply the domestic model for doing business to each international market you are involved in.

1 2 3 4 5 6 7 8 9 10

You always start from the local market conditions and build your business practices around these—taking very little for granted.

___

5. Overall leadership to make it happen

You are preoccupied with task management—constantly trying

1 2 3 4 5 6 7 8 9 10

You are focused on results—you clarify expectations

to explain to your subordinates the steps they need to take. | _____ | about the desired end results and let your people figure out how to get there.

You exercise a command-and-control model of leadership.

1 2 3 4 5 6 7 8 9 10

You lead through articulating clear goals, then coaching, counselling, and cheerleading people to achieve them.

You prefer to wait for all the analyses, reports, and studies to come in before taking a position about the issues facing the organization.

1 2 3 4 5 6 7 8 9 10

You are comfortable sketching out a rough-and-ready vision of where the organization needs to go and using actions as a way to test and refine the vision and the overall direction.

You are constantly worried about giving people more than they can handle—considering everything else on their plate.

1 2 3 4 5 6 7 8 9 10

You are comfortable putting out exceptional challenges to people—even if you have no clue how people will deliver on them.

You promote a keep-your-head-down policy—one mistake can derail a career.

1 2 3 4 5 6 7 8 9 10

You create an environment in which coming up with and exploring new ideas is encouraged and rewarded.

Notes

Preface
1. See "Making the Deal Real: How GE Capital Integrates Acquisitions," by Ronald N. Ashkenas, Suzanne F. Francis, and Lawrence J. DeMonaco, *Harvard Business Review,* Jan.-Feb., 1998.

Chapter One
1. The Sears example is based in part on D. R. Katz, *The Big Store: Inside the Crisis and Revolution at Sears* (New York: Viking Press, 1987).
2. "Letter to shareholders," *GE Annual Report,* 1993.

Chapter Two
1. Exodus 18:17–26.
2. H.F.J. Porter, "The Realization of Ideals in Industrial Engineering," *Transactions* (ASME), 1905, *27,* 352–353.
3. W. F. Muhs, "Worker Participation in the Progressive Era: An Assessment by Harrington Emerson," *Academy of Management Review,* 1982, 7(1), 99–102.
4. S. Haber, *Efficiency and Uplift* (Chicago: University of Chicago Press, 1964), p. 124.
5. See F. J. Roethlisberger and W. J. Dickson, *Management and the Worker* (Cambridge, Mass.: Harvard University Press, 1939) for a full report of the Western Electric research.
6. D. M. McGregor, "The Human Side of Enterprise," *Management Review,* Nov. 1957, p. 9.
7. W. Bennis, "Organization of the Future," *Personnel Administration,* Sept.-Oct. 1967.
8. J. Huey, "The New Post-Heroic Leadership," *Fortune,* Feb. 21, 1994, p. 44.
9. D. Smith and R. Alexander, *Fumbling the Future, How Xerox Invented, Then Ignored, the First Personal Computer* (New York: Morrow, 1988).

10. We are indebted to professor Edward E. Lawler III and his associates at the University of Southern California who first suggested the importance of these four dimensions. For further information, see E. E. Lawler III, *High-Involvement Management: Participative Strategies for Improving Organizational Performance* (San Francisco: Jossey-Bass, 1986).

11. L. Dyer and D. Blancero, "Workplace 2000: A Delphi Study Working Paper" (Center for Advanced HR Studies, School of Industrial & Labor Relations, Cornell University, 1992).

12. Compare J. H. Shea and R. C. Ochsner, "Top Executive Compensation: Science or Witchcraft?" *Compensation & Benefits Management,* Autumn 1984, *1*(1), 59–65.

13. D. Ulrich and D. Lake, *Organizational Capability: Competing from the Inside/Out* (New York: Wiley, 1990).

Chapter Three

1. See R. Ashkenas, "Beyond the Fads: How Managers Drive Change with Results," in C. E. Schneier (ed.), *Managing Cultural and Strategic Change* (New York: Human Resource Planning Society, 1995), pp. 33–53. Also see R. G. Eckels and N. Nohria with J. D. Berkley, *Beyond the Hype: Rediscovering the Essence of Management* (Boston: Harvard Business School Press, 1992).

2. The concept of organizational capabilities is drawn from Ulrich and Lake, 1990.

3. See G. Will, *Men at Work: The Craft of Baseball* (New York: Macmillan, 1990).

4. R. W. Stevenson, "Watch Out Macy's, Here Comes Nordstrom," *New York Times Magazine,* Aug. 27, 1989.

5. Tony Rucci was senior vice president of human resources at Baxter Healthcare. He is currently executive vice president of human resources at Cardinal Health.

6. D. Ulrich, "OASIS: An Empirical Study of Strategy, Organization, and Human Resource Management," presentation at the Academy of Management, 1986.

7. R. Eichinger and M. Lombardo, *Twenty-Two Ways to Develop Leadership in Staff Managers,* Report #144 (Greensboro, N.C.: Center for Creative Leadership, 1990); M. W. McCall Jr., M. Lombardo, and A. Morrison, *The Lessons of Experience: How Successful Executives Develop on the Job* (Lexington, Mass.: Lexington Books, 1988).

8. W. Tornow (ed.), *Human Resource Management Journal,* 1993, *32*(2–3) (special issue on 360-degree feedback).

9. R. S. Kaplan and D. P. Norton, *The Strategy-Focused Organization: How Balanced Scorecard Companies Thrive in the New Business Environment* (Boston: Harvard Business School Press, 2000).

Chapter Four

1. A. Smith, *The Wealth of Nations* (New York: Viking/Penguin, 1986; originally published 1776).
2. Personal communication from Bruce Phillips, Apr. 1994.
3. R. L. Ackoff, *The Democratic Corporation* (New York: Oxford University Press, 1994), p. 95.
4. R. J. Kramer, *Organizing for Global Competitiveness: The Matrix Design,* Report #1088–94-RR (New York: Conference Board, 1994), p. 39.
5. J. Galbraith, *Competing with Flexible Lateral Organizations* (Reading, Mass.: Addison-Wesley, 1994).
6. M. Bellmann and R. Schaffer, "Freeing Managers to Innovate," *Harvard Business Review,* June 2001, pp. 32–33.
7. See J. Kochanski and P. Randall, "Rearchitechting the Human Resources Function at Northern Telecom," *Human Resources Management,* 1994, *33*(2), 299–315.

Chapter Five

1. An excellent source for accounts of these tools and how to use them is M. Brassard, *The Memory Jogger Plus* (Methuen, Mass.: Goal/QPC, 1989).
2. J. Katzenbach and D. Smith, "The Discipline of Teams," *Harvard Business Review,* Mar.-Apr. 1993, pp. 111–120.
3. J. D. Thompson, *Organizations in Action* (New York: McGraw-Hill, 1976).
4. T. Teal, "Service Comes First: An Interview with USAA's President Robert S. McDermott," *Harvard Business Review,* Sept.-Oct. 1991, pp. 116–127.
5. S. J. Frangos with J. Bennett, *Team Zebra: How 1500 Partners Revitalized Eastman Kodak's Black & White Film-Making Flow* (Essex Junction, Conn.: Oliver Wright, 1992).
6. Much of the material in this section is based on D. Ulrich, "Shared Services: Reengineering the HR Function," *Human Resource Planning Journal,* 1995, *18*(3), 12–24. Robert Gunn also supplied us with information based on his consulting work, as reported in R. W. Gunn, D. P. Carberry, R. Frigo, and S. Behrens, "Shared Services," *Management Accounting,* Nov. 1993, pp. 22–28.

7. R. L. Huber, "How Continental Bank Outsourced Its 'Crown Jewels,'" *Harvard Business Review*, Jan.-Feb. 1993, pp. 121–129.

8. The Honeywell International company snapshot as found in "Catch the Next Wave—2001 Think Tank," *Gunn Partners*, 2001.

9. Many of the ideas in this section are drawn from D. Ulrich, M. A. VonGlinow, and T. Jick, "High Impact Learning: Building and Diffusing Learning Capability," *Organizational Dynamics*, Winter 1993, pp. 52–66.

10. C. Argyris, "Teaching Smart People How to Learn," *Harvard Business Review*, May-June 1991, pp. 99–109; C. Argyris, *Reasoning, Learning, and Action: Individual and Organizational* (San Francisco: Jossey-Bass, 1982); C. Argyris, *Overcoming Organizational Defenses—Facilitating Organizational Learning* (Boston: Allyn & Bacon, 1990); C. Argyris and D. A. Schön, *Organizational Learning: A Theory of Action Perspective* (Reading, Mass.: Addison-Wesley, 1978).

11. For more information about Motorola's program, see J. Miraglia, "OEP: Motorola's Renewal Process," *Tapping the Network Journal*, Spring 1990, pp. 2–6. Also see T. Jick's Harvard Business School case study, "Bob Galvin and Motorola, Inc." (Boston: Harvard Business School, 1987).

12. D. Ulrich, M. A. VonGlinow, and T. Jick, 1993. For a short summary of the report, see "Briefing from the Editor," *Harvard Business Review*, Mar.-Apr. 1995, p. 10.

Chapter Six

1. J. Womak, D. Jones, and D. Roos, *The Machine That Changed the World* (New York: HarperCollins, 1990), pp. 138–139.

2. J. A. Carlisle and R. C. Parker, *Beyond Negotiation* (New York: Wiley, 1989), p. 5.

3. R. F. Lynch, *Business Alliances Guide* (New York: Wiley, 1993), p. 7.

4. Lynch, 1993, p. 18.

5. For a brief history of strategic alliances, see Lynch, 1993, pp. 8–15.

6. P. Drucker, "The Shape of Industry to Come," *Industry Week*, Jan. 11, 1982, p. 55.

7. R. Normann and R. Ramirez, "From Value Chain to Value Constellation: Designing Interactive Strategy," *Harvard Business Review*, July-Aug. 1993, pp. 65–66.

8. M. Best, *The New Competition* (Cambridge, Mass.: Harvard University Press, 1990), p. 20.

9. Womack, Jones, and Roos, 1990, p. 194.

10. Best, 1990, p. 274.

11. P. Senge, *The Fifth Discipline* (New York: Doubleday, 1990).

12. S. Strom, "K-Mart Shifting Cost Burden to Toy Makers," *New York Times,* July 29, 1993, p. D5.

13. "E-Management Survey: Enter the Eco-system," *Economist,* Nov. 11, 2000, pp. 30–34.

14. Carlisle and Parker, 1989, p. 5.

15. *Work-Out Roundtable Gazette* (an internal publication of GE Appliances), July 7, 1993, p. 4.

16. "E-Management Survey," 2000.

17. See D. Ulrich, "Tie the Corporate Knot: Gaining Complete Customer Commitment," *Sloan Management Review,* 1989, *30*(4), 22.

18. P. Engardio (New York), S. Hamm (New York), F. Keenan (New York), D. Welch (Detroit), and W. Zellner (Dallas), "E-Biz: Down But Hardly Out," *Business Week,* Mar. 26, 2001, pp. 126–130.

19. L. Thurow (ed.), *The Management Challenge: Japanese View* (Cambridge, Mass.: MIT Press, 1985).

20. S. K. Yoder and G. P. Zachary, "Vague New World: Digital Media Business Takes Form as a Battle of Complex Alliances," *Wall Street Journal,* July 14, 1993, p. A4.

21. Yoder and Zachary, 1993.

22. Lynch, 1993, pp. 174–175.

23. Drucker, 1982, p. 57.

24. Lynch, 1993, p. 23.

25. Dr. Seuss, *One Fish, Two Fish, Red Fish, Blue Fish* (New York: Random House, 1960).

26. Yoder and Zachary, 1993.

Chapter Seven

1. See, for example, Lynch, 1993.

2. T. Jick, "Customer-Supplier Partnerships: Human Resources Bridge Builders," *Human Resource Management,* 1990, *29*(4). Quote on pp. 440–441.

3. Jick, 1990, p. 442.

4. See R. H. Schaffer, *The Breakthrough Strategy: Using Short-Term Successes to Build the High Performance Organization* (New York: Harper Business, 1988), pp. 187–188.

5. See Ulrich, 1989, for more on these and other examples.

6. Normann and Ramirez, 1993, p. 67.

7. Schaffer, 1988, pp. 189–190.

8. Huber, 1993.

9. C. Duff, "Nation's Retailers Ask Vendors to Help Share Expenses," *Wall Street Journal,* Aug. 4, 1993, p. B4.

10. "E-Management Survey: Enter the Eco-system," *Economist*, Nov. 11, 2000, pp. 30–34.
11. Normann and Ramirez, 1993, pp. 66–67.

Chapter Eight

1. "The Discreet Charm of the Multicultural Multinational," *Economist*, July 30, 1994, pp. 57–58.
2. D. Milbank, "Asian Tigers Are on the Prowl in Europe," *Wall Street Journal*, Oct. 26, 1994, p. A16.
3. B. R. Schlender, "Matsushita Shows How to Go Global," *Fortune*, July 11, 1994, pp. 159–163.
4. J. Welch, "Productivity: Lessons from General Electric," *Boardroom Reports*, Nov. 15, 1994, p. 8.
5. Delta & Pine Land example is from *Business Week*, June 11, 2001, p. 119.
6. For the Lila Pause and Barilla examples, see C. Rohwedder, "Eurobrands Take Hold Across Borders," *Wall Street Journal*, Apr. 28, 1993.
7. Rohwedder, 1993.
8. Company capsules for Exxon Mobil, Motorola, and Coca-Cola as found on Hoovers Online [http://www.hoovers.com].
9. C. Tovar, "The (World Wide) Web They Weave," *Wall Street Journal*, Apr. 3, 2000, p. B12. The story includes a dense half-page diagram that shows how AOL is connected to 91 other organizations by ownership, equity share, or partnership.
10. C. Crystal, "Do You Measure Up?" *International Business*, Nov. 1992, pp. 60–62.
11. Background information about ABB is drawn from M.F.R. Kets de Vries, "Making a Giant Dance," *Across the Board*, Oct. 1994, pp. 27–32.
12. J. M. Stopford and L. T. Wells, *Managing the Multinational Enterprise* (New York: Basic Books, 1972), cited in C. Bartlett and S. Ghoshal, *Managing Across Borders* (Boston: Harvard Business School Press, 1989).
13. P. Evans, "Management Development as Glue Technology," *Human Resource Planning*, 1992, *15*(1), 85–105. (Paul Evans is professor of organizational behavior at INSEAD, a French business school.)
14. Bartlett and Ghoshal, 1989.
15. Bartlett and Ghoshal, 1989.
16. H. Wendt, *Global Embrace* (New York: Harper Business, 1993), p. 40.
17. "The Elusive Euro-Manager," *Economist*, Nov. 7, 1992, p. 83.
18. S. H. Rhinesmith, *A Manager's Guide to Globalization* (Homewood, Ill.: Business One Irwin, 1993).
19. G. Hedlund, "The Hypermodern MNC: A Heterarchy," *Human Resource Management*, 1986, *25*, 9–35.

20. D. Hightower, personal communication.

21. Dennis Hightower has since become a professor at the Harvard Business School.

22. Cultural study is discussed in C. Lorenz, "Learning to Live with a Cultural Mix," *Financial Times*, Apr. 23, 1993, p. 11—an article based on F. Trompenaars, *Riding the Waves of Culture* (London: Economist Books, 1993).

23. "The Discreet Charm of the Multicultural Multinational," 1994.

24. Johnson and Associates, *How International Are You and Your Company?* (Brussels: Management Centre Europe, 1994).

25. P. Carey, "Foreigners on the Board," *International Business*, Oct. 1994, pp. 24–26.

26. Carey, 1994.

27. Evans, 1992.

28. Evans, 1992.

29. D. Milbank, "It's Not Easy Being the Little Guy Overseas," *Wall Street Journal*, Sept. 15, 1994, p. A11.

Chapter Nine

1. R. Donkin, "Cultural Restraints on Missionary Zeal," *Financial Times*, Sept. 30, 1994, p. 12.

2. M.F.R. Kets de Vries, "Making a Giant Dance," *Across the Board*, Oct. 1994, pp. 27–32.

3. D. Savona, "When Companies Divorce," *International Business*, Nov. 1992, p. 6.

4. J. Main, "Making Global Alliances Work," *Fortune*, Dec. 17, 1990, pp. 121–126.

5. P. Evans, "Management Development as Glue Technology," *Human Resource Planning*, 1992, *15*(1), 85–105.

6. F. Gee, T. Jick, and S. Paine, *Clifford Chance: The Merger (A)* and *Clifford Chance: International Expansion (B)*, case study (Fontainebleau, France: INCITE, 1993).

7. P. L. Zweig, "Sachs' Spectacular Road Trip," *Business Week*, Nov. 8, 1993, pp. 56B-E.

8. "The Discreet Charm of the Multicultural Multinational," *Economist*, July 30, 1994, pp. 57–58.

Chapter Ten

1. See R. S. Kaplan and D. P. Norton, "Putting the Balanced Scorecard to Work," *Harvard Business Review*, Sept.-Oct. 1993, pp. 134–147.

2. For more on this subject, see Ashkenas, 1995. Another perspective is provided by R. Schaffer and H. Thomson, "Successful Change

Programs Begin with Results," *Harvard Business Review,* Jan.-Feb. 1992, pp. 80–89.

3. M. Beer, R. Eisenstat, and B. Spector, "Why Change Programs Don't Produce Change," *Harvard Business Review,* Nov.-Dec. 1990, p. 159.

4. N. Nohria and J. D. Berkley, "Whatever Happened to the Take Charge Manager?" *Harvard Business Review,* Jan.-Feb. 1994, pp. 129–137.

5. J. Lawlor, "Faxes Taxing Office Life," *USA Today,* Apr. 20, 1994, p. 1.

6. H. Mintzberg, "The Fall and Rise of Strategic Planning," *Harvard Business Review,* Jan.-Feb. 1994, pp. 107–114.

7. R. Ashkenas and T. Jick, "From Dialogue to Action in GE Work-Out," *Research in Organizational Change and Development,* 1992, *6,* 267–287.

8. S. Kerr, "Toward Natural Acts in Natural Places," in *Launching and Leading the Boundary-less Organization: Work-Out Best Practices,* an unpublished collection of GE Company working papers, July 1990.

9. J. R. Katzenbach and D. K. Smith, 1993.

Index